LIBRARY OF RELIGIOUS BIOGRAPHY

Edited by Mark A. Noll, Nathan O. Hatch,
and Allen C. Guelzo

The LIBRARY OF RELIGIOUS BIOGRAPHY is a series of original biographies on important religious figures throughout American and British history.

The authors are well-known historians, each a recognized authority in the period of religious history in which his or her subject lived and worked. Grounded in solid research of both published and archival sources, these volumes link the lives of their subjects — not always thought of as "religious" persons — to the broader cultural contexts and religious issues that surrounded them. Each volume includes a bibliographical essay and an index to serve the needs of students, teachers, and researchers.

Marked by careful scholarship yet free of footnotes and academic jargon, the books in this series are well-written narratives meant to be *read* and *enjoyed* as well as studied.

LIBRARY OF RELIGIOUS BIOGRAPHY

available

Billy Sunday and the Redemption of Urban America
Lyle W. Dorsett

The Divine Dramatist:
George Whitefield and the Rise of Modern Evangelicalism
Harry S. Stout

William Ewart Gladstone:
Faith and Politics in Victorian Britain
David Bebbington

Aimee Semple McPherson: Everybody's Sister
Edith L. Blumhofer

Sworn on the Altar of God: A Religious Biography of Thomas Jefferson
Edwin S. Gaustad

Charles G. Finney and the Spirit of American Evangelicalism
Charles E. Hambrick-Stowe

Blaise Pascal: Reasons of the Heart
Marvin R. O'Connell

Emily Dickinson and the Art of Belief
Roger Lundin

Thomas Merton and the Monastic Vision
Lawrence S. Cunningham

Thomas Merton
and the Monastic Vision

Lawrence S. Cunningham

WILLIAM B. EERDMANS PUBLISHING COMPANY
GRAND RAPIDS, MICHIGAN / CAMBRIDGE, U.K.

© 1999 Wm. B. Eerdmans Publishing Co.
255 Jefferson Ave. S.E., Grand Rapids, Michigan 49503 /
P.O. Box 163, Cambridge CB3 9PU U.K.

Printed in the United States of America

04 03 02 01 00 99   7 6 5 4 3 2 1

Library of Congress Cataloging-in-Publication Data

Cunningham, Lawrence.
    Thomas Merton and the monastic vision / Lawrence S. Cunningham
        p.   cm.   — (Library of Religious biography)
    Includes index.
    ISBN 0-8028-0222-2 (pbk.: alk. paper)
    1. Merton, Thomas, 1915-1968.   2. Trappists — United States
Biography.   3. Monks — United States Biography.   4. Monastic and
religious life.   I. Title.   II. Series.
BX4705.M542C86   1999
271′.12502 — dc21
    [B]   99-34656
                                                                 CIP

Contents

Foreword

THERE IS AN ADAGE THAT SAYS "IT TAKES ONE TO KNOW one." That, I believe, is the source of the wisdom in this volume by Lawrence S. Cunningham. Through his long association with monks, he knows what it is to be a monk and has acquired something of the monastic spirit himself. Cunningham brings that vision to his presentation and evaluation of Thomas Merton and his writing. The constant reminder in this book is that Merton produced all his various works while he continued to live a full monastic observance. Scholar, professor, writer, and intuitive monk that Cunningham is, he understands the extraordinary discipline required to be so involved with the task of writing on such varied topics and still to be immersed in the unrelenting rhythm of monastic living.

I had the real blessing of being introduced to monastic life by Father Louis, as Merton was known within the Gethsemani community, when he was Novice Master at the monastery. My first meeting with the Novice Master revealed how he juxtaposed his vocation as monk, including his service in the community as Novice Master, with his stature as a well-known writer. Having arrived, somewhat unannounced, at the monastery to enter the community on the feast of Saint Augustine, I was asked to stay in the retreat house for several days. A week later I was told to be in my room after the evening meal because the Novice Master was coming to interview me. At the designated time there was a knock on the door and a rather unimpressive person introduced himself as the Novice Master. He was easy to talk to as he asked all the questions that are a usual part of such interviews. Near the end of the interview, the Novice Master asked how I had heard of monasticism. I told him that I was a product of Catholic schools and a student of history, and added that I had read all of Thomas Merton's published books and the writings of Father Raymond, another Gethsemani monk who wrote spiritual books in a somewhat different genre. He asked what I thought of the authors. I said that they both portrayed monastic life somewhat romantically but I found Merton's style more congenial. The Novice Master responded that what we read is very important, so one must choose wisely and approach critically. Needless to say I was surprised and disconcerted the next morning when the Father Guest Master asked me how the meeting with Thomas Merton went. Later in the day when I was taken into the novitiate and met Father Louis all I could say was, "At least you know what I think about your work."

Throughout the two years of my novitiate and the time after the novitiate when I served as Father Louis's assistant, I witnessed firsthand how the monastic life was paramount in his perspective. His conferences were very well-prepared. His interaction with the novices, though somewhat circumscribed by the discipline of the monastic community, was always very personal and respectful, and demonstrated genuine concern for the well-being of the novice. On a number of occasions when Father Louis was engaged with some person of renown in the guest house, he would excuse himself to honor a regular spiritual direction appointment with a novice.

Though many of his diary entries are concerned with the complex relationship between himself and Abbot James Fox, he never betrayed any hint of these difficulties to the novices. In fact, Father Louis was adamant on matters of obedience and respect for authority. I had my own difficulties with Abbot James and sought out Father Louis to support my position, but he in no uncertain terms made it known where my obligations were if I considered myself a monk.

I attended his conferences and had almost daily contact with him during the period when he was anguishing about going to another monastic community and during some of his struggles regarding the ban on his writing about peace issues. Never in that time did Father Louis make any direct comments or even veiled innuendoes about his conflicts and difficulties. In retrospect it is clear that some of the topics about which he wrote during those days did indeed have a connection with his personal struggles.

All this is to underscore the recurring theme in this book, that Merton's many and varied interests were experienced and commented upon from within the context of a seriously lived monastic life. Perhaps we can see in the almost petty complaints of the diaries something of his effort to be honest and his resistance to the image that the ecclesiastical world and the realm of popular piety tried to impose on him. The diaries so often will contain the most anguished complaints, only to be followed by an entry a day or so later acknowledging his own pettiness.

What Merton did for monastic life, in addition to his example of lived experience, was to expand its horizon. Merton himself came to the monastery with the narrow perception that outside the walls of the monastery all was sin and evil. While living out a serious monastic discipline combined with a willingness to learn from all sources, he soon came to the realization that the truth of the gospel is very alive in many different places and ways of living. He always insisted that in discerning their vocations the novices be open to the realization that there are many mansions in the Kingdom of God. He never portrayed the world in terms of sin. What Merton taught was that we must be authentic persons wherever we are. To be that authentic person no one can stagnate, neither in the monastery nor in the world, if that is where one chooses to live the gospel. We must always be searching that further horizon. As Merton described the journey in the *Asian Journal*, after speaking with a Buddhist hermit, "The unspoken or half-spoken message of the talk was our complete understanding of each other as people somehow *on the edge* of great realization and knew it and were trying, somehow or other, to go out and get lost in it — and that it was a grace for us to meet one another." Merton was always learning and always respectful of the truth in other persons and traditions. This is one of the gifts he gave the Gethsemani community.

Lawrence Cunningham has done the brother monks of Father Louis, Thomas Merton, a real service. He has reminded us of the example of one who lived a serious monastic discipline and did not hesitate to engage any element of our varied world to find there the authentic truth that is necessary to live a contemplative life. Cunningham also has a message from the works of Merton for all persons. He quotes Merton from a foreword to a Latin American edition of his works in the final lines of this volume: "Without contemplation, without the intimate, silent, secret pursuit of truth through love, our action loses itself in the world and becomes dangerous."

It is with gratitude that I offer these few words to introduce the work of an author who understands what it is to be a monk. Lawrence Cunningham's study supplies the context for all who read and study Merton's writings. Merton's work is that of a person who lived a dedicated and disciplined life in order to be true to his deepest self. Only from that perspective was he able to comment on such an array of subjects with freshness of insight and the wisdom of life.

Abbot Timothy Kelly
Gethsemani Abbey
15 August 1999

Preface

THIS STUDY OF THOMAS MERTON IS ONE VOLUME IN A series devoted to religious biography edited by Mark Noll, Nathan Hatch, and Allen Guelzo. To them and to my editor at Eerdmans, Charles Van Hof, the author is deeply in debt.

Work on this spiritual biography began during my sabbatical year after having completed six years as chair of the University of Notre Dame Theology Department. The University and the College of Arts & Letters in particular receive my thanks for making Notre Dame such a congenial place to teach and do research. A travel grant from the college's Institute for Scholarship in the Liberal Arts allowed me to attend the 1998 meeting of the International Thomas Merton Society, held in England at Merton's old public school at Oakham. Special thanks goes to John Cavadini, my successor as departmental chair, for his constant solicitude for all of us who teach in the department. I have also benefited mightily from the friendship and advice of my fellow author, Keith Egan, who teaches theology at Saint Mary's College, our neighbor across the road. Keith was especially helpful in instructing me on the thought of Saint John of the Cross. Thomas O'Meara, O.P., has been generous in sharing with me some works from his own library of Mertoniana.

My interest in Thomas Merton has always been richly nurtured by the hospitality extended to me by the monastic community of Our Lady of Gethsemani in Kentucky. Both the environment of the place itself and the memory of Father Louis (as Merton was known in the community) — especially by those who had him as a novice director — were invaluable. At the abbey, one senses Saint Bernard of Clairvaux's observation that Cistercians are "lovers of the place and the Rule."

Acknowledgment is gratefully made to the Thomas Merton Literary Trust and to Anne McCormick, its administrator, as well as the Abbey of Gethsemani, for permission to cite from Merton's work.

For over twenty years Brother Patrick Hart of the Abbey of Gethsemani has been a steadfast friend. His generosity with materials, his willingness to read and comment on work, and his unparalleled knowledge of Merton — as a fellow monk, as Merton's secretary, and as an author — has sustained many of us who have written about Merton.

Brother Patrick entered the monastic community of Gethsemani in 1951 after doing undergraduate studies at the University of Notre Dame and having spent time as a religious brother of the Congregation of the Holy Cross. He has never forgotten his days at Notre Dame. It is only fitting that this book be dedicated to him as a token of our long friendship and to honor his half century as a Cistercian monk — from one "Domer" to another.

Prologue

ONE MAY READ THE FIRST NINE BOOKS OF AUGUSTINE'S *Confessions* as the author's intense search for the solution to two intertwined spiritual problems, one intellectual and the other moral. After Augustine, as an adolescent, read Cicero's now lost treatise called the *Hortensius,* he decided to embrace philosophy which meant, in his day, not merely to study an academic subject but to adopt a way of life in search of the truth. That way of life led Augustine, through many a turn, to Christianity — largely under the twin influences of the person and preaching of bishop Ambrose of Milan and the writings of the Neoplatonists where, as he said famously in the *Confessions,* he found everything except the name of Christ. Nonetheless, despite this intellectual conversion, Augustine still had to confront the moral untidiness of his own personal life summarized in his famous prayer "Lord, make me chaste but not just yet!"

All Christian autobiography owes a certain debt to Augustine's *Confessions.* James D. Fernandez's study of Spanish religious autobiography (*Apology to Apostrophe* — 1992) notes four stages in the genre: (1) a description of the old unredeemed self; (2) a picture of the new, redeemed self; (3) address to an audience of human readers to edify or convert; (4) and, most crucially, an address to God who is seen as the

1

Ideal Reader. What Fernandez writes in terms of Spain (think of Teresa of Avila's *Mi Vida*) holds for most other types of the genre including that produced by Thomas Merton.

If those twin trajectories of moral and intellectual searching can be seen as the threads that led Augustine to the Christian life, then it is almost plausible to accept the late Monsignor Fulton Sheen's somewhat florid judgment that Thomas Merton's *Seven Storey Mountain* (1948) was a modern version of the *Confessions*. The superficial parallels are attractive. Both Augustine and Merton wrestled with the intellectual demons of their respective times and both had to put some framework of moral order into their personal lives. Both wrote about their spiritual journey in that most fictive of forms, the spiritual autobiography. After all, as some critics of the genre have maintained, autobiographies are a kind of imaginative reconstruction; that backward glance by which persons seek to find the dynamics to explain how and why they reached a certain point in their lives. Such glances, of course, are a selective filtering out as well as a gathering in of those moments that make up a life. Both Augustine and Merton, finally, would end their spiritual autobiographies just as they begin their lives as public churchmen.

The Augustine/Merton parallels, without exaggerating their exactitudes, do not stop there. Both had somewhat feckless fathers and both grieved the loss of powerful mothers, although Merton had his only as a pained childhood memory, since she died when he was only six. Both found, on reflection, that their intellectual formation was both a shaping and mis-shaping experience even though both found their vocations through books and returned the favor by producing prodigious amounts of writing. Both went to "good schools" and, along with their academic peers, sought a brilliant career through the mastery of language. Augustine saw himself as a public person in the role of rhetor while Merton envisioned a life in the professoriate after the model of his own teacher at Columbia, Mark Van Doren. Both, in the process of their education, were not immune from the fleshly temptations that make up so much of education away from home. For Augustine it was the steamy sinks of Carthage while for Merton it was the refined decadence of Cambridge University in England and the Depression culture of New York City in the 1930s.

When they turned from their original career path they did not abandon their fundamental trust in the power of language to persuade, illumine, and yes, convert. Both would look back on their writings and pass judgment on them, although Merton would be harsher than Augustine since the latter treated himself rather gingerly in the *Retractiones* and Merton, at one point in his life, would be brutal enough to judge some of his early writing as "trash." Finally, both had a strong mystical streak in their makeup, with their mysticism, at times, breaking forth into their writing.

Augustine, after his conversion, led the life of an activist bishop who retreated into periods of contemplative retreat as befitting one who lived in a quasi-monastic community for which he had written a rule. The newly converted Merton, by contrast, chose the contemplative life but found himself inexorably drawn into the world of public affairs, even though for the best part of his mature life he remained within the cloister walls of his rural monastery in Kentucky. Like Augustine, Merton carried on a far-flung correspondence and writing program while remaining rooted in the quotidian rhythms of a daily life organized around the seven offices that constitute the celebration of the monastic liturgy.

One can only speculate what Augustine would have made over the fact that it was his *Confessions* that deeply touched Thomas Merton as he sought religious clarity. The good bishop of Hippo would have undoubtedly raised an eyebrow had he also known that Merton read *The Confessions* in the 1930s while at Columbia University at the suggestion of an odd little Hindu guru with a doctorate from the University of Chicago. Bramachari had suggested the saint's work (as well as the *Imitation of Christ*) when the young student of literature desired to learn something about mysticism after reading Aldous Huxley's *Ends and Means*. The guru wisely understood that one should begin the spiritual quest by knowing one's own tradition first.

Not overly much should be made of these suggested parallels between the lives reflected in *The Confessions* and *The Seven Storey Mountain*. Nor is it clear that Merton consciously modeled his autobiography on that of Augustine, although it is true that hardly any spiritual autobiography in the West has ever escaped its formative power. The closest stylistic parallel between the two works is that they are both cast largely in the form of a prayer — which is at least one of the meanings of the word "confession." The other sense of "confession" is, of

3

course, admission of moral failure. Finally, a "confession" is a profession of faith. This polyvalent sense of the word should not be overlooked.

The literature of Christian conversion is littered with tales of young restless people who change their lives or have their lives changed as a result of the books they read, the crises they encountered, or the profound dissatisfactions they hoped to palliate. Christian conversion stories almost reflexively think back to the *Confessions* since it is the template of the genre. Not every conversion story is a dramatic epiphany experienced on the road to Damascus; but every conversion story, like every good spiritual autobiography, seems like a variation of the *Confessions* (the first of the genre, as Georg Misch has argued in his monumental history of autobiography in the West) in that a person goes back over his or her life to mark the unfolding moments which led up to the time when one is able to utter the words "I believe." In that sense, at least, a life's story seen in retrospect is almost always read as a life under the eye of providence.

The Seven Storey Mountain (1948) was such an account. Merton looked back on his life (he was in his early thirties when it was published) in order to detect the impulses that led him, first to Christian belief, and then, somewhat implausibly, to join the Order of Cistercians of the Strict Observance, known more familiarly as the Trappists, as a monk in the monastery of Our Lady of Gethsemani outside the town of Bardstown, Kentucky. Merton lived as a monk at that monastery for twenty-seven years to the day when, again implausibly, he died of accidental electrocution (or a heart attack triggered by an electrical shock; for complicated legal reasons, his body was never autopsied) at a Red Cross guest house outside of Bangkok, Thailand. His body was returned to the monastery on a U.S. Air Force plane along with the bodies of young American soldiers who had lost their lives in the war in Vietnam — a war which he passionately resisted by his witness and through his pen. *The Seven Storey Mountain* attempts to account for the odd web of circumstances that led from his birth in Europe to a relatively obscure monastery nestled among the hills of Kentucky.

Thomas Merton was born in Prades, France, on January 31, 1915, the son of Owen Merton (1887-1931), an expatriate painter from New Zealand, and Ruth Jenkins Merton (1887-1921), an American of

Quaker background whose family lived on Long Island, New York. A second son, John Paul, was born in 1918 in New York while the family stayed with Ruth's family on Long Island. John Paul was to die in 1943, shot down over the English Channel while serving with the Royal Canadian Air Force. John Paul makes only cameo appearances in *The Seven Storey Mountain*, but those moments are touching in their affection — an affection tinged with a certain guilt at the way the elder brother neglected the younger in their childhood days. John Paul, ready to depart for service with the Royal Canadian Air Force, became a Catholic after brief instruction by one of the monks at Gethsemani. His death, an agonizing ordeal as he floated in the English Channel with a broken back, would find expression in one of Merton's most celebrated short poems, whose final stanza begins with an expression of deep sorrow and rocklike faith: "For in the wreckage of your April Christ lies slain / And Christ weeps in the ruin of my spring. . . ."

Ruth died in 1921 of cancer when Merton was only six. Owen Merton returned to France, after various wanderings in Bermuda and a painting expedition to Algeria. During their Bermuda sojourn Owen Merton had a love affair with the American novelist Evelyn Scott. Extant correspondence from that period proves that the young Tom was devastated by his mother's death. Evelyn Scott described the boy in a letter as "morbid and possessive," making Owen, the father, also "morbid about Tom through various things that happened in connection with Ruth." What those "various things" were is not clear, but one of them surely must have been his mother's decision not to see the boy when she was dying in the hospital, opting instead to send him a letter of farewell. Years later Merton would describe his childhood as one of pain and extreme loneliness. In *The Seven Storey Mountain* there is the poignant description of the six-year-old Tom standing in the shade of a backyard tree at his grandparents' home puzzling out his mother's final letter, leaving him, as he wrote, not with the tears of a child but with "something of the heavy complexity and gloom of adult grief and was, therefore, more of a burden. . . ."

Young Tom, as an adolescent, was sent to live at a French Protestant boarding school, the Lycée Ingres in Montauban. Owen Merton's plans for building and maintaining a home in the village of St. Antonin in France did not work out, and he announced that the family would move to England. This news was greeted with immense

5

relief by the young boy, who was miserably unhappy and as a for-eigner was frequently bullied at his French boarding school, even though one side benefit was an increased facility in speaking French. Tom was promptly enrolled in an English preparatory school and then, in 1929, at Oakham, an English boarding school of a modestly solid reputation. At the time when Merton was a student at Oakham his father had already been diagnosed with an inoperable brain tumor which would kill him in 1931. At sixteen, then, Merton found himself an orphan. Merton recalled his father's death with the same sadness that attended his mother's death. He experienced, as he wrote, a sense of isolation as he realized after receiving a telephone call at school with the news that he was "without a home, without a country, with-out a father, apparently without any friends, without any interior peace or confidence or light or understanding." His only close rela-tives (his maternal grandparents) lived on the other side of the Atlan-tic in Long Island, New York. It would only be in the last decade of his life that Merton would make contact with his paternal relatives in New Zealand.

When Merton was eighteen he finished his studies at Oakham. The school archives still preserve the manuscript of his prize-winning literary essay, and his name appeared with some regularity at the end of articles he wrote for the *Oakhamian*. A further testimony to his con-siderable intelligence was his winning a scholarship by examination for Clare College at the University of Cambridge, where he was to study modern languages. His Cambridge experience was short-lived. His year at Cambridge seems to have been marked by inattention to study and zeal for life in the local pubs. Finally, Merton evidently got a young woman pregnant and, because he was either threatened by a paternity suit or unable to marry the woman (class differences?), his guardian and the administrator of Owen Merton's estate promptly dispatched him back to the United States to live with his maternal grandparents on Long Island. His American exile was a kind of relief, for, apart from reading Dante in depth, he found his Cambridge expe-rience a terrible waste and, morally, a disaster.

The subsequent history of mother and child is unknown. What settlement young Merton's guardian made for them has never come to light. One rumor had both mother and child subsequently dying in the London blitz; but William Shannon, a careful Merton biographer,

6

thinks that this is a "deus ex machina" explanation to erase the memory of these persons from Merton's biography. The only thing we know for sure is that in the will Merton wrote when he became a monk, he left a bequest that his guardian should pay to a person "mentioned in letters" if "that person can be found." Beyond that, we know nothing more about this sad episode in Merton's life or of the subsequent history of either mother or child.

After Merton arrived in New York he enrolled as a sophomore at Columbia University for the January term of 1935, with the intention of studying literature. Given the tenor of the times it does not surprise us that he joined, for a very brief period (in fact, he attended one meeting), the Young Communist League (under the somewhat risible party name of Frank Swift). But he also fed his enthusiasm for jazz, joined a fraternity, worked for both the campus newspaper and the humor magazine, drew mildly risqué cartoons and illustrations, and took a range of courses in languages and literature. His love for hanging out in bars with his friends had evidently not been slaked, despite his unhappy experiences in England. Photographs from the period show him nattily turned out in three-piece suits, acting very much the big man on campus.

If there was an economic depression in those years it did not seem to have any effect on Merton other than his short period of toying with leftist politics. His passion for Marxist politics may have been short-lived, but his interest in writing and literature and the music of the 52nd Street jazz clubs or the clubs in Harlem never waned. Years later, as a monk, he would find time, when in Louisville, to go to the public library and listen to jazz records. In his hermitage he even spent some time playing the bongo drums. He had a weakness, it seems, for the classic jazz of the Thirties as well as an interest in bebop.

When he left the maternal home on Long Island where his grandparents lived (they would both die before Merton entered the monastery) Merton moved, characteristically enough for someone of his bohemian leanings, to Perry Street in Greenwich Village. Through student publications at Columbia University he made some friends who would remain so until his death. These would include Robert Giroux, who would later be his editor and one of his literary executors; Bob Lax, his closest friend, who would go on to be a poet; Ed Rice, later a writer, magazine editor at *Jubilee*, the modish Catholic magazine that was a regular outlet for Merton's writings, and author of one of the first biographical studies of Merton; Ad Reinhardt, who gained future fame as an abstract expressionist painter of the New York School and who would later nurture Merton's interest in art by sending him papers, Chinese calligraphy brushes, and other art supplies. It is also worthy of note that Merton left Columbia University just a few years before the founding members of the Beats — Allen Ginsberg and Jack Kerouac — would matriculate. Their paths would intersect indirectly later through the avant-garde poetry published by Lawrence Ferlinghetti's City Lights Press in San Francisco.

One of the most influential friendships he developed was with Mark Van Doren, a legendary professor of literature as well as a fine poet and critic at Columbia, who made an enormous impact on Merton's intellectual life and would go on to become a lifelong correspondent and sometime visitor to the monastery. It was Van Doren, singled out for elaborate praise in *The Seven Storey Mountain,* who brought the young student into intimate contact with the world of literature, guiding him through the classical tradition and encouraging his interest in writers like Donne, Blake (about whom Merton would later write an MA thesis), and Hopkins, and the modernist canon of Pound, Eliot, Joyce, etc. Van Doren, a meticulous reader of literature, taught his students that literary study was a way of life and, further, that this way of life had moral consequences.

Merton never lost his faith, partially learned from Van Doren, in the capacity of poetry to express moral and religious truth. In the last decade of his life he would turn to experimental poetic forms to express both his own sense of the contemplative life and to connect with the great social issues of the day, but those experiments had behind them the solid education he received at Columbia University. Merton and Van Doren exchanged letters after Merton became a monk, and when traveling, Van Doren would visit the monk in Kentucky. Merton always recorded the fundamental elements of their conversation, but it was always patent that Van Doren still remained the monk's teacher.

The very things Merton studied for his major led him to other areas of study. Years after Merton entered the monastery he wrote an essay reflecting on his university experience. In the essay, he declared that the greatest thing Columbia had done was turn him loose "in its library, its classrooms, and among its distinguished faculty." Merton

8

goes on to say, "I ended by being turned on like a pinball machine by Blake, Thomas Aquinas, Augustine, Meister Eckhart, Coomaraswamy, Traherne, Hopkins, Maritain, and the sacraments of the Catholic Church." Merton left Dante off that list, but it was, in fact, his close reading of *The Divine Comedy* which led to his interest in religious experience and to scholasticism.

One can map with some precision the literary journey that led Merton to find entry into the Catholic Church. A friend encouraged him to read Aldous Huxley's *Ends and Means,* with its argument that there is a spiritual substratum to the material changing world, a substratum that took the form of a *philosophia perennis.* This notion that there was a transcultural structure of transcendent experience hidden under all religious systems made a profound impact on him. The *philosophia perennis* accepted the historical limits of religious traditions but insisted that under all of them was a substratum of religious experience which was mystical, recoverable, and, ultimately, the bedrock of truth itself. Huxley, then, provided Merton with the notion that the religious search was an authentic and deeply human one.

Merton then encountered Etienne Gilson's *The Spirit of Medieval Philosophy,* which revolutionized Merton's thinking about the nature of God. Gilson's explication of the scholastic notion of God's *aseitas* — a scholastic neologism which refers to God as Being itself — stunned him with the force of a revelation. Merton saw this concept of God as putting everything in the cosmos into some kind of meaningful whole. Everything and everyone is contingent upon the Eternal One who is the reason of his own existence.

This intuition about God as self-subsistent being from which flows all other being, discovered in reading Gilson, is movingly described in *The Seven Storey Mountain* as a kind of intellectual and spiritual epiphany. He recounts how he bought Gilson's book at the Scribner bookstore on Fifth Avenue but was initially horrified when he discovered it bore the then customary "imprimatur" indicating that a theological censor found nothing antagonistic to Catholic faith in its pages. Despite that discovery, Merton read the book with care. In a letter to Gilson ten years after Merton entered the monastery, he thanked the French scholar for being, along with the writings but, especially, the friendship of Jacques Maritain and "a few others," the reason he became a Catholic.

9

We have already referred to the Hindu guru, Doctor Bramachari, who insisted that Merton read the literature of his own tradition before tackling the Upanishads and other texts that had so influenced Aldous Huxley. Bramachari was enough of a scholar and disciplined enough in Indian mystical thought to know that a promiscuous and random study of an alien tradition would not bring instant religious enlightenment. He wisely saw that one should begin with one's own inherited tradition. He recommended that the young student read Augustine's *Confessions* and the classic late medieval devotional work of Thomas à Kempis, *The Imitation of Christ.* When Merton got to Calcutta in 1968 he made an attempt to connect with Bramachari, who had an ashram near the city, but he failed to do so. He remembered him with both affection and gratitude as an authentic religious person and as an occasion for his own religious conversion. The brief encounter with Bramachari on the Columbia campus would be the first of many sympathetic contacts he would have with representatives of Eastern wisdom, but he would still be grateful to him, mainly, for the guru's insistence that he learn his own tradition before plunging into the tradition(s) of others.

Merton graduated from Columbia in 1938 and immediately enrolled for MA studies at the university with the intention of writing a thesis on the poetry of William Blake. He submitted his MA thesis in 1939 on the topic "Art and Nature in William Blake," which, characteristically enough, "read" Blake's theory of art through the lens of the aesthetics of Saint Thomas Aquinas as mediated through the writings of Jacques Maritain.

It was also in this year that he began to pray and occasionally hear Mass at the red-doored Catholic Church of Corpus Christi, which was on the northern edge of Columbia's campus around the corner from the Jewish Theological Seminary and across the street from Union Seminary. He was to write later that what most powerfully struck him about going to church was that there always seemed to be people of various kinds there deeply in prayer. In the fall of that year he began to receive instructions from one of the parish priests, Father George Ford. They would meet regularly at the parish for catechetical instruction, and on November 16th he was received into the church.

While it is easy to map his intellectual progress towards the church, it is more difficult to understand his interior life. Nor does Merton himself help much towards that understanding. Almost everything he would later write had an autobiographical edge, but he was, paradoxically, rather reticent about his personal interior life. Born and christened into a nominal Anglican family, he tells us that his first serious religious impulses came during a vacation in Italy, in the summer between finishing his public school education at Oakham and entering Cambridge. In Rome he was terribly moved by the Byzantine mosaics of Christ that he saw in the Roman churches, mosaics like those found in the apses of Santa Prassede, Saints Cosmas and Damien, and in the other Roman basilicas. It was then, he would later write, that he first came to know this person called Christ. It is noteworthy but little remarked on that Merton's first encounter with Christ, through the tradition of Byzantine mosaics, showed Christ as he was understood by the theology of the high christology characteristic of the Byzantine world: Christ as the Word through whom both creation and re-creation occurs. It was a christology that would remain with Merton during his entire adult life. In order to find the biblical sources of his understanding of Christ, one would do well first to examine the prologue of Saint John's Gospel. It was this figure of Christ who is both Word and Wisdom, through whom the world is created and sustained, that gave him a fundamental contemplative principle both for his life of prayer and his conviction about the spiritual unity of humanity. It was this Christ, of course, that stands behind the Byzantine *pantocrater* figure that fundamentally moved Merton. However stirred he was by the image of Christ at that time, though, that mood certainly fell away by the time he matriculated to Cambridge, only to be reawakened in his maturity.

Merton's more explicit attraction to Catholic Christianity developed from a number of different roots. Partially, it was a matter of aesthetics. In poets like the nineteenth-century British Jesuit (and convert) Gerard Manley Hopkins he saw a fusion of deep love for beauty with an intense awareness of the presence of God in the world. Hopkins taught him to see the presence of God and the creative Word which is Christ in the world of nature closely observed. The influence of Hopkins ran deep in Merton; he paid both explicit and implicit tribute to the Jesuit's poetic vision both in his own poetry and in his writings on aesthetics. For Merton, a major part of the conversion process was intellectual.

Furthermore, he encountered Thomism at a time when it was undergoing a vigorous revival thanks to the labors of mainly French scholars like Jacques Maritain and Etienne Gilson. The scholastic emphasis on reason in relationship to faith, its doctrine of natural law, its coherent theory of aesthetics in general and a theory of beauty in particular, and its vigorous resistance to the givens of the Enlightenment were a powerful allure for a whole generation of intellectuals who despaired of meaning and order in a world which, famously, came to be called a waste land. This thomistic synthesis, especially as articulated by sophisticated thinkers like Maritain, provided a holistic framework for understanding faith in relation to culture. This kind of thomistic thinking, to borrow a phrase from Maritain, could construct an "integral humanism." This integral humanism was promoted as a bulwark against the worst excesses of the Enlightenment. Maritain, after all, contrary to the conventional wisdom, did not see Descartes as the beginning of modern philosophy; he saw him as the decay of authentic philosophy.

Finally, Merton had instincts that were instinctively mystical, if one can judge from those writers who most nourished his mind and heart during these days. It is not accidental that he wrote his thesis on the prophetic visionary, William Blake, and intended to do his dissertation on the Jesuit poet Gerard Manley Hopkins. We catch glimpses of that mystical temperament in some of the entries he made at this time in his journals. In 1940, while visiting Cuba shortly after his conversion to Christianity, for example, Merton listened as a group of children in a church cried out the opening words of the creed "Yo creo . . . I believe." At that moment something went off inside of Merton "like a thunderclap," and without any change in his senses: "I knew with the most absolute and unquestionable certainty that before me, between me and the altar, somewhere in the center of the church, up in the air (or any other place because in no place) . . . was at the same time God in all His essence, all His power, God in the flesh and God in himself, and God surrounded by the radiant faces of the thousand million uncountable saints contemplating His glory . . . to say that this was the experience of some kind of certainty is to place it, as it were, in the order of knowledge but at the same time . . . as much an experience of loving as of knowing something and in it knowledge and love are completely inseparable." Lines like those and the many prayer fragments one finds in his journals are clear indications that his religious conversion was not only intellectual and moral but deeply experiential.

With his MA in hand in 1939 and talk of war in the air, Merton, like many of the young, had to decide what to do with his life. Merton thought seriously enough about the priesthood to make application to join the Franciscan Order and was initially accepted to join the next novitiate class. In the interim he taught English at the Franciscan-sponsored Saint Bonaventure's College (now University) in the upstate town of Olean, New York, which was, incidentally, the home town of his closest friend, Bob Lax. That happy coincidence permitted the two (and some of their friends) to spend vacation periods using a cottage in Olean where they would read, write, and enjoy the pleasures of the countryside.

His application to join the Franciscans, at first tentatively accepted, was then rejected after he had a conference with a friar in New York. The news devastated Merton. Did Merton confess about his child in Great Britain? The only clue we have is that in a letter to his abbot in 1942 he says that he and his Franciscan advisor decided that he should not enter the Order because of something that had happened in his past life. Evidently, the Franciscans were cautious about accepting a novice in their order who might well turn out to have parental responsibilities for which the community might have to respond to, since the Franciscans, like all religious communities, vowed their individual members to poverty.

In the summer of 1941 he spent some time as a volunteer at a Catholic settlement known as Friendship House in Harlem, and seriously considered living there permanently as a volunteer serving the needs of the Harlem community as a lay Christian in a life of poverty and service. Friendship House had been founded by an expatriate member of the Russian nobility, the Baroness de Hueck, who, herself a convert to Catholicism, would become a lifelong friend. It was clear that wherever his future rested it would somehow involve his new-found Christian faith. At Saint Bonaventure's University he had begun to read regularly the canonical hours of the breviary, spent time in mental prayer each day, and attended daily Mass. He read seriously in theological literature and, as his now published journals indicate, took copious notes on some of the Latin treatises of the Franciscan Saint Bonaventure and Duns Scotus (both had influenced Gerard Manley

Hopkins) as well as, prophetically, a treatise on the love of God *(De Diligendo Deo)* written by the Cistercian saint, Bernard of Clairvaux.

What finally focused Merton's vocational choice, however, was a Holy Week retreat he made at the Abbey of Gethsemani in Kentucky in the spring of 1941. He got the idea for making this retreat from a teacher of scholastic philosophy, Dan Walsh, who taught part time at Columbia. It was Walsh who guided his study of medieval philosophy, which Merton undertook as part of his general education in literature. Years later, Walsh would move to Kentucky and be ordained a diocesan priest. He is buried in the "secular" cemetery on the abbey grounds. What the young convert saw at the monastery captured his imagination. "This," he wrote melodramatically in his journal, "is the center of America. . . . This is the only real city in America — in a desert."

Years later Merton would chide himself for such baroque spiritual posturing, but at the age of twenty-six, tortured by his own guilt, passionate in his newly found faith, prompted by the zeal of the convert, and convinced that the Cistercian round of silence, work, penance, and prayer would center what he saw as his tattered life, he seriously entertained the thought of joining the community of monks permanently. With war looming on the horizon he did not have the luxury of leisurely meditations about his future. The draft was a real possibility; a possibility that deeply disturbed a young man whose inclinations were pacifist.

Over the summer and fall, events moved quickly. He was declared eligible for the draft after a first round deferment because of some minor health issues. He found encouragement from the Cistercians in his correspondence with them when he wrote about another visit. In their answers back they said that they would take him as a postulant when he came to make his Christmas retreat at their guest house. He decided that a life as a volunteer in Harlem, strongly urged by the Baroness, was not for him even though the experiences there touched him deeply. Years after the summer Merton spent in Harlem, the late Eldridge Cleaver in his own autobiographical memoir *Soul on Ice* remarked that no white person ever wrote as deeply about Harlem as Merton did in *The Seven Storey Mountain.* By that fall Merton destroyed or gave to friends his unpublished novels, distributed his books and possessions to his friends, bid farewell to his brother John

Paul who had dropped out of Cornell University to join the Canadian Air Force, and in early December he took the train for Kentucky.

In 1969 one novel written in the period before he entered monastic life would be published under the title *My Argument with the Gestapo* while two novel fragments are also known; they bear the titles: *The Labyrinth* and *The Man in the Sycamore Tree*. Merton's friend Ed Rice would borrow that latter title as the one he used when he wrote a biographical memoir of his deceased friend.

Merton entered the guest house of Gethsemani as a guest postulant on December 10, 1941, three days after the bombing of Pearl Harbor, and twenty-seven years to the day of his death in Thailand. This writer remembers vividly seeing the news of Merton's death in the papers on the same day that there was an announcement of the death of a theologian Merton admired mightily, Karl Barth. Merton passed from the guest house into the cloister as a postulant on December 13th — the feast of the martyr, Saint Lucy. Merton, always sensitive to symbolism, saw the celebration of that feast as a sign; Lucy's name meant "light" and, according to the legend attached to her name, gave her earthly sight in martyrdom for the sight of God. That her feast day coincided with the December gloom of winter would lead Merton later to praise her in a poem in which he petitions: "Show us some light, who seem forsaken by the sky: / We who have so dwelt in darkness that our eyes are screened and dim / and all but blinded by the weakest ray . . ." ("An Invocation to Saint Lucy"). The point, of course, is that it was on her feast and through her intercession that Merton, in fact, always felt that he received his sight.

What I have described in these few hurried pages makes up the bulk of Merton's spiritual autobiography, *The Seven Storey Mountain*. He ends his book as he enters the life of Gethsemani. Like Augustine, who finished the autobiographical part of the *Confessions* as he was ready to leave Rome's port of Ostia for the great adventure of his Christian life in North Africa, Merton ends with what would prove to be almost exactly the first half of his life. He spent roughly twenty-six years "in the world" while he would spend the next twenty-seven in the monastery. The epilogue to *The Seven Storey Mountain* sketches very briefly Merton's first years in the monastery, but it ends rather abruptly with the Latin epigram *sit finis libri, non finis quaerendi* — "here the book ends but not the search."

15

The standard biographies of Merton treat these early years in some detail while probing the nuances of those early experiences, searching for keys to explain his later life and spirituality. What was the impact of the loss of his mother at the age of six? What scars did he suffer as a lonely child in an austere French Protestant boarding school abandoned by a frequently absent father who himself would die during Merton's adolescence? What did it mean to be completely orphaned as an adolescent? What significance rests on his lack of a stable home either in terms of culture or domesticity? Did his somewhat rootless upbringing add to his desire for monastic stability? How did his misadventures in Cambridge affect him in his later life? Was his desire to enter a penitential order connected to those events? What were the precise characteristics of those deep spiritual experiences that he had in Rome and in Cuba? Did his near hysterical collapse when the Franciscans rejected his application provide a symptom of the inner guilt he felt? Does his rootlessness as a young person shape his personality and contribute to the restlessness he often experienced in the monastery? Who was this expatriate whose life was shaped by France, England, and the United States? Did a partially Quaker background from his mother's side of the family lead him to value social justice and the stance of pacifism? Did his interest in Gandhi — about whom he wrote, as a teenager, an admiring essay, and who visited England when Merton was a schoolboy at Oakham — add impetus to his instinctive pacifism? Was his conversion part of the pattern of many converts of the period, who sought in the seeming stability of the Catholic Church a bulwark against the chaos of a world racked by economic depression and political instability? Did Merton seek a God in place of the god(s) that had failed?

These are all questions that have been debated, analyzed, and written about at great length elsewhere. Excessive preoccupation with one or other of these elements seems to result in the worst kind of psychological reductionism. Although this writer has felt no need to rehearse these issues in any detail, when such circumstances might shed light on a specific issue later in life they will be brought to the fore. My intention is to begin my study of Merton where his major autobiography ends off, i.e., with his entrance into, and full embrace of, the monastic life. My story begins there because of a deep personal conviction, stated in more than one place, that if one does not understand Merton as a monk, one does not understand Merton at all.

This approach may seem somewhat narrow at first glance, but monasticism in general and the culture of monasticism in particular is a complex phenomenon in Catholic Christianity — a phenomenon that has been mediated to the larger Christian (and non-Christian!) world in our time most effectively by Merton himself. My desire, in short, is to show that the prolific works which flowed from Merton's pen and the impact that those writings and his person had and continue to have can only be understood against the background of his contemplative experience as a Trappist monk. Indeed, if this book can be said to have a thesis, it is that one simply cannot understand Thomas Merton if one does not understand him as a monk.

Getting to that monastic reality means that one must cut through the clichés and stereotypes of monastic life (hoods, cloisters, silence, chant, and all the other epiphenomena emphasized in popular culture) to reflect more deeply on the reality of monasticism. Monasticism is a living tradition, not a museum of past observance. Here we might recall the wittily wise words of a contemporary European Cistercian, Dom Andre Louf:

> What is a monk?
> A monk is someone who every day asks:
> "What is a monk?"

Louf's question is the leitmotif that will run through these pages for the very simple reason that no monk but Merton ever asked that question so persistently, a question that involved not only his own sense of identity but his identity in relationship to the larger world about him. As his understanding of how to respond to the question "what is a monk?" changed, so did the direction of his writing, the interests he took up, and the styles he pursued. This is not to say, as some have alleged, that there were abrupt and definitive transitions in his life. Reading the whole corpus of his now published journals or working through a volume of his letters in chronological fashion reveals a person who deeply imbibed monastic ideas, refined them through experience, and saw their application in a changing society. Merton began to study the classical monastic sources as a novice in 1941 and he was still reading them in the year of his death in 1968. The question of his identity as a monk, the monastic formation he received, and the works that he wrote exist in a symbiotic relationship. It is sketching out and following the development and the nature of that relationship which provides whatever unity this present study may possess.

Many books, dissertations, and essays have been written about Thomas Merton. My only consolation in adding to the already mountainous literature is the one offered by Saint Augustine as he began the *De Trinitate*. Many books on the same subject, Augustine wrote, may help in illuminating an aspect of a subject hitherto studied. My intention is to focus on Merton as a monk not in the abstract but against the cultural background of the American experience, and in the midst of the vast upheavals of the Roman Catholic Church.

One of the reasons why Merton is such an intriguing figure is that he lived and wrote while participating in the life and culture of one of the most ancient and traditional institutions of the West: Roman Catholic monasticism. What strikes me as most pertinent about Merton's life is that he was like the good householder Jesus described in the gospel: one who was able to bring forth both old things and new. There is a delicious paradox operating here: a person becomes deeply involved in the cultural struggles of his day while having made a conscious decision to flee from the life of that culture. The paradox becomes less stern when it is recalled that fleeing from culture is in itself a kind of judgment on the culture, as figures as diverse as Socrates and Henry David Thoreau have shown.

This work will follow the trajectory of Merton's life from his entrance into the monastery until his death twenty-seven years later. No attempt will be made to follow every event in his crowded life; such information is easily attainable in either the published biographies or by a careful reading of the now published private journals. My intention is far more modest: to see the development of his life against the background of his monastic education and the events of the times as they impinged on that education. To say it another way: my intention is to scrutinize the "signs of the times" through the lens of Merton the contemplative monk. Readers who wish to find more detailed biographical information can consult the bibliographical essay that serves as the final chapter of this book.

1 The Making of a Monk

A saeculi actibus se facere alienum
[To make oneself a stranger to the world's business]

The Rule of Benedict

ALMOST EVERYONE WHO SPEAKS OR WRITES OF THE AB-
bey of Gethsemani, located just south of Bardstown, Kentucky,
where Thomas Merton became a monk in 1941, describes the life there
as "medieval." Looking at photographs of the monks and their milieu
at that time would lend credence to this description. The monks, in
their hooded robes and heads shaved with a monastic crown, worked
the fields, cut wood to heat their house, used great draft horses for
their farm work, spent long hours in the monastic choir with great
Psalters set out in front of them, maintained a rule of silence, ate
sparsely of a vegetarian diet, kept a daily schedule that began long before dawn, and finished as the sun went down, the monks going off to
bed on straw pallets in small cubicles in a large dormitory. They baked
their own bread, cobbled their own heavy work boots, made cheese,
raised livestock even though they did not eat meat, and grew their

food as if modern shops did not exist. The monks wore rough monastic habits complete with a sort of ancient undergarment and rough leggings in lieu of socks. Their clothing was made in the tailor shop of the monastery. They earned a good deal of their income from agriculture, as they had for centuries, relying on great Percheron horses for most of their work. The monastery was heated (to the degree that it was heated at all) by wood that they culled from their own forests. Most of these customs, in fact, were done in imitation of their Cistercian ancestors of the twelfth century.

Nonetheless, to describe that life as "medieval" fails to appreciate the many layers of custom, tradition, and what the monks called "usages" that, like the strata of an archaeological dig, were both much more recent and much more ancient. The genealogy of the monastic life of Gethsemani in 1941 could be described, in brief, as the tail end of a long, involved series of historical moments. Gethsemani itself had been founded in 1848, but behind that relatively new foundation was a much longer history. The life of the Cistercians of the Strict Observance derived from a reform of Cistercian life initiated in the seventeenth century by Armand-Jean Bouthillier de Rancé (died 1700), who began this reform at the decadent French monastery at La Trappe (hence the name Trappist). De Rance's reform, in turn, was a purification of a late twelfth-century reform of Benedictine life begun in France in 1098 at the Burgundian abbey of Citeaux and carried forward by Saint Bernard of Clairvaux and his companions. Benedictine monasticism, in turn, derived from a Rule of Life penned by a sixth-century Italian monk, Benedict of Nursia, who, as he tells us in the Rule, derived his theory of monasticism from the writings of earlier monastic writers like the Cappodocian writer, Basil the Great, and John Cassian. Cassian, in turn, mediated to the West the wisdom of the great desert monks of Palestine and Egypt with whom he had been in contact during visits there in the fourth century. Benedict's Rule also utilized much of an earlier Rule by an unknown writer (called simply the Rule of the Master), which Benedict modified. In the Carolingian period the Rule of Benedict was adopted (and loosely adapted) by most monasteries in the Frankish Kingdom, even though Celtic monasticism still thrived in Ireland and in those monasteries founded by the Irish monks. Monasteries in the Byzantine empire, of course, had an independent evolution rooted in the Rule of the fourth-century Cappadocian theologian, Basil the Great.

At the beginning of the twentieth century Adolf von Harnack named monasticism as one of the institutions that marked the end of primitive Christianity and the rise of "catholicism" — in von Harnack's mind, a deformation from the spirit of the gospel. More recent research, of course, has a far more benign view of monastic origins, with some tracing it to ancient institutions like the place of widows in the New Testament church of the pastoral epistles, even though the precise character of these earliest ascetic communities is hard to describe in detail. The one thing that is clear, however, is that those impulses and communities which would be called in time "monastic" had long and deeply rooted life in the Christian tradition.

To put the matter plainly, Merton entered a community whose tradition went back at least a millennium and a half in the West but whose more recent usages dated to the seventeenth century, with some modification made in subsequent years. The Abbey of Gethsemani itself had been founded in 1848 by French monks uprooted by the constant turmoil in France in the wake of both the Revolution and the Napoleonic era. When they settled in Nelson County (Kentucky) they found there an old Catholic community that had settled there before the revolutionary war as an expansion of Lord Calvert's Maryland settlement.

The abbot of the monastery when Merton first came to Gethsemani, Dom Frederic Dunne, was the first native-born American to become (in 1893) a choir monk at the monastery. Gethsemani itself, now over 150 years old, became the source for other monastic communities founded in Latin America and in Georgia, Utah, South Carolina, New York, and California. Monastic foundations grow by a kind of spiritual cell division. A vigorous monastery will make a foundation, and when that foundation is stable it will become an independent abbey, maintaining its links to the mother monastery by visitations from the founding house. Merton was among many who entered Gethsemani in the 1940s — so many, in fact, that foundations had to be made (in Georgia, Utah, and South Carolina) during the same decade to allow for breathing space in the monastery.

The daily life of the monastery as Merton first experienced it followed an ancient pattern. The monks began their first service of

Matins at 2:00 in the morning, breaking some hours later for a quiet interval and a time for the priests to say Mass. Services then punctuated the rest of the day: Lauds at dawn; Prime at the first hour; Tierce at the third; Sext at the sixth; None at the ninth. Vespers were celebrated in the late afternoon and Compline just before retiring. Within that liturgical framework of public prayer, whose outlines were set forth by Benedict in his Rule, the monks attended a community Mass in the morning and had long periods of time for work or study both in the morning and afternoon. They ate one main meal with small collations of food in the morning and evening. Their schedule varied a bit according to the season, with a rest period in the summer during the heat of the day and a later rising during winter. Feast days would mean more time in church, and except for Lent and Holy Week, a bit more food in the refectory. Monastic fasts were more or less severe depending on the time of the year.

The life in a Trappist monastery was self-consciously rigorous and penitential. The diet was vegetarian, with meat provided only for the elderly or the sick. Dom Frederic was a Trappist formed in the old style. It was said of Dom Frederic, half humorously, that he had two basic rules for the community: "Do what you are told" and "Do what you are told." When he became abbot, among his first acts was to abolish the Easter morning "treat" of two fried eggs as needlessly extravagant!

The monastic community itself was divided into choir monks, who were also destined for priestly ordination, and lay brothers (this second rank of monks was actually a Cistercian innovation developed in the twelfth century), who were not obliged to be in the liturgical choir, did not aspire to ordination, and did most of the manual and craft labor in the monastery. When Merton entered the monastery these two groups led quite separate lives, with their own novitiates, places in church, dining and sleeping areas, etc. The choir monks wore white habits with a belt and a black scapular. The lay brothers, unlike the choir monks, were bearded and wore rough brown habits. In place of the monastic liturgical hours, the brothers had simplified offices of recited prayers. The entire community, however, lived an enclosed life. The priests had no pastoral duties outside the monastery itself. Their self-contained community was a place for prayer, solitude, and penance.

It is important to note that over this basic monastic style of life there had been encrusted, with the passing centuries, an overlay of devotions and observances, exercises of piety that accrued to the monk's life either in the medieval period or as a result of the new forms of spirituality that arose especially in the post-Tridentine period of baroque Catholicism. At Gethsemani this devotional life had, naturally enough, a strong French tone to it. The monastic year was punctuated by post-Reformation devotions like Days of Recollection, Forty Hour Devotions, annual retreats (a custom assumed from the Jesuits who made retreats popular), dedication of various months to Mary (May and October), private and communal recitation of the rosary, following the stations of the cross, eucharistic adoration, benediction of the Blessed Sacrament, and other devotional practices which had accumulated in the life of Catholic piety over the centuries but which became characteristic of Catholicism after the period of the Protestant Reformation. To the standard liturgical offices were superimposed shorter offices (developed in the medieval monasteries) for the dead and in honor of the Blessed Virgin Mary. The monastery church itself, until later renovations took place, was clearly demarcated between the choir for the monks, an area for the lay brothers, and a tribune for lay congregants and guests. The monastic enclosure was vigorously maintained with signs warning non-monks not to enter the enclosure (for female intruders there was a threat of excommunication).

Furthermore, monastic life was highly clericalized. It was expected that each choir monk would go on for priestly ordination unless he chose to leave the choir in order to be part of the separate status of lay brother. Historically, monastic and priestly vocations were quite separate well into the early medieval period. Saint Benedict did not wish many priests in his monastery and was himself a lay person. Among the fourth-century desert monks there was a saying, recorded in Cassian's *Institutes*, that a monk should avoid women and bishops; the former might lure one from the monastery while the latter might attempt to ordain one to the priesthood. It was only with the slow evolution of sacramental practice and a changing concept of the Mass in the church that priestly ordination became expected of monks, so that by the Middle Ages priestly ordination became the norm rather than the exception for monks.

One of the reforms of contemporary monasticism is to clearly in-

sist that the monastic vocation does not necessarily mean a priestly vocation. A monk may go on to the priesthood only if he feels a call to do
so. In actual fact the nonordained members of the monastic community at Gethsemani today outnumber those who are ordained by a ratio of two to one. The net result of all of these historical accretions was
that the monastic life was very full and the daily schedule crowded,
engaging the choir monks in nearly seven hours of liturgical prayer in
addition to the recitation of the rosary, the celebration of Mass, and
cloister processions — in addition to study and work. One of the constant complaints that Merton had of Cistercian life as he first experienced it, criticisms begun very early in his monastic career, was the
lack of time given to silence, contemplative prayer, and periods for the
ancient practice of monastic *lectio* — the prayerful reading of sacred
scripture. He found the life of Gethsemani very regimented in those
early days, with ever shortened "intervals" so designed to keep the
community busy. The old austere Trappist superiors always felt that
the worst situation for a monk was one of idleness. When Merton once
asked his first abbot the secret of the holiness of a recently deceased
lay brother, he expected a pious homily; but the answer was characteristic and brief: "Brother always kept busy." Traditional monastic literature encouraged "sacred leisure" *(sacrum otium)*, but, it seems, the
old-fashioned Trappist superiors distrusted leisure, sacred or otherwise.

It is important to keep this full daily schedule in mind in order to
appreciate how much personal discipline Merton possessed to produce such an enormous body of published work in the short amount
of daily time available to him. Until he retreated to the hermitage in
the 1960s, he had at best three hours a day for his personal work. He
himself would say in his journal that he had only two hours to write if
he kept to his desire for another two hours of private prayer, reading,
and meditation. Often that latter period spilled over into his writing,
at least in the journals which would later become material for his published work. Those hours were interspersed within the normal monastic day during which, after he was a fully professed monk, he was
obliged to contribute his fair share of labor in addition to his teaching
duties.

To become a monk was not simply to join an organization. It was
to be initiated into a style of life and a culture that was commonly

called "life under a rule" *(vita regularis)*. Like all aspirants, Merton spent some time as an observer until he was admitted to the novitiate under a master who would instruct him in monastic thought, the rule of life, the cycle of prayer, and the more general culture of monasticism. When entering the monastery, the monk was given a new name as a sign that he had left the world for a new life. In Merton's case it was Louis, even though around the monastery he was later more familiarly known as "Louie" or "Uncle Louie" or, among the young or the fastidious, "Father Louis." To his lay friends he was simply "Tom."

If, after that two-year novitiate of testing, the community voted favorably, the novice was permitted to take temporary vows (for three years) of poverty, chastity, obedience, stability (i.e., a promise to live in the monastery as a member of the community), and "conversion of manners" — which is to say, a sincere attempt to be continually turned to a life of Christian perfection. Trappists did not take vows of silence as so often is alleged, even though they tried to keep silence in the monastery by a system of sign language. For monks destined to the choir, theological studies were undertaken which would lead to ordination to the priesthood after the taking of solemn vows. This theological training, almost without exception, took place in the monastery; Trappists did not maintain separate seminaries. A few monks might be sent to Rome or elsewhere for special studies required for monastic life, but in general, priestly formation took place in the house, almost always in very small classes that were like tutorials, the candidates working through the courses in theology, scripture, canon law, et cetera, stipulated by canon law as the curriculum for priest-candidates.

In those early years as a monk, Merton, with the encouragement of his abbot, published four volumes of poetry: *Thirty Poems* (1944); *A Man in the Divided Sea* (1946); *Figures for an Apocalypse* (1948); and *Tears of the Blind Lion* (1949). For all of his old-fashioned austerity, Dom Frederic knew that Merton was a person of talent, and despite his own early penchant for monastic denial, he encouraged the young monk to use his gifts to the full.

Leafing through those early poems, with all four volumes now assembled in the posthumous *Collected Poems* (1977), one sees both the influence of his years of literary study in the poetry's formal rhyme schemes, the attempts at metaphysical wit, and the echoes of Hopkins

and Blake as well as the pleasure that Merton took in his monastic milieu. The poems are filled with paeans of praise for the life of prayer;
the joy of being separated from the world; the satisfaction with the
clean aesthetic of Cistercian simplicity; and the conviction that the
monastery had provided him with a true home — a home of grace, purity, and protection from the pollution of the decadent world in which
he once lived. Nowhere was this theme of *fuga mundi* — the monastic
doctrine of "flight from the world" — more baldly stated than in his
poem "A Letter to My Friends" (written in the monastery's guest
house soon after he arrived at the monastery) with the subtitle "On Entering the Monastery of Our Lady of Gethsemani, 1941." In part it
reads:

> More than we fear, we love the holy desert,
> Where separate strangers, hid in their disguises,
> Here come to meet, by night, the quiet Christ.
>
> We who have some time wandered in those crowded ruins,
> (Farewell, you woebegone, sad towns)
> We who have wandered like (the ones I hear) the moaning trains,
> (Begone, sad towns!)
> We'll live it over for you here.

If we were to inquire into the reasons why Merton entered the
monastic life and what compelled his fidelity to that decision after he
entered, the evidence from his journals, poetry, and the volume *Seven
Storey Mountain* would suggest three motives.

First, Merton very much desired a life spent as far away from and
in contrast to the life he had lived before entering the monastery. In the
traditional parlance of Catholic spirituality, he wanted to "give up" the
world for the sake of God. His writings well into the 1950s are full of
his disgust with contemporary secular culture. Like T. S. Eliot, he saw
the modern world as corrupt and deracinated, and clearly, his own
past disordered life was evidence of what the corrosive acids of modernity (to borrow a phrase from the late Walter Lippmann) can do to
a person. In fact, this sense of disgust with the world was an attitude
with which Merton himself would have to wrestle when he looked
back on his early monastic years. The monastery would give wide

scope for such feelings; monks not only fled the world, but their asceticism encouraged them to shun the world — *contemptus mundi*. In a sense, this contempt for the world in Merton's case was also contempt for as well as a judgment upon his own earlier life.

Second, Merton desired to live a life of penance for his own sins and as a necessary condition for a fuller life of contemplative prayer. It was not a rhetorical flourish for Merton to call his spiritual autobiography *The Seven Storey Mountain*. The clear allusion, after all, was to Dante's ascent of the purgatorial mount as the seven deadly sins, beginning with pride, were burned away in anticipation of arrival at the Garden of Eden. Merton wrote that he took his first step up that purgatorial mountain at the time of his baptism.

Monastic literature often described the monastery as an Edenic garden (the *hortus claustralis* — the cloister garden) where monks waited to be called back to God. Dante, in turn, borrowed the imagery of that ascent from monastic literature. The category of "deadly sin" itself came from the writings of the fourth-century monastic writers Evagrius of Pontus and Cassian, via Gregory the Great to Dante. One had to erase those sins before one could enter into the contemplative life. The entire idea of the spiritual ascent, indeed, had its own antecedents in the ascetical literature of antiquity from Gregory of Nyssa's *Life of Moses* to John Climacus's *The Ladder of Monks*. Merton, a close reader of Dante as far back as his adolescent days, would have naturally gravitated to this great poem of purification and union with God, a work he had studied in Italian in his university days. It is also worthwhile noting again that the monastery in medieval literature was often compared to an earthly paradise — the so-called *paradisus claustralis* — even though, faithful to Dante's understanding, this paradise was only a preparation for the ascent to the heavens.

Monastic enclosure and monastic observance were not ends in themselves. They were considered a necessary condition for, and a matrix out of which would come, contemplative union with God. The contemplative life as a life spent for God was the final and most important reason why Merton became a monk. He desired to live a life of prayer and praise. Visitors to Gethsemani today will see carved over the entrance gate to the monastery cloister the declaration "God Alone" — this is not a pious slogan but a capsule statement of what monastic life was all about. In the theological milieu in which Merton lived, it was taken as a given that this pursuit of the contemplative life was the more perfect way to live as a Christian. Christian writers going back to the third-century exegete Origen of Alexandria loved to point to the story of Martha and Mary in the gospel by identifying themselves as contemplatives in line with Mary, who sat at the feet of the Lord, as opposed to the "activist" Martha, who was, as Jesus said, "busy about many things."

It would be one of the great contributions of Thomas Merton to Catholic life that he would help in time to overcome the sharp dichotomy between action and contemplation, between separation from the world and love for the world. It would be his further gift to the believing world to argue that contemplative prayer was not an occupation for the spiritually elite but available to all persons of faith. Those contributions were for the future. In the 1940s Merton not only worried in print about whether he should give up writing poetry, as poetry could only lead to "natural" contemplation; he also agonized over the issue of whether he should leave the Cistercians for the more austere and largely eremitical Carthusians, who led a life of solitude and total withdrawal from the world. Merton's desire for solitude and some respite from the unremittingly communal life of the Cistercians would be a theme in his writings until the day he died.

His novitiate year finished and his temporary vows taken, Merton began his theological studies for the priesthood. Since the monks did not get sent out to seminaries, or, as in many religious orders, get provided with a separate house of formation, his studies consisted largely of tutoring under a priest in the monastery in the scholastic treatises of dogmatic and moral theology, as well as an introduction to a smattering of canon law and the other courses needed by a priest. Merton spends little time discussing this course of study as part of his formation, but it seems to have been rather routine and perfunctory. This education consisted basically of a priest appointed as professor who would lead students through the approved scholastic manuals of the time. Merton would later lament his ignorance of moral theology while attempting to remedy it by fitful attempts at independent study. Moral theology, after all, in Merton's day, was designed to help future priests become better confessors, and in time he would be a confessor like every other priest in the house. In his correspondence Merton would always show a certain diffidence when queried about private moral issues, since his training in moral theology had been so narrowly focused in the monastery.

Even before he was ordained to the priesthood (on Ascension Thursday in 1949) Merton noticed how odd it was that monks, in their early formation, were educated for the priesthood and not for the monastic life. In a memorandum written in 1948 to the new abbot Dom James Fox, who succeeded the late Dom Frederic, he proposed a curriculum of study that would focus on the tradition of monastic thought and theology rather than, or alongside, the standard fare served up for candidates for the priesthood. He wanted young monks to read the early monastic authors, the great Cistercian writers of the Middle Ages, as well as those writers (like Anselm of Canterbury) who came out of a monastic milieu. It did not occur to him then that one could be a choir monk without going on for ordination, so the problem his program could not overcome was how to integrate his ideal program of studies along with the requirements of study, stipulated by canon law, for the priesthood.

Today, and this in no small part because of Merton and monks of a similar persuasion, those who enter the monastery do so with the clear idea that they are to become monks, and only when necessity or calling occurs do these monks go on for ordination to the priesthood. What had been a difficult problem has now been solved by a clearer understanding that a call to the ordained priesthood may come for some only as something beyond their vocation to be a monk. One other benefit of making this distinction is that the present constitutions of the Cistercians were written for both men and women monastics; with the few exceptions of regulations for priests, the monastic life is the same for women and men.

In addition to his round of studies and his other works, Merton was encouraged to write by his abbot even though Merton himself had been tempted to give up writing as part of his new vocation. This form of work was not seen as incompatible with his monastic vocation. The Cistercians had a noble history of great writers. It was Etienne Gilson who wrote of the first generation of Cistercians that those twelfth-century monks, many superb Latin stylists, gave up everything for God except the art of writing well. The Abbey of Gethsemani already had in its community a popular writer in the former Jesuit, Father Raymond Flanagan, who in his lifetime at Gethsemani would pen over twenty books, many of them best sellers in Catholic circles. The Irish Trappist, Dom Eugene Boylan, an older contemporary of Thomas Merton, was a well regarded writer on spiritual topics and was widely read on both sides of the Atlantic.

Within the Order itself, there was a recognized need for scholars who would work on the monastic heritage as well as the need for experts on the liturgy, history, and spirituality of the Order. Merton was already in contact with those European monastic scholars in the 1940s because of his own interest in monastic theology and spirituality, and because of his considerable linguistic gifts. He spoke Italian, French, and Spanish; he was a superb Latinist; and he had a smattering of Greek and some German. In his later years, he also studied Portuguese with one of the monks in his community who was from Brazil. He promised himself that he would learn Russian and he even made some desultory stabs at Chinese, although this latter study never went beyond some facility in penning ideograms.

In the early period of his monastic life Merton wrote or translated a number of monastic brochures and books along with writing a rather pious biography of a French Trappistine nun in Japan under the title of *Exile Ends in Glory* (1948) and another biography on the life of the medieval nun, Saint Lutgarde, under the title *What Are These Wounds?* In 1967, when Merton made a "fever chart" of his writing, he would place these works with a great downward spike towards his worst books; subsequent critics have had no reason to challenge that judgment. He also worked on a huge compilation of lives of the Cistercian saints, which never saw the light of day except as a mimeographed manuscript that circulated in some of the monasteries in this country. All these labors were done in obedience to the judgment of his superiors that he should write to help people to be better Christians and "to pray better." Some of these works done in the 1940s (like his translation of Dom Chautard's highly popular *The Soul of the Apostolate*) were done anonymously.

Even before his ordination to the priesthood, Merton was entrusted with scholarly work by his abbot, Dom Frederic, who encouraged the young monk to study the monastic fathers. Merton spent many hours reading Saint Bernard and the other early Cistercians. His 1947 volume *The Spirit of Simplicity* (a translation and commentary on a Cistercian volume published by the general chapter of the Order in 1946) betrays careful study of the writings of Saint Bernard of Clairvaux. As Basil Pennington has pointed out in a number of addresses, reading Bernard in the 1940s was no easy task. The critical edition of the saint's writings was not yet available, and Merton was obliged to plow through the forbidding double columns of Migne's *Patrologia Latina* to study the saint's works. This early grounding in the classical texts of Cistercian monasticism would serve him in good stead in his future work. His habit of reading such works would remain with him for the rest of his life.

In 1948, a year before his ordination to the priesthood, Merton found out that the manuscript of *The Seven Storey Mountain*, which he had sent off in 1946 to his friend (who would become his long-time editor and literary agent) Naomi Burton (Stone), who in turn had sent it to Merton's old Columbia classmate Robert Giroux, would be published. This news came after two years of wrangles with the Cistercian censors and his own rewriting. Giroux would later relate that when he suggested publishing the work to the publisher he was asked if it "would lose money." When told that it would probably not lose money but it might not make much, Mr. Brace (of Harcourt, Brace) gave Giroux permission to see it through to publication but declined an invitation to read the manuscript himself. Merton received his first copy of the book in July, 1948, in anticipation of a fall publishing date.

The Seven Storey Mountain began its life as a book without much fanfare. It received very few reviews (but when the reviews came they were uniformly enthusiastic) but it had a vigorous word of mouth reception. By the time of his ordination in May, 1949, it had sold 100,000 copies and by the end of the year it had become a publishing phenomenon. Giroux remembers an order for 10,000 copies from bookstores for one day during the Christmas season. It continued as a best seller with a total run of 600,000, and in time, translations in all of the major languages of the world. By the time Merton was ordained to the priesthood he was a best-selling author, even though this fact was little known by the members of his own community.

It is worth pausing for a second to note how curious it is that Merton's book should have achieved such popularity. As I have noted elsewhere, popular religious books were often best sellers in the immediate post–World War II period. People sought meaning in a world weary of war and frightened by Cold War threats of renewed hostilities. But the messages of these books could not have been more distant than those found in the autobiography of this thirty-three-year-old monk.

To make my point let me simply cite three extraordinarily popular works written in the first decade of the postwar period, each, conveniently enough, by authors who were, respectively, Jewish, Catholic, and Protestant: Rabbi Joshua Liebman's *Peace of Mind;* Monsignor Fulton Sheen's *Peace of Soul;* and Norman Vincent Peale's *The Power of Positive Thinking.* Furthermore, American Catholic life was in a vigorous "bricks and mortar" period of expansion, with little serious interest in the retiring life of monks despite the fact that veterans were flocking to the monasteries. The *beau ideal* of American Catholicism was Bing Crosby's Father O'Malley, or the pixie of an old Irish priest played by Barry Fitzgerald in the popular film "Going My Way," or the silver-haired orator Monsignor Fulton Sheen, who would make his name as a television star after a successful career as a professor of philosophy at the Catholic University of America and a stint as a very popular "radio priest."

Each of those best-selling books (Peale's was more than a best seller; it was a publishing phenomenon) had at least one thing in common — a characteristic noted half a century ago by the writer Will Herberg. They were all upbeat, affirmative, typically American in their optimism, and, as even their titles indicate, oriented towards the therapeutic. These books reflected the needs of a generation that had gone through the world war and were now entering into what *Time* magazine's Henry Luce had called "the American century." Indeed, Sheen's book was most likely written as an answer to *Peace of Mind;* Sheen's antipathy to psychoanalysis was well known but his spirituality was, nonetheless, upbeat and sunny. What Sheen made of Peale's Pelagian effusions is not known.

Merton's book, by contrast, offered a quite different form of therapy to his readership. He preached withdrawal from the world, penance, silence, the life of prayer, the silent ascent to God, and a sternly prophetic NO to modern culture. The one thing that it did not propose was the ideal of the successful and happy life. That this rather uncompromising message struck a chord is patent. Although it would be an exaggeration to say that his book triggered an explosion of interest in the monastic life (many veterans had already sought out the monastery in the waning years of the war) it certainly did contribute to a fascination with the life of the spirit and further opened the floodgates of those seeking life in monasteries. It is the rare literate Catholic of a certain age who cannot remember when he or she read *The Seven Storey Mountain;* many a priest or nun will affirm that Merton's book had a strong influence on their own religious vocation. I myself remember quite clearly reading it as a high school student in the 1950s, and the enormous impact it had on my life.

The Seven Storey Mountain was a book of pilgrimage and conversion. Such works, as the critic Anthony Padovano has noted, had a long and noble history in America. It was a rare home in the nineteenth century that did not own a copy of the book that practically defined the genre: Bunyan's *Pilgrim's Progress.* Christian readers enjoyed a certain *frisson* in reading about the life of a person who turned from sin and evil to a life of graced conversion. The converted sinner (the worse the sin, the better) was a staple of the evangelical tent meeting, and the theme was equally popular in the penny press of Catholicism. Evangelicals loved converted drunks; Catholics were enamored of converted communists. Catholic popular piety produced copious amounts of such literature, including the work of Merton's confrere at Gethsemani, Father Raymond, who penned a series of books about religious conversion and subsequent entrance into Trappist life, with somewhat lurid titles like *The Man Who Got Even with God.*

What distinguished Merton's book from the lot was that it told a tale that was so thoroughly modern. Here was the story of a hard-drinking, cigarette-smoking, jazz-loving, left-leaning, poetry-talking, bilingual, New York intellectual with European roots who chucked it all for the monastic life. The only thing missing was any specific details about his sex life. The Trappist censor had enough problems with the picture of his rather bohemian life in the final version of the manuscript, and the romantic dalliances were blue-penciled out as lacking in edification.

One result of the slow but enormously positive reaction to *The Seven Storey Mountain* was a flood of "fan" mail as well as letters from all kinds of people sharing with Merton their own religious journeys. His notebooks were filled with laments (and the pleasure) of receiving so much mail in response to his book. In time he had to avoid working in the guest house or saying Mass for the retreatants in order to avoid autograph seekers or picture takers. The plain fact of the matter was that after the publication of this runaway best seller, Merton was a public person, and at least in Catholic circles, a celebrity. The only place where he remained relatively unknown as a literary celebrity was the monastery itself, which knew little of what was going on in the outside world.

The Seven Storey Mountain made Merton a household word, at least among Catholics. His name and that book are inextricably intertwined, even though he himself knew it to be an imperfect work. Years later he would complain.of being the equivalent of a poster child used by nuns in parochial schools, caricaturing himself as striding out of New York, tramping out to Chicago and Louisville with a copy of Saint John of the Cross in his pocket and a Bible open to the Book of the Apocalypse. To be sure, there is an element of the judgmental in this work as well as a touch of the pious zeal that often afflicts new converts. He would later blush at his harsh assessment of Protestantism and his corresponding Catholic triumphalism. For all its weaknesses (even with cuts it is a somewhat prolix work) it is still read as a classic of conversion literature. A close reading of the text reveals a deeply passionate style of writing as well as a finely wrought series of vignettes of the writer's life, both in Europe and in the United States.

What *The Seven Story Mountain* did not reveal, however, was that however much he committed himself to the monastic life, Merton did not find unalloyed joy in the monastery. He felt overworked; his health was not always the best; he complained of the business of the place; he yearned for the more solitary life of the Carthusians; and he worried whether he was indeed a contemplative. His theological studies were terribly unsatisfactory. When he heard about his coming ordination as a subdeacon, he fretted in his journal that the local archbishop might find out how little theology he knew. Months before his ordination to the priesthood in 1949 he confesses in his journal that he finds it very hard to write theology, mainly because he does not know any. In the technical sense of knowing the manual tradition of scholasticism, this was probably true. To exacerbate matters even more, he suffered — as he did all of his life — with recurring physical problems. He was plagued with dental problems, bursitis, skin eruptions, and other physical annoyances that could be traced partially to his frequent worries about his nervous stamina. After his priestly ordination, the stern style of life in a Trappist monastery brought him close to a nervous collapse. His superiors took his health problems seriously enough to mitigate his Trappist diet somewhat.

Merton also realized that life in Gethsemani was not as perfect as it might have appeared from the outside. He decried the business, the crowded conditions (by 1950 there were two hundred persons in the community despite the earlier foundations in Georgia, Utah, and a projected one in South Carolina). The new abbot (James Fox; Abbot Dunne had died while making the Georgia foundation) had a kind of "open door" policy in accepting novices which, as might be expected, meant that a number of spiritually unstable persons would try their hand at the monastic life only to become severely neurotic or even psychotic under the pressures of monastic living.

Despite these problems, fears, anxieties, and doubts, his journals are also filled with lyrical patches in which he finds his life in the monastery profoundly moving. He speaks of going along with his head, haunted with good words like "solitude, obscurity, emptiness, *munditia cordis* (cleanness of heart), a virgin spirit." He would repeat those words as a form of meditation, and in time, would turn those meditations into finely wrought essays on the spiritual life. He exults in those days when the work of the monastery is suspended for days of recollection, allowing him to meditate, pray, and find a quiet spot away from the activities of the community. He relished the moments when he could walk in the woods for solitary prayer (there is a good book to be written on Merton's reflections on the world of nature; he was a fine nature writer) or to do manual work. He looked back with fondness on his days working in the fields with the other monks as they cut corn, gathered tobacco, planted seedlings in the woods, or reaped from the gardens. He maintained a keen interest in tree planting for many years, even serving in the informal office of monastery forester. His forestry interests also allowed him some much needed solitude in Gethsemani's woods.

The success of *The Seven Storey Mountain* only intensified the demand for writings. He accepted some invitations but continued to work on projects either done in obedience to his superiors (as his 1949 history of the Reformed Cistercians, *The Waters of Siloe*) or as a result of his own interests; he had the encouragement of his confessor and his superiors to write works that would help people to pray better and love God more. Between 1948 and 1953 Merton published three books: one would be completely rewritten well over a decade later; one was a failure (as Merton himself was well aware); and the third was not only a success as a work but for Merton marked a new way of spiritual and theological writing.

The same year *The Seven Storey Mountain* was published, Merton also saw his book *Seeds of Contemplation* come into print under the imprint of Jay Laughlin's New Directions publishing house. New Directions would become a favorite outlet for his more creative writing down to the time of his death, and Jay Laughlin would become a close personal friend. Their friendship began after Mark Van Doren sent Laughlin the poems that became Merton's first volume of published poetry. The friendship continued by letter and by Laughlin's visits to the monastery for the rest of Merton's life.

Seeds of Contemplation (1949; a revised edition appeared in the same year from the same publisher) is not a very good book even though Jay Laughlin turned it out in an elegant fashion, complete with a then fashionable burlap cover and very refined typefaces. In his preface to the work, Merton says that he intended the book to be a series of short chapters (there are twenty-seven of them) done in a pithy, aphoristic style, with little attempt to hold the separate chapters together in any methodical way. He justified this approach because Blaise Pascal, Saint John of the Cross, Guigo the Carthusian, and even Thomas à Kempis in his *Imitation of Christ* had done spiritual writing in the fashion of short pithy meditative chapters. *Seeds of Contemplation* was, in fact, the fruit of his meditation on spiritual works made in the context of his monastic observance.

If there is a thesis behind the book, it is simply this: God sends us germinal impulses across space, time, and history which rest in our being. If we cultivate them these "seeds" will grow into a conscious love for God. Unfortunately we cannot nurture these seeds so that they bloom into love for God because the seeds are overcome by the evils within ourselves and within the world. The path to loving union with God, according to Merton, is summed up in the challenge with which he brings his book to a close: "Let us throw off the pieces of this world like clothing and enter naked into wisdom."

There is nothing intrinsically heretical or heterodox or even idiosyncratic about this book. Indeed, it contains much that was drawn from the traditional literature of Christian perfection. One hears echoes of a certain reading of Saint John of the Cross and other apophatic mystics who emphasized the "dark" way of imageless prayer. In fact, despite its unsystematic character, one can detect the classical doctrine of ascent through the stages of purification, illumination, and union as classical sources beginning with Origen described the three steps of the spiritual life. Spiritual union with God is impossible without first burning away the sins and impulses to sin resident in every human heart.

Nonetheless, when one reads the book closely it is clear that Merton is caught up into using a certain stark menu of dialectical ideas that tend to polarize into opposing positions. In this work, nature combats grace; the world is in opposition to faith; the supernatural resists the natural; sin opposes grace, etc. There is little space for, or interest in, the community or the works of justice. The book has a kind of highly charged spiritual individualism about it and is suffused with a rather pessimistic vulgar Augustinianism. In that sense, Merton accepted the then conventional wisdom of the separation of nature and grace which plagued a good deal of neo-scholastic writing in this period.

Seeds of Contemplation derived from Merton's own prayer life, his thinking about the problem of contemplation, his rejection of the world, and a rather narrow understanding of the relationship of grace and nature. It would require more than a decade of prayer, study, and experience before Merton would see how unsatisfactory that work was. When he revised the work again and republished it a decade later under the title *New Seeds of Contemplation* (to be discussed in its proper place) he would fully understand, to borrow the critique of William Shannon, that he had produced, in the original version, an immature and naive book.

Merton himself would say, in the preface to *New Seeds*, that when the book was first written "the author had no experience in confronting the needs and problems of other men" but in the intervening years he had confronted "other solitudes" like the loneliness, the perplexity, and the simplicity of young monks, of people outside any monastery, the loneliness of people outside any church. What Merton had developed, in short, was a sense of compassion and a method for integrating his experience of God in prayer without denying the presence of

God in the created world and among his fellow human beings. In *New Seeds,* Merton came to understand that the fullness of the contemplative life would come only when one moved away from radical individualism into a deep personalism.

While working on *Seeds* Merton also assembled notes for a book on the theology of Saint John of the Cross. His journals are full of observations about his mounting notes, his false starts, and his perplexities as he attempted to come to grips with the writings of the great sixteenth-century Spanish mystical doctor. During his first years in the monastery Merton studied Saint John assiduously, an interest that he had developed long before he entered the monastery (he notes in his pre-monastic Cuban journal his attempts to find John's work in Spanish while traveling around the island). Merton was especially taken with the short paragraphs of John's counsels (the *cautelas* or "cautions" and the *avisos* or maxims) and his spiritual advice; but, poet that he was, he also read John's poetry with evident delight. He was also encouraged by the use to which T. S. Eliot had put John in the writing of the *Four Quartets.*

John of the Cross is not an easy writer to engage, both because of the profundity of his thought and the complexity of his finished work. The saint gives us a precious window into his method of composition in the preface to *The Spiritual Canticle.* John writes that he had certain deep experiences in prayer which he then tried to articulate in poetry. After writing the poetry he wrote commentaries on the poems using his university education as a scholastic theologian. From that brief description it would seem to follow that one should try to read back from the poetry to get at the experience, as the commentary is yet another step away from the experience. Merton, like most readers of John, tended to put most of his energy into reading the commentaries.

Alas, too many persons, Merton among them, wrestled not with the poems but with the doctrinal glosses on the poetic experiences. It is curious that Merton almost never discusses the poetry of John in *The Ascent to Truth.* One plausible reason for this omission may be his own youthful conviction that poetry was a prelude to but not coterminous with mystical prayer — a view he would later change. When *The Ascent to Truth* (the original title had been *The Pillar and the Cloud*) was published in 1951, Merton produced a rather abstract treatise on the path(s) of contemplative prayer according to the mind of John of the

Cross, using the language of scholastic theology. His discussion of John would at times become entangled in Merton's attempts to deal with the largely philosophical literature (Merton was openly dependent on the work of Jacques Maritain in this work) describing the workings of grace in the life of the mystic. This literature itself depended on the whole framework of thomistic epistemology and the then current theories of grace (many of them elaborated in the baroque age as a counterweight to the issue of grace both among the Reformers and, later, the Jansenists).

Rereading this book in preparation for this study, I was struck by a number of things. First of all, it is a book that has certain insistent theses. One is Merton's argument that an authentic understanding of authentic contemplation could only come by seeing it in the light of a correct understanding of both philosophy and theology. Such an approach serves as a safeguard against pseudo-mysticism (e.g., of Freud, Marx, and Nazi ideology) and an extravagant reliance on "signs" of mysticism such as visions, inner locutions, and other "mystical" phenomena. Like Saint John of the Cross, Merton was very dubious about such extraordinary phenomena. In fact, he was very unhappy with any link that could be erected between extraordinary phenomena and mystical prayer itself. His crusade against pseudo-mysticism was part of Merton's general revulsion at modern culture. He saw in the fascination with forms of Marxist thought a kind of degraded political mysticism, a mysticism that had brought suffering to so many who could not resist the ecstasy of political worship of charismatic figures.

His resistance to the more baroque forms of "Christian" mysticism more than likely reflected his own experience in the monastery observing some of the overly pious and not very stable postulants who came to enter the monastery. Like his mentor, John of the Cross, Merton warned against these things. Merton, importantly, was coming close to realizing something that more recent scholarship has come to emphasize, namely, that mystical prayer should not be confused with extraordinary phenomena. Union with God in love, he wrote, is not like being part of a Wagnerian opera after which, he sarcastically concludes, "the soul pirouettes gracefully back into the body and the mystic comes to himself to discover that he is surrounded by a hushed admiring circle of his fellow religious . . . including one or two who are surreptitiously taking down notes of the events in view of some future process of canonization." Only readers of the more excessively pious volumes of past Catholic hagiography, with their stock imagery of ecstasy and levitation, will recognize the sarcastic sting of those remarks.

Second, Merton, following a long theological tradition that goes back again to the third-century theologian Origen, distinguishes acquired wisdom (available to all disciplined thinkers, Christian or not) and infused wisdom, which is the gift of God by which we see (or, as the case may be, "not see") dimly the reality of God who is the source of wisdom. The latter is a gift from God and cannot be attained by human work and sweat. Infused wisdom or contemplation comes only as freely given grace to the person who is "disposed" to receive it by giving up all, by purifying the senses and mind to be ready for the gift. It is, in the technical sense of the term, a grace. The true contemplative does not become so through effort but through patient purified waiting for the gift of God. In that process one must, of course, avoid the twin temptations of quietism and its opposite, frenetic action. Even at this early stage of his career, it is worth noting, Merton had a favorable view of non-Christian Eastern contemplative efforts because he understood that yogic practices were not an end but only a path towards enlightenment.

A French Carmelite translated *The Ascent to Truth,* which was published in France in 1958. Merton wrote a preface for that heavily edited translation in which he confessed that he had too much to say about philosophy in the original work and that were he to write the book over it would have had a lot more to say about scripture and the fathers and less about the role of reason in the mystical journey. He then provides what has been the most common and correct judgment about this work, which he would later rank as "fair" on his 1967 fever chart. He would have done better, he wrote, "to concern myself a little less with scholasticism which is not the *true intellectual climate for a monk"* [my emphasis].

One continuing influence of John of the Cross for Merton was the saint's custom of writing out short meditative phrases or maxims (*avisos* in Spanish) that could be used as a meditative preparation for contemplative attention. Merton enjoyed crafting such phrases, meditating on them himself, and enlarging them for future publication. He would compose short phrases (in Latin) and hand them to young monks as texts for meditation.

Merton did a good deal of his writing in a vault that contained many of the old books and manuscripts collected by an earlier abbot. As early as 1946 Merton drew up a list of projects at the request of the Father General of the Order relative to writing projects he intended to do, based at least in part on the library holdings at Gethsemani (many of these rare works are now on extended loan to the library of Western Michigan University). This list of works (many of which never saw the light of day) included translation, the compilation of bibliographies, studies of various monastic writers, etc. While he never completed most of these tasks it is a fact that right up until the final year of his life he did turn out essays, studies, volumes, translations, pamphlets, and reflections on a wide range of monastic themes. He contributed regularly to monastic journals both here and abroad; and he was diligent in acquiring books on monastic history, liturgy, and theology for the Gethsemani library.

Merton had also kept a journal from his pre-monastic days, and he remained faithful to this task after he entered the monastery. From those private notebooks he would draw materials and publish them, in somewhat different form, beginning with one of his finest works, *The Sign of Jonas* (1953). That volume was not only one of the best-written works he ever produced; it also marked — almost single-handedly — the beginning of a new genre of theological reflection: the journal as theological treatise. In the words of the Merton critic Elena Malits, he made the use of the word "I" respectable in theology.

To read *The Sign of Jonas* is to go back over materials and events we have already discussed. The journal, divided into six large parts with an epilogue, covers Merton's life from 1946 to the middle of 1952. Since the raw journals from which Merton drew his materials are now published, it is a fascinating exercise to compare the original entries with the finished product.

His purpose in publishing a journal (a rather novel genre that met with more than some resistance from religious superiors within the Order) is clearly set out in the prologue to the book. First, he discovered that in writing *The Ascent to Truth* he failed to reach ordinary readers, who found his language too abstract; concomitantly, he failed to convey what is most personal and moving in spiritual experience. In other words, Merton searched for a new style of writing useful for his need to communicate. Hence, his desire to sketch out the spiritual movements within his own life in order to give his readership some sense of the attracting power of God's love. The second reason for writing the book is alluded to in the title. During the period 1946-1952 Merton felt strong urgings to leave the Cistercians for the greater solitude of Carthusian life. Like Jonah (Merton uses "Jonas" — the spelling of the Catholic Douai-Rheims translation then widely read in Catholic circles) he attempted to move in a direction opposite from where God was calling him. In his solemn profession and his subsequent ordination to the priesthood, he finally saw where God was calling him. The monastic fathers often used the symbol of Jonah praying in the belly of the sea monster as a sign for their own lives hidden away in prayer. Thus, at the end of the prologue Merton writes that he is especially sealed with this great sign . . . finding himself "traveling towards my destiny in the belly of a paradox."

Each of the six major sections of the book are introduced by an italicized introduction providing necessary biographical background about his path towards monastic profession and all that it involved: his writing chores, his priestly ordination, his various discomforts — including bouts of ill health and a near nervous breakdown after ordination (Merton suffered from ill health most of his adult life), and his intellectual and spiritual study, as well as closely observed descriptions of daily monastic life and reflections on the natural environment of Gethsemani.

The entries in the journal are dated, and range from a few lines to several pages. The paragraphs are studded with passages from the liturgy, references to books he is reading and his reactions to them, as well as snatches of outbursts of prayer or finely sketched characters who live in or come into contact with the Gethsemani community. One senses the tensions within the house now bursting, with more than two hundred monks and the need to care for them.

Through his friendship with Jay Laughlin at New Directions he was well supplied with literary works. *The Sign of Jonas* is interwoven with monastic references and comments on James Joyce, Dylan Thomas, Rainer Maria Rilke, Robert Lowell, Gertrude Stein, T. S. Eliot, and Henry Miller (with whom he would later enter into correspondence). He delighted in his solitary walks in the woods where he would go to pray in his free time, and he found some peace and quiet in the vault, cluttered with "little magazines" and monastic tomes, where he had a small office space in which to work. After his priestly ordination he would begin to give conferences to the novices, and his reading in scripture and spiritual literature would grow apace. He treasured the quiet moments when he could find a quiet place to sit while he read slowly something like Eliot's *Four Quartets* — a poetic work that had a profound influence on him.

The Sign of Jonas was a personal book; it described a life refracted through the personal experience called "I." Precisely because of its somewhat disjointed nature, readers must seek out its leitmotifs and recurring preoccupations. Close readers of Merton will see threads that will eventually lead to his later work. For example, his reflections on solitude recur in this work, but his thinking on this subject would only crystallize when he published *Thoughts in Solitude* (1958), a work that would have its own long gestation period.

The epilogue to *The Sign of Jonas* is entitled "Fire Watch, July 4, 1952." It is perhaps the best piece of poetic prose that Merton ever wrote, but more importantly, it was a summary of his most optimistic and deeply felt response to his early life as a monk and as a contemplative. The epilogue was a carefully crafted and meditative essay, as a comparison between it and some of the earlier versions in the notebooks demonstrates.

Gethsemani had had its unhappy experiences with destructive fires more than once in its history. A college the monastery once ran at the turn of the century burned, an event that was seen as providential in freeing the monks from a task for which they were not called. Barns regularly caught fire. Given the crowded conditions in the monastery, a fire in the abbey itself would have been a disaster. Accordingly, each night a monk was designated as a "fire watcher." While the community slept, this person would stay up and watch for potential fires, shod with sneakers and carrying a flashlight, punching into a time clock as the hours passed.

In a very complex description, filled with symbolism and metaphor, Merton made his rounds of the monastery buildings, triggering memories of certain events in his past life as he passed through the scullery, chapter room, library, novitiate, and so on. His narrative has several motifs beloved of the Christian spiritual tradition. His journey through the monastery is both a going down and a rising up (themes found as a regular refrain in the book of the prophet Jonah), a journey in which he is a watcher like those described by the psalmist and the prophet Isaiah. The theme of going up and going down is traditional in ascetical literature. In a sense *The Seven Storey Mountain* is a volume of ascent (going up the purgatorial mountain) while *The Sign of Jonas* is a going down (into the belly of the sea monster). In "The Fire Watch" there is a constant play between going down and going up as he makes his rounds as a fire watcher.

The apex of his nightly rounds is a climb into the bell tower of the monastic church: "the door swings out upon a vast sea of darkness and of prayer. Will it come like this, the moment of my death?" The monk-watcher sits looking over the silences of the night and prays in the presence of God ("Do You remember the place by the stream? Do You remember the time of the forest fire?") and affirms the omnipresent God who sustains the world ("There is no leaf that is not in Your care. . . . There is no concealed spring that was not concealed by You"). He continues with a long meditative hymn of praise for the variegated world God has given us until the first cracks of dawn begin to appear. The prologue ends: "There are drops of dew that show like sapphires in the grass as soon as the great sun appears, and leaves stir behind the hushed flight of an escaping dove."

The Sign of Jonas was an enormous success, building on Merton's fame as the author of *The Seven Storey Mountain*. It also provided Merton a vehicle for expressing his spiritual ideals in a format congenial to his own temperament and his self-understanding as a contemplative monk. *The Sign of Jonas* went through three printings in four months and was a main selection of four different book clubs. Merton's fame was such — at least outside the monastery; inside he was more or less a non-celebrity — that he still could not celebrate Mass or serve in the monastery's guest house because of autograph seekers. In his notebooks he wryly comments that when he went to Louisville to get his citizenship papers there was only one person — a tonsured monk in a black clerical suit from a rural monastery — who had to worry about the attention of reporters. He was also the only person who was queried about his leftist political connections during his days at Columbia University, to the bemused shock of the ladies from the D.A.R. who were there to hand out flags to the new citizens.

It was clear enough within the community and within the Order that Merton had formidable gifts. He was appointed master of scholastics in 1951, which meant that he was responsible for the education of the young monks who were in vows and destined for the priesthood. The thousands of pages of unpublished conference notes done in mimeographed format now housed in the Merton archives are mute testimony to how seriously he carried on his pedagogical tasks. He would continue to add to these outlines after he became novice master in 1955. Because of his linguistic gifts, he would be called on to act as a translator when official visitations came to Gethsemani either in the person of the General of the Order or the Father Immediate, delegates from the mother house from which Gethsemani had sprung (Melleray in France), since neither spoke English.

Merton managed this monastic labor in tandem with the demands made on him as an author who had to deal with editors, publishers, and the myriad requests that came to him for essays or reviews. In a truculent moment in the mid-1950s he grumbled that people must have thought that he "sweated articles out of his pores" when yet one more urgent demand came to him for an article to contribute to an Italian journal.

In the decade between his entrance into the monastery and the publication of *The Sign of Jonas* Merton more or less made his peace with life at Gethsemani, even though he never lost his desire for greater solitude and a more peaceful atmosphere. His temptation towards the more solitary life of the Carthusians or for a more solitary life in another place would be a leitmotif in his writings until the day he died. His notions of what monasticism was all about began to mature. Many of his criticisms of life as he experienced it began to crystallize and, always obedient, he took steps to refine monastic life for himself and for his young charges in the scholasticate. He pleaded for more free time in the daily horarium. He bargained for more space away from the crowded confines of the monastery buildings so that time could be spent in the woods, with their silence and their beauty. This meant the right to roam the monastery acreage beyond the concrete block walls that had been erected earlier in the century to mark off the canonical cloister. He insisted that a distinction be made between the canonically necessary course of studies mandated for priests and an education more adapted for monastic formation, while taking the lead in developing such a curriculum.

More importantly, Merton slowly began to refine his concept of the meaning of contemplation and its place in the monastic life. He rejected older, somewhat aberrant, notions that the purpose of the monk's life was to do penance for the sake of penance, just as he resisted the idea that the monk's duty was to supply prayer for the church the way a boiler supplies steam to run a ship. Merton, in other words, did not conceive of his life as only one of surrogacy — praying for those in the world that did not pray. He did not see the asceticism of the monastic life as an end in itself but as a way of being prepared for union with God in love. He also rejected this search for contemplative union as an elite enterprise available only to those who live the "life of perfection." Finally, he saw that his early conviction of monastic life as a mere rejection of the world and its sinfulness was at best naive, or at worst a projection of his own inadequacies and fears onto the life of monasticism itself.

In the prologue to *The Sign of Jonas* Merton described himself as journeying towards his destiny "in the belly of a paradox." He himself probably never fully realized how paradoxical his situation was. He sought the monastic life because he desired hiddenness and solitude, but his writings brought fame and demands. His desire to flee the world, while physically a fact as he lived in the rural country of Kentucky, nonetheless brought him into contact with religious seekers, people from the world of letters and art, social activists, and, beginning in the 1950s, religious seekers from all of the world's religions. His thirst for imageless union with God coexisted with his wide-ranging reading and his insatiable desire for a deeper understanding of contemporary culture.

The first generation of the desert monastics of the fourth century described their life as a striving for the "angelic" (*bios aggelikos*), but Merton learned that monastic life, like life in general, is burdened by the very real demands of getting by each day and the strains of living with others. His years in the monastery taught him to practice toleration for the foibles of his brethren, the caprices of his superiors, and the sheer tedium of living a life that was tied to a cycle of prayer, work, and study. Merton responded to those mundane realities in turn by complaint (mainly to himself in his diaries) and, when monastic realities were concerned, by arguing for change.

46

2 The Conversion of a Monk

The monk should be like the Seraphim: All Eye.

A Saying of a Desert Father

B Y THE TIME MERTON WAS ORDAINED TO THE PRIEST-hood in 1949 he was already a celebrity. In 1949 *Life* magazine did a picture layout featuring Trappist monks leaving the Abbey of Gethsemani to make a foundation in Utah, but framed the story by consideration of Gethsemani's most famous monk, Thomas Merton, whose autobiography was still a best seller.

Merton's writing reached the American Catholic public at a most propitious time. There was a genuine Catholic revival going on in the postwar church. Encouraged both by theological movements on the continent and the cautious approval of Pope Pius XII, there was a renewal of interest in the serious study of scripture, in the reform of the liturgy, and of new ways of making the church present in the world. The pope had issued encyclicals on all of these topics beginning in the early 1940s. The Benedictine monks at Collegeville, Minnesota's Saint John's Abbey had not only been encouraging more participation in the liturgy but had linked that desire to a vision of social justice. Their journal *Orate Fratres* (later *Worship*) was the outlet for liturgical renewal in the church. In the postwar period both the Catholic Theological Society of America (which had only been founded after the war) and the Catholic Biblical Association began a more vigorous attempt to provide the United States a more sophisticated approach to theological study. Lay movements like The Catholic Workers attempted to live out new ways of being Catholic. There was real enthusiasm for designing and implementing university curricula that would express a genuine Catholic humanism. Catholic writers like George Bernanos, Graham Greene, Evelyn Waugh, Flannery O'Connor, and others made it seem as if there were a real renaissance in Catholic culture taking place. Catholic publishing houses like Sheed & Ward in New York and Bruce in Milwaukee had initiated a vigorous publishing program that was reaching a literate lay audience. The G.I. Bill would result in a burgeoning life on Catholic campuses as well as a better educated Catholic laity.

One of the enduring stereotypes of American Catholicism, however, was that it was all of a piece — characterized by an authoritarian hierarchy, a stern parish clergy, and a compliant laity. In fact, in the American Catholic Church of the postwar period there were any number of initiatives going on, not all of them clerically directed, keenly interested in religious and intellectual renewal. Many of these initiatives were encouraged by the renovation of Catholic life in Europe, especially in Belgium, France, and to a lesser degree, in Germany.

Merton would be a natural player in many of these new currents. After all, he was deeply immersed in the life of the liturgy. He was, like all monks, a daily meditator on sacred scripture; his natural penchant for literature and his increasing desire to mediate monastic wisdom to the larger world made him a natural participant in this burgeoning of Catholic life. Furthermore, as someone who was bilingual, he read the new theology coming out of France with ease and with a gift for translating its insights into an understandable vernacular. His notebooks were filled with citations from such writers as Yves Congar, Jean Danielou, Henri de Lubac, and the other writers who were associated with such (then) avant-garde publications as *L'Esprit, Istina, La Vie Spirituelle, Irenikon,* etc. Merton, in turn, became a steady contributor to Catholic periodicals in this country: *Commonweal, Cross Currents,*

Thought, Worship, Jubilee, The Catholic Worker, and other such outlets of the (scattered) Catholic renewal.

As the 1940s came to an end, Merton had already lived the monastic life for nearly a decade. He had made his solemn vows and received priestly ordination. In the world outside the monastery he had gained more than a certain fame after the publication of *The Seven Storey Mountain.* Despite some health problems, he was still a young man, and with certain small mitigations of diet, he led a full monastic life. His appetite for writing was still keen even though he was often called on to write "out of obedience" works that for him were a personal distraction.

In the 1950s Merton published about nine books after the appearance of *The Sign of Jonas* in 1953. Some of these were works done out a spirit of piety, like his reflections on the Cistercian saint Bernard of Clairvaux (*The Last of the Fathers* — 1954) or his eucharistic reflections issued under the title *The Living Bread* (1956). *The Last of the Fathers* consisted of a long meditation on an encyclical letter Pope Pius XII wrote on Saint Bernard as an anniversary tribute. Merton's original contribution to this volume reflected the enormous effort he had put into the study of Bernard's writings. He produced a new book of poems: *The Strange Islands* (1957) and two years later did a volume of *Selected Poems* (1959).

The 1955 publication *No Man Is an Island* was dedicated to the monastic students (i.e., the "scholastics") and newly ordained priests of the monastery. In his "Author's Note" to the book, Merton said that in his desire to share with the reader "my own reflections on certain aspects of the spiritual life" he was, as it were, writing a sequel to his previous volume, *Seeds of Contemplation.* He also said that much of the material would be familiar to his own students, who had been the audience for many of the themes found in the book.

No Man Is an Island consists of a prologue and sixteen chapters in which Merton explored certain fundamental notions of the spiritual journey. He took pains to make his observations germane to those who were not monks, but the main themes of the work were standard topoi in the monastic lexicon: solitude, recollection, silence, asceticism and sacrifice, purity of intention, and so on. *No Man Is an Island* is not widely read today, but it deserves attention if for no other reason than its frequently striking aphorisms. One reiterated caution that Merton employs is to warn the reader against any encounter with the real world. The interior life, he writes, only becomes possible when people understand the "value and beauty in ordinary things, to come alive to the splendor that is all around us as creatures of God."

He spent a fair number of pages in *No Man Is an Island* on the necessity of intelligent discrimination between true interiority and the false interiority of false asceticism, psychological rigidity, and casting the ascetic life in the pure negativity of not doing things. He has a stunning chapter on the necessity of "remembering God," in which he casts the whole Christian life in the coming to awareness that we can know God because God has always known us. In a distinction he will later turn to repeatedly, Merton argues that as we come to such an awareness we do so using the resources of tradition. Tradition, however, is not the same as convention; the latter can be death dealing, while the former brings life.

The other deeply felt work he wrote in this period came from his continuing reflections on the meaning of a solitary existence. *Thoughts in Solitude* (1958) had a slow evolution from his meditations on short spiritual texts, his correspondence with other contemplatives, and his wide-ranging reading both in the classical sources and in contemporary philosophers, poets, and fiction writers who took up the then popular existentialist themes of loneliness, alienation, and the meaning of the individual in mass society. In that sense, *Thoughts in Solitude* is cut from the same cloth as *No Man Is an Island.* His thinking on the value and place of solitude was much in debt to his careful reading of the Swiss writer and physician, Max Picard, whose *The World of Silence* was influential in his thinking.

Thoughts in Solitude is one of the best spiritual works that Merton ever wrote. It had a meditative pace, and the style contributed to a cloistered spirit. It remains today as a favorite meditation text for many people of prayer. Part of the reason for its continuing success is that it can serve as a meditation manual for prayer without imposing any rigid "system" of meditation. The book can simply be taken up and read in a ruminative fashion to achieve the quiet that is essential for prayer. In this period of his life it was the kind of work he very much desired to do: the elaboration of fundamental spiritual insights into prose meditations and prayers in order to help others see the fruits of the contemplative life. Merton said in the preface to *Thoughts in Solitude,* that his intention was to write of one's solitude before God, the dialogue in silence with God, and the interrelation of our personal solitudes with that of others. It is also pertinent to note that his need to speak of personal solitude was a kind of antidote to the overweening demand for submersion of the personal in a world of totalitarian governments. In this enterprise (anticipating his increasing interest in the broader world of religious experience) he places his concerns in the company of ancient Oriental thinkers like Lao-Tse and the Zen masters, as well as more modern voices like Henry Thoreau, Martin Buber, and, of course, Max Picard.

Merton's preoccupation with solitude was not merely a personal concern for him. Both as a master of students and a novice master he was convinced that the monks of Gethsemani needed some measure of physical solitude — some space for quiet and prayer. In that period the monks were obliged to stay within the monastic enclosure, which was the part of the monastic grounds bound by the walls erected in the early part of the century. Only out of necessity did the monks go out of the enclosure into the vast acreage the monastery possessed. It was one thing to go into the woods to cut firewood for fuel; it was unthinkable that a monk would go there simply to be alone. Merton wrote to Abbot James a number of memoranda around 1950 suggesting the building of a monastic "grange" or a chapel or some place out in the woods where a monk or a small group of monks could go to get away from the noise of the abbey, to pray and meditate and be still. Solitude for Merton was always a combination of exterior silence and interior silence. He felt that the cramped life of the abbey — then filled to capacity with monks — was too much like a crowded urban area. He was also constantly irritated by the noise of a busy monastery as it went about the business enterprises that provided its monks with income. At this stage of his life he was not so much thinking of permanent hermitages but of places of retreat and silence that would foster the interior silence he considered crucial for the life of contemplation.

If one were to look at Merton's published work in the 1950s it would be easy to judge that his preoccupations followed trajectories already established in the decade before. He says in the preface to *Thoughts in Solitude* that what he wrote had matured in his thinking all through the previous decade. Despite this continuity, however, the period of the 1950s was a time of deep change in Merton's thinking, a

51

change radical enough to be called a "conversion" (or, perhaps better, a series of conversions) which explains the title of this chapter. The full extent of that change only became apparent when Merton published (in the 1960s), in a somewhat rewritten fashion, gleanings from his private journals for the previous decade: *Conjectures of a Guilty Bystander* (1966). With the full publication of his personal journals we can now more fully appreciate how Merton's understanding shifted and matured in those seemingly placid years of the Eisenhower administration.

This conversion, or perhaps, series of conversions, happened at a number of different levels. First, there was a shift in his thinking about his role as a monk vis-à-vis the intellectual world of his day. More importantly, there was a change in the way he conceived of the monastic life in general and his own monasticism in particular. Indeed, one could imagine this decade as a time when he meditated profoundly on the issue of solitude and community if one understood this tension in the broadest of terms: How does the solitary life of the contemplative monk intersect with the larger Christian community and with the world of culture more generally understood? This is a topic he would wrestle with until the day he died, and it must be understood more broadly than a simple desire to find a monastic tradition like the Carthusians or Camaldolese, who put greater stress on the eremitical life.

These broad issues were important to him personally, but they were also important for him as a director of novices in the monastery. With the flood of applicants entering monastic life in the aftermath of World War II, Merton felt it crucial to understand not only why he was a monk but to be able to articulate that monastic vision for those who were under his care. A master of novices had to be sensitive to the varied gifts of those who entered the monastery (many were military veterans) as well as discerning enough to weed out the neurotics and emotionally unstable who sought refuge from the complex world in the cloister. As a mature monk once phrased it to me, there are many people who wish to enter the monastery to punish themselves, and if allowed to enter, they end up punishing the community! However great these problems happened to be, it was crucial that mature candidates coming into the monastery be directed by people who understood something about the world that shaped them and the ideas that motivated them.

This need for some degree of psychological expertise partially explains why Merton began a somewhat schematic study of psychology, and enjoyed the chance afforded him in 1956 to go to Saint John's Benedictine Abbey in Collegeville, Minnesota, to attend a conference on sharpening psychological skills for the better training of novices. During the conference, which he attended with his confrere John Eudes Bamberger, a trained psychiatrist, he received an unpleasant tongue lashing by the psychiatrist (and convert to the Catholic Church) Gregory Zilboorg, who accused Merton of being a self-promoter and a dabbler in psychology, a man who wished to stand in the middle of Broadway with a sign announcing that he was a hermit. Merton returned from that conference somewhat chastened, wondering, in his private journal, to what extent Zilboorg had made a case against him. One thing that happened as a result of this fateful meeting was a dampening of his Freudian enthusiasms. The essay he wrote on Freud, the fruit of his studies, was put on the shelf, only to be published after his death. Despite his unhappy experience at Collegeville, he was still convinced that lack of psychological understanding could result in terrible pain for those who came to the monastic life if formation in that life was not balanced and sane.

One question that haunted Merton personally was how to keep in balance the relationship of his own quest for contemplative solitude in a monastery, his restlessly inquiring mind, and his natural instincts as a poet and essayist. How does a monk live apart from the world but not be indifferent to it? How does one live out the traditional monastic flight from the world without making that flight into a gesture of indifference or callous contempt for the world? Many of these questions imposed themselves on him simply because so many demands for articles, essays, and advice poured in as he became more known as a writer and spiritual teacher. The issue became this: What responsibility did he owe to that world "outside" when the world asked him to share the fruits of his contemplation? To put the matter a different way: Did his call to be a monk mean that the call was only for his own Christian life and salvation, or did it mean that his life as a monk was a gift of God that was also to serve others? And further, what did he have to say to the world of unbelief, the world of intellectual culture about which he had a passionate interest? Did a monk have a legitimate role in the arenas of ideas?

As Merton matured as a monk he would confront such issues on a number of levels. It was in the 1950s that Merton, well before the openness deriving from the Second Vatican Council, began to formulate ideas and strategies that would not only allow him to enter into dialogue with Christians from other traditions, but would also help him learn how to relate to other cultures and to religions that were not Christian.

All of these ecumenical and interreligious probes had, at their root, certain hard-won convictions that derived from his own monastic practice but which, to many other monks, seemed daring and idiosyncratic. Much of his correspondence with his religious superiors in the fifties (and especially with the French General of the Order, Dom Gabriel Sortais) was an attempt to explain himself and his sense of what he was doing in terms of the traditional understanding of monasticism. This misunderstanding also spilled over into the many discussions and arguments he had with his Cistercian censors, who felt that some of his writing was not seemly for a cloistered monk.

We can trace out a number of intellectual trajectories in the 1950s which, while they seem disparate, led him nonetheless to certain common intellectual principles.

Largely as a result of reading the fathers of the church, Merton became interested in those Russian Orthodox intellectuals who, from their exile in Paris, wrote works of a theological nature. Merton's notebooks, beginning in late 1956, are studded with quotations from the works of Vladimir Soloviev, Nicholas Berdyaev, Sergius Bulgakov, Paul Evdokimov, Vladimir Lossky, and other Russians who were associated, in one fashion or another, with the Saint Sergius institute and seminary in Paris. Merton loved their emphasis on Christ as Wisdom, on the role of the Holy Spirit in the world, their love for the "dark" mysticism of the Greek fathers, their appreciation for monasticism, their integration of liturgy in theology, and their vision of christology as deeply implicated in the creation, maintenance, and final destiny of the cosmos. He further admired their willingness to engage in social criticism from those deep theological roots. He read these authors critically (Merton saw, rightly, a tendency in Berdyaev towards a kind of Christian gnosticism) but with a great deal of sympathy. In these Orthodox thinkers he found a theology free from abstractions and fundamentally shaped by liturgy, tradition, and the life of prayer. Even though these figures were lay writers, their theology was very monastic; indeed, Evdokimov worked out a theory he called "interiorized monasticism," of how one might transpose monastic values into the lay world. While writing from a quite distinct position as an Orthodox thinker, his ideas were somewhat parallel to Merton's own concerns.

In April of 1957, in the period when he was most intently engaged with these Russian thinkers, he penned some lines in his notebook (he would later reproduce these lines in his *Conjectures of a Guilty Bystander*) that represent, in my estimation, a critical moment in Merton's intellectual and spiritual maturity. In reaction to some lines in Berdyaev's *Le sens de la création* Merton wrote:

> If I can unite in myself, in my own spiritual life, the thought of the East and the West of the Greek and Latin Fathers, I will create in myself a reunion of the divided church and from that unity in myself can come the exterior and visible unity of the church. For if we want to bring together East and West we cannot do it by imposing one upon the other. We must contain both in ourselves and transcend both in Christ.

In that brief passage Merton articulates a strategy for a contemplative approach to openness to the Other. He recognized that if he could be transparent to other attempts to engage the mystery of God in Christ then he, in turn, would have the right to speak to others in sympathy and understanding. This approach, natural enough for a contemplative, was a form of interior dialogue. Such an approach would later come to be known as "deep dialogue." It is not accidental that Merton came to these ideas at a time when he was also reading the foundational book of interior and exterior dialogue: Martin Buber's *I and Thou*. Merton slowly began to realize more fully that the world of "God seekers" was not at all confined to Catholic cloisters. In realizing this, he started a conscious campaign to become engaged either directly or indirectly to work for the greater good of humanity, and in doing so, to deepen his own contemplative life.

That he started with these Orthodox thinkers is easy to explain. French Catholic thinkers in the twentieth century had a long and intimate relationship with such writers, as Christian theologians, philosophers, and historians from tsarist Russia flooded France after the

Revolution of 1917. There was a flurry of intellectual interchange between Catholic theologians like Lambert Beaudoin, Henri de Lubac,
Yves Congar, and Jean Danielou and their Orthodox counterparts,
made the more easy by their mutual love for the patristic tradition.
In the French theological journals of the period, one finds contributions by these and other Orthodox thinkers. Belgian monks like Lambert Beaudoin and journals like *Istina* were deeply engaged with
such thinkers as part of an ecumenical effort to bridge the fissures
caused by the split of the churches of West and East in the eleventh
century. The Benedictine monastery of Chevetogne was founded
precisely as a bridge between East and West. Merton grew to know
these efforts because of his facility with, and love for, French Catholic culture. It is worth noting in passing that while such interests
were considered daringly ecumenical in the 1950s, some of the Russian writers Merton was then reading have now been cited by Pope
John Paul II in his encyclical letter *Fides et Ratio* (1998) as models for
those who wish to synthesize deep philosophical learning and intense Christian faith.

This strategy of interior dialogue was not limited, in Merton's
view, to theological exchange. Largely as a result of his interest in the
Russian Orthodox theological tradition, he began to read the Russian
poet and novelist Boris Pasternak, whose work he came across quite
accidentally while browsing through literary journals in the public library in Louisville on one of his infrequent trips into the city. When
Doctor Zhivago was published in English, Merton saw in the novel's
deep structure many of the themes that he loved in reading Orthodox
theology: the Christ-Wisdom element in the world of Russia, the re-
demptive possibilities in suffering, and the mysterious working of
grace in human conversation. He wrote to Pasternak, sending some of
his own poetry and prose, and the two entered into a limited exchange
of letters (Pasternak was in deep political trouble with the Soviet authorities, especially after winning the Nobel Prize in 1958) through the
intermediary of Pasternak's American editor Kurt Wolff. In that limited exchange, however, Merton saw meaning for his own life as a
monk: conversation between those who deeply love the Truth and
pursue that Truth in a serious and purified way. Merton saw this exchange not only in terms of exchange between two people but as a way
of creating, as he himself wrote, "our interior bond that is the only ba-

sis of true peace and true community. External, juridical, doctrinal, etc. bonds can never achieve this."

What Merton saw as a way of entering into dialogue with Russians of good will (we were, at this time, in the midst of the Cold War, when dialogue between Russians and Americans was relatively rare; it was, after all, the period of the suppression of the Hungarian freedom fighters) was not limited to that part of the world. In the same period, a brilliant young poet — like Merton, a Columbia University graduate — from an aristocratic Nicaraguan family, Ernesto Cardenal, entered Gethsemani as a novice. Cardenal would later find fame as a poet revolutionary and minister of culture in the Sandinista government of Nicaragua, but in this period his instincts were monastic and literary. Merton welcomed him as a kind of soul mate at Gethsemani even though Brother Lawrence (his monastic name) was very much Merton's junior.

It was through Cardenal that Merton become acquainted with Central and Latin American poets and cultural critics. He began to translate their poetry, write to them, and send work to their journals. Through Cardenal he also received an education in the ways of Central and Latin American dictatorship, as many members of Cardenal's family were anti-Somozan to the core. This exchange would remain a lifelong interest of Merton. Again, he saw this interest as not only compatible with his monastic vocation but central to it. He saw that his life could serve as a conduit for the deep fruits of prayer and contemplation to others while he, in turn, would be nourished by these contacts.

Writing in 1958 to the Ecuadorean sculptor and writer Jaime Andrade, he wanted to commission a statue of the Virgin and Child for his novices "that would tell the truth about God being 'born' Incarnate among the Indians of the Andes. Christ poor and despised among the disinherited of the earth." This conviction was reinforced by the number of men from Latin America who wrote him seeking entrance into the Gethsemani community. Such exchanges were an antidote to North American prejudices against Latino culture, which Merton detected among his own novices. He wrote furious lines in his journals about the teasing that a Filipino novice took by well-meaning novices who jollied the young man about his "brownness." This insensitive racism (innocent though it may have been) represented for Merton a deep flaw in American culture.

Again, Merton thought that these encounters with Latin Americans (mostly by the exchange of letters and offprints) were a bridge between the North and the South, with his hope being that every act of reconciliation and understanding would lessen tensions between the two hemispheres and mitigate the indifference of the rich North to the plight of the impoverished South. He had an almost instinctive reaction against the patronizing attitude of those who thought that America meant only North America.

Merton was so serious about this enterprise that he spent a good deal of energy in the late fifties dreaming of leaving Gethsemani to found a primitive monastery in Latin America, where he would combine a life of solitude with an intellectual apostolate. His journals for this period are full of entries about places he might go, how much land would be needed, what the horarium of such a monastery would look like, etc. He pored over atlases and eagerly wrote to people in various Latin American countries. His plans were abetted by the encouragement of a Benedictine in Mexico, Dom Gregorio Lemercier, who wanted him to come and live at his Benedictine monastery at Cuernavaca outside Mexico City until he could settle on a permanent place of residence. Indeed, the Belgian-born Lemercier actively campaigned to get Merton to leave Gethsemani; he thought Merton's talents were being suppressed by the conservative life of the Gethsemani monastery. Lemercier's encouragement was abetted by the enthusiasm of some of the younger monks at Gethsemani, who felt they also would like to join this as yet unnamed community. As one might imagine, Lemercier's visits to Merton at the monastery were not welcomed by Abbot James.

Merton was so taken by this idea of a monastic settlement in Latin America that he even wrote Rome about an exclaustration (i.e., a document allowing him to leave his stable monastery) while attempting, without much success, to keep his plans from his abbot, Dom James Fox, who was decidedly unsympathetic to the whole scheme. In the end, after much secret letter writing, private complaining in his journal, and considerable scheming, Rome said "no" to his grand plan; but it is clear that even apart from this authoritative closure the whole idea was wildly romantic and hopelessly impractical. First of all, Merton was neither very practical (he could not even drive a car) nor in robust health. Second, he would not have survived well in the culture of

Latin America. As Jaime Andrade told him in a letter, Merton and his putative community would have been intellectually and culturally whipsawed between a rigidly reactionary Catholic hierarchy and an anticlerical and Marxist intellectual class. The end result, Andrade judged, would be frustrated isolation. Finally, Merton never thought through how he would finance such a community. Merton's unofficial theological advisor, the French Jesuit scholar Father Jean Danielou, insisted that Merton stay where he was and use his gifts as he had been using them.

In the end, when Rome said no to his plan, Merton accepted the decision, writing that he would have to find solitude "outside geography." Despite the practical setback of a Roman veto, he continued corresponding with poets south of the border, translating their works from Spanish and Portuguese and finding homes for their works in the United States. In his spare moments he could not even resist drawing up plans for a primitive monastery and developing various schedules for the monastic day, despite the resistance to the foundation.

Even though Merton's monastic foundation never got off the ground it is still worthwhile reading Merton's concerns in this period. One can see, in the workings of his original mind, a kind of preview of what would become one strand of Latin American liberation theology, namely, the marriage of a radical spiritual vision and a passionate concern for the poor. In that sense, he was vaguely formulating what would become explicit in the landmark work of Gustavo Gutiérrez, whose *A Theology of Liberation* (ET: 1970) was the manifesto of Latin American liberation theology, even though Merton by temperament and education never gave his ideas any extended economic reflection. By contrast, Gutiérrez saw that his own early work was too oriented towards social criticism and required a deeper spirituality. His *We Drink from Our Own Wells* (ET: 1983), with the title taken from Saint Bernard of Clairvaux, was his attempt to write a work on liberation spirituality. It is a work with which Merton would have resonated had he lived to see its publication. Merton's own love for and concern about the life and culture of Latin America would persist right down to the year of his death.

One must also conclude that part of Merton's imaginary alternative monastic schemes came from his own discontent with the somewhat rigid and crowded life he led at Gethsemani. The very success of the monastery (ironically enough attained, in good part, because of the fame of his own writing) with its busy farm and factories created an atmosphere that Merton felt inimical to the contemplative life. He often expressed irritation at the noise, machinery, and business of what, in a cynical moment, he called this "Jesus loving, All American, go getting house filled with pseudo-contemplatives." He feared that the success of the various monastic enterprises brought, as a result of that success, too much emphasis on work, productivity, and income at the expense of quiet, silence, and a simple lifestyle. The success-oriented leadership of Dom James Fox combined with the abbot's saccharine spirituality ("All for Jesus through Mary with a smile") chafed Merton's religious sensibility. He took no great pleasure in the success of the monastery's many enterprises and he could be especially irate at the number of noisy machines that were purchased to increase their efficiency. Among his unpublished poetry was a sarcastic parody of Joyce Kilmer's "Trees," which contains these lines: "Poems are naught but pent up breeze / Big bucks are made with Trappist chee$e. . . ."

The abbot, whatever little sympathy he may have had for some of Merton's interests, had enough good sense to allow this high-strung intellectual monk some breathing space. One sign of that confidence is that he went to Father Louis frequently to make his own confession. Beginning early in the 1950s Abbot James provided him the use of a little shack out in the woods behind the monastic barns, a shack that Merton called "Saint Anne's," as a tiny shelter for periods of recollection, prayer, and being silent. That time of recollection plus his genuine love for the novices and the joy he experienced in teaching and directing them were the anchor points of his life, despite days of unrest and moodiness that show up in his journals. Merton could wax lyrical at his joy in having just a few hours alone at Saint Anne's, where he would go to pray and read or simply sit still and watch the world of nature. The little shack of Saint Anne's became his favorite solitary haunt, replacing his perch in the loft of the monastery's horse barn, where as a young monk he would go to get away from it all. It was interesting to learn, on a recent visit to the monastery, that the little shack, for a long time a bit of a shambles, was being fixed up by a monk who on occasion puts it to the same use that Merton did four decades go.

It was in this same period of the 1950s that Thomas Merton

60

would enter into a correspondence with a man who would prove to be a major influence on his life, the Zen Buddhist master from Japan, D. T. Suzuki. Again, it was the desire to enter into deep dialogue that prompted this renewed interest in (he had read some studies written by Suzuki when still a student at Columbia) and love for the Zen tradition that prompted these contacts. It is not difficult to see why the Zen tradition would prove attractive to the monk. The austere aesthetics of Zen was a counterpoint to the traditional Cistercian emphasis on simplicity and spareness. Zen monasteries emphasized meditation, withdrawal, and techniques for reaching new levels of consciousness. Merton would frequently note in his writings that he had a deep appreciation for the seriousness with which Zen practitioners embraced the disciplined life of withdrawal. It should also be noted that there was then a modest renaissance in Zen studies in the Catholic world (quite independently of Merton's interest), most conspicuously represented by the work of the English Benedictine monk Aelred Graham, whose *Zen Catholicism* (1958) was, in the English-speaking world, a pioneering effort in introducing the world of Zen into anglophone Catholic culture. Similar work was being done by Jesuits in Japan associated with their university (Sophia) in Tokyo.

There was a further, more theological, reason why Merton felt an affinity for Zen. Following a long tradition of Catholic theology, Merton felt that at the core of every human person God was present by indwelling, and that the serious seeker for God could touch that deep center. Thus, he wrote in *Conjectures of a Guilty Bystander* that "at the center of our being is a point of nothingness which is untouched by sin and by illusion, a point or spark which belongs entirely to God, which is never at our disposal, from which God disposes of our lives. . . . This little point of nothingness and of absolute poverty is the pure glory of God in us." It was bringing that deep center — what he called, at times, borrowing from Louis Massignon in a somewhat untranslatable French phrase, the *point vierge* — to consciousness that Merton saw as the goal of the contemplative life. Since Zen had as a fundamental goal the penetration of illusion to the non-Self he saw an affinity with the Christian contemplative path. Since Zen, further, saw itself as a tradition that emphasized discipline and technique it did not have strong theological demands on those who wished to learn its way. In other words, one could find in Zen a technique and an aesthetic without em-

61

bracing "Buddhist" doctrine. Hence, it was an attractive tradition for spiritual seekers and many, not monks alone, would seek out its teachings in the postwar period.

To cultivate this friendship with Suzuki, Merton asked the elderly scholar to write an introductory essay for a collection of translations that Merton was making of the sayings of the desert fathers. Merton saw in those simple tales of the early ascetics wisdom tales not unlike those found in the Buddhist tradition of the short tale called the *mondo*. As it turned out, Suzuki's introduction did not appear at the head of *The Wisdom of the Desert,* which Merton finally saw through to publication. Nonetheless, it was a way for Merton to make a connection between himself and someone for whom he had a deep reverence.

It was precisely those affinities that led Merton to write about Suzuki in his journal lines strikingly reminiscent of his thinking about both his dialogue with the Russian Orthodox theologians and the Latin American poets: ". . . if I can meet him [i.e., Suzuki] on a common ground of spiritual Truth, where we share a real and deep experience of God, and where we know in humility our own deepest selves . . . then, I certainly think that Christ would be present and glorified in both of us and this would lead to *a conversion of us both . . .*" [Merton's emphasis].

Who is this Christ to which Merton refers? All through the fifties Merton meditated on the Wisdom mentioned in Proverbs 8, developed in the Pauline epistles to the Colossians, Ephesians, and in the Gospel of John: that Wisdom who was with the Father from the beginning, through whom the world was created, and in whom all things were sustained. It was the Wisdom that was the subject of his magnificent prose poem "Hagia Sophia" with its resonances of the Bible and Orthodox piety. Structuring the poem partially on the monastic hours of the day, Merton sees biblical Wisdom as the Spirit of Christ and perhaps even more:

> All the perfections of created things are also in God and therefore He is at once Father and Mother. As Father He stands in solitary might surrounded by darkness. As Mother His shining is diffused, embracing all His creatures with merciful tenderness and light. The diffuse shining of God is Hagia Sophia. We call her His "glory." In Sophia His power is experienced only as mercy and love.

(When the recluses of fourteenth-century England heard their church bells and looked out upon the wolds and fens under a kind sky, they spoke in their hearts of "Jesus Our Mother." It was Sophia that had awakened their childlike hearts.)

Merton's emphasis on the cosmic Christ and the Wisdom of God as suffusing the whole universe and the works of human beings helped him at a time when Catholic scholastic theology argued about the salvation of the non-Christian and the relationship of non-Catholic Christians to the Catholic Church. Merton, whose interest in scholastic theology was tangential at best, worked out his own theory of grace based largely on the fruits of his own deep prayer life and his willingness to look for those God seekers who struggled to speak and live the Truth. He would spell out his attitude towards this whole issue in a somewhat fiery tract he wrote in 1961 entitled "A Letter to Pablo Antonio Cuadra Concerning Giants." The "giants" in the title were Gog and Magog from the prophet Ezekiel, whom Merton identified with the two superpowers, the Soviet Union and the United States. In that long screed against the Cold War antagonisms of the day he said that it is true that the "visible church" (i.e., the Catholic Church) alone has the mission to sanctify and teach, but "no man knows that the stranger he meets coming out of the forest in a new country is not already an invisible member of Christ and perhaps one who has some providential or prophetic message to utter." He goes on to criticize those missionaries who went in the past to Asia, Africa, and elsewhere only to teach and not to listen, while concluding, "God speaks and God is to be heard, not only on Sinai, not only in my own heart, but in the *voice of the stranger*. That is why the people of the Orient, and all primitive people in general, make so much about the mystery of hospitality" [Merton's emphasis].

Merton comes to the issue of the salvation of the non-believer and the whole vexatious question of God's grace outside Christianity not as a systematic theologian nor as a professional ecumenist. The eruption of these questions in his writings derived from his evolving conviction that his vocation was to enter into deep contemplative dialogue with other seekers on a one-to-one basis, seeking out those commonalities that all who pursued the truth found. He was aided in this quest by his conviction and experience that Christ as the Word, Christ as Wisdom, permeated the entire cosmos.

This slow development of his understanding of how he might speak to a larger intellectual world did not mean that Merton wanted to turn the entire monastery into some kind of spiritual think tank. He recognized that many men and women enter monastic life in order to have the milieu within which they can pray and work in silence and solitude. He had enormous love and deep respect for the simple monks who lived at Gethsemani and other houses. What he did try to articulate for himself and for his superiors was the idea that a sustained dialogue with the world of intellectuals was not incompatible with but could be integrated into monastic life. He argued, directly and indirectly, that the monastic tradition was large enough to make a place for those who felt that they could have a voice in this larger world, and further, that they would use their voice in a way fully compatible with monastic solitude and withdrawal.

Merton's conviction about the importance of an intellectual life for some contemplatives was most clearly formulated in a letter he wrote to Pope John XXIII in 1958, in which he offered the congratulations of his novices upon the pope's recent election to the papacy after the death of Pope Pius XII. In that letter he then sets out what he considers to be his special vocation as a monk:

> It seems to me as a contemplative I do not need to lock myself into solitude and lose all contact with the rest of the world; rather this poor world has a right to a place in my solitude. It is not enough for me to think of the apostolic value of prayer and penance; I also have to think in terms of the contemplative grasp of the political, intellectual, artistic, and social movements of this world — by which I mean a sympathy for the honest aspirations of so many intellectuals everywhere in the world and the terrible problems they have to face. . . . Most Holy Father, with the encouragement of friends and a number of priests and bishops, I am beginning to think seriously of the possibility of a monastic foundation, whose purpose would be to exercise a contemplative apostolate of this kind. . . .

It is important to note that Merton was making this argument about the relationship of monastic life and the intellectual world (what he once called an "apostolate of friendship") at the precise period in American Catholic history when a ferocious debate was going on triggered by a famous essay by Monsignor John Tracy Ellis about Catholics and the intellectual life. Ellis's thesis was that American Catholics had been so defensive about their faith and so concerned about the "brick and mortar" issues of caring for a largely immigrant church that they had neglected the intellectual life. That neglect resulted in an under-representation of Catholics in public life, in the scholarly world, and in the world of intellectuals.

There is no need to rehearse here the correctness of the debate triggered by Monsignor Ellis's essay or of the vast literature it produced, either to support the thesis or critique it. Suffice it to note that in the precise decade in which that debate took place, a monk already possessed of some fame, in a rural Kentucky monastery, was developing, from one particular angle of Catholicism, a powerful apologia for intellectual engagement. Furthermore, he was putting that program in motion through an indefatigable exchange of letters, ideas, publications, and conversation with people on three continents. It was a form of intellectual engagement that centered itself not in a university setting but from the cloister of a rural monastery.

In this decade, without making an exhaustive catalogue, we can note a long correspondence between Thomas Merton and his old mentor from Columbia University days, Mark Van Doren, on literature; an exchange between himself and Jacques and Raissa Maritain on spirituality and philosophy; any number of letters to Latin American poets and writers, including the beginning of a long exchange between himself and Victoria Ocampo, who would publish much of Merton's writings in Latin America. He also exchanged visits with the expatriate artist and printer Victor Hammer, who would set in print some of Merton's shorter works at his printery in nearby Lexington and with whom he had fruitful conversations on art. He maintained in the same period exchanges of letters with Jay Laughlin, his publisher at New Directions in New York, and with Robert Giroux of the Harcourt, Brace publishing firm, as well as old classmates Ed Rice and Robert Lax. Finally, there was an extended exchange of ideas with Erich Fromm (whom Merton called an "atheist mystic") going back to 1954. That correspondence well illustrates Merton's capacity for dialogue even when the two participants stood for radically different foundational issues.

One of the most interesting exchanges of letters, begun in the

1950s, was between Thomas Merton and the Polish expatriate Czeslaw Milosz. Milosz at this period still lived in Paris as an exile from his native land, but would eventually come to America where he taught Slavic literature at the University of California at Berkeley. Milosz would win the Nobel Prize for literature in 1988. Their correspondence has now been published. It is an exchange of immense interest, begun with Merton's letter of appreciation for Milosz's famous book *The Captive Mind*. Milosz was every bit Merton's intellectual equal, feeling no hesitation in offering a salutary critique when he found Merton's religious musings too facile or not well enough thought out. Coming from a believer it was helpful for Merton, who did most of his study of Marxism, modern alienation, and the search for the transcendent in modern culture without the aid of living conversation partners. As Merton would say in a letter written to Milosz in 1959, "Even as a Catholic I am a lone wolf, and not as independent as I might seem to be, yet not integrated in anything else either."

All of these exchanges — most of them by letter even though old friends like Ed Rice, Bob Lax, Jay Laughlin, Bob Giroux, and Mark Van Doren would sometimes visit the monastery — illustrate Merton's key conviction that he had something to say as a contemplative; that he brought a different angle of vision to the more pressing questions of the day. There is not the slightest apologetic thrust to these letters. In this fashion, he was able to exercise what he once described as an "apostolate of friendship." Since Merton was not free to travel and visitors found Gethsemani a difficult place to get to he found the exchange of letters, offprints, books, pamphlets, etc. as a way of carrying on a dialogue with people. The hefty volumes of his correspondence are mute testimony to how seriously he took this task.

A preoccupation with literary matters was not always appreciated in the monastic community. The abbot groused about monks reading fiction which, Merton said in his journal, he always referred to as "love stories." Dom James could not understand how a monk could find time to read a fat novel like *The Brothers Karamazov*; the abbot was fastidious both about filling up a monk's day and suspicious of any "secular" distractions in the monastery. At times, in the daily chapter room meeting he would issue oblique and not so oblique warnings about wasting time on novels and "secular" music. Wisely, he dispensed Merton from these strictures since he knew that his novice master was more than disciplined about his work in the monastery. Nonetheless, he had grave doubts about how these various intellectual interests meshed with traditional monastic life.

Merton, by turn, believed that this somewhat narrow vision was harmful to the many young monks who came to the monastery with good intellectual formation and a thirst for learning. He saw too many potential monks driven from Gethsemani by a too rigid conception of work and prayer, and by a narrow vision of the contemplative life as one of suffering, penance, and the cross. The great task was to integrate that desire for deep contemplative living into authentic monastic observance.

Monastic life was no sideline for Merton. While he carried on his intellectual enterprises he was also still very much a part of his monastic community. In his capacity as master of novices he was responsible for vetting potential candidates for the monastery (aided in this endeavor by the naval veteran, Father John Eudes Bamberger, who was a medical doctor and had been sent by the abbot to be trained as a psychiatrist) and for bringing young monks into monastic culture in the novitiate. His days, then, were spent in a round of liturgical exercises, classes, writing, and participation in the general life of the monastery. He was also in correspondence with monks from around the world, dealing with issues of monastic research and renewal. He carried on a lengthy correspondence with the European monk-scholar Jean Leclercq and with the French Jesuit, Jean Danielou. Danielou became a sort of spiritual and theological advisor to him during the period when Merton sought to leave Gethsemani for Latin America, but he also kept Merton *au courant* on matters theological. Brother Patrick Hart's edition of Merton's letters on monasticism *(The School of Charity)* reproduces over 120 printed pages of letters Merton wrote between 1950 and 1960 on aspects of the monastic life. Most of this vast correspondence deals with issues of reforming the monastic life by seeking a better grasp of the meaning of monastic usages, by inquiring more deeply into the very meaning of monasticism in the Christian tradition, and by studying in depth the writings of monastic theologians.

The meaning of monasticism was not simply an exercise in intellectual speculation for Merton. He had devoted his life to this way of being and he never stopped inquiring into its meaning and mystery. It was in the 1950s that he had almost an instantaneous intuition into his own monastic life, one that would radically change the way he thought of who a monk was and how the monk ought to live. He described this moment of insight in his notebooks of the time and then, in a more reflectively rewritten fashion in *Conjectures of a Guilty Bystander*. The epiphany at "the corner of Fourth and Walnut" is now so celebrated that some scholars see it as an axial moment in Merton's life. That is probably an exaggeration, but it was a moment that did give Merton a new understanding into his monastic existence. Here is the beginning of the *Conjectures* version, which is somewhat rewritten from his earlier journal entry:

> In Louisville, at the corner of Fourth and Walnut, in the center of the shopping district, I was suddenly overwhelmed with the realization that I loved all these people, that they were mine and I theirs, that we could not be alien to one another even though we were total strangers. It was like waking from a dream of separateness, of spurious self-isolation in a special world, the world of renunciation and supposed holiness. Not that I question the reality of my vocation, or of my monastic life: but the conception of "separation" from the world that we have in the monastery too easily presents itself as a complete illusion: the illusion that by making vows we become a different species of being, pseudo-angels, "spiritual men," men of the interior life, what have you.

The fundamental point of that passage is simple enough: by becoming a monk a person cannot think that he is cut off from the life, travails, and concerns of other human beings. To flee from the world — a traditional monastic desire — cannot mean to ignore the world, to hate or disdain it, or to be indifferent to it. To think that a person can abdicate from the world and its needs is, in Merton's word, an "illusion." He then uses some traditional monastic language which, if understood incorrectly, fosters that illusion. Monks are not bodiless; they are not angels even though the early monks strove for the "angelic life" (*bios aggelikos* was the Greek phrase). They cannot fool themselves by arguing that they are interior persons or "spiritual men" (*viri spirituales* was the medieval Latin term for the ascetics) and, by making that argument, turn themselves away from the world and its needs. By using the traditional monastic vocabulary Merton was determined to "deconstruct" pernicious meanings attached to the vocabulary over the years.

Merton went on in this passage to note that even though monks may flee the world, they are, whether they like it or not, part of the world — which includes war, race hatred, mass media, big business, technology, and so on. To pretend that such a world does not exist in the name of contemplative living is not only illusory but immoral. Furthermore, to see the world and its people through the eyes of the contemplative makes it imperative to let those people know that the monk is with them, to help them see that they are made in God's image, even though, in a lovely phrase, "There is no way one can tell people that they are walking around shining like the sun."

The implications derived from this epiphany on the streets of Louisville ramifies out in a number of different directions. In the first place, it aided Merton to see how monastic ascesis must be free from any morbid hatred of the flesh or disdain for the ordinary business of human living. If monks are not angels then they must live as flesh-and-blood human beings tied to all other men and women in the world. Second, this sense of connectedness meant that Merton needed to foster in his life a wider and thicker sense of human community, a sense made more easy because of his love for the doctrine of the Communion of Saints and for seeing the church as the "Mystical Body of Christ." However much the monk might love solitude, solitude must never be confused with individualism.

One could make the argument that Merton's desire to be in interior union with Orthodox thinkers and a conversation partner with a whole range of people in Latin America, Europe, and Asia was an attempt to found a community that would cross boundaries of space and diverse thought patterns in order to foster the transcendent character of human experience. Such an enterprise (far deeper than the now fashionable "networking," which finds its meaning in venues for self-aggrandizement) would encourage honesty, social criticism, and fidelity to the prompting of the spirit of God.

Third, and most importantly, this sense of solidarity towards and membership in the large human family gave him a theoretical underpinning for his growing need to express himself on matters of social justice in a world that was becoming more conscious of racial divisions, the threat of atomic warfare, and the growing social and economic tensions both between the Great Powers and the nations struggling against colonial power. After all, Merton wrote these words about an apostolate of friendship while the first struggles for racial integration were happening in the South, when the Hungarians had risen up against their Soviet masters, and the countries of Africa were breaking their bonds with colonial powers in places as different as Algeria and Ghana. Over all these events, of course, loomed the widening arms race as atomic weaponry gave way to hydrogen bombs and more nations began to enter into the nuclear weapons "family." It was also the period in which the antagonisms between West and East were at their height.

The insight that Merton received at this time would be aided immeasurably as he continued to study Buddhism; what Merton was struggling to articulate was not totally unlike the Buddhist notion of compassion for all living things — a compassion available to those who had become enlightened through contemplative insight and disciplined living. After all, the Buddhist concepts of mindfulness and compassion had deep resonances within the Christian tradition in general and the monastic tradition in particular. Buddhism had the further attraction of being (especially in its Theravada strain) heavily monastic in its orientation.

This greater sense of human solidarity did not undermine his conviction about the necessity of contemplative withdrawal or his own commitment to solitude. In fact, in that same extended passage about his epiphany in downtown Louisville, he wrote that it was precisely from the angle of his own monastic life that he could see others in the core of their reality, the person "that each one is in the eyes of God."

Despite these heavy intellectual and devotional duties, Merton still found time to enjoy hours of solitude in the woods, in the little shed dedicated to Saint Anne. His journals of the period fairly exult in the quiet and stillness that those hours afforded him. He took that time also to become a close observer of nature. His notebooks are full of observations of bird life (he used a manual for identification and had the use of a pair of binoculars), and he had a keen interest in the monastic forests; he often took his novices for brush clearing or seedling planting expeditions.

True to his poetic impulses (and deeply influenced by his love for the poetry of Gerard Manley Hopkins, who was to have been his dissertation topic) Merton saw in the natural world and its inhabitants the hidden grace of God, the movement of Sophia-Wisdom, and a clear hint of the cosmic redemption of Christ. A good study could be written on how Merton blended the close observation of nature with his sense of contemplative prayer. Nowhere is that sense of God's presence in nature more apparent than in the opening verses of a prayer that he wrote on the eve of Pentecost Sunday, later reprinted in *Conjectures:*

> Today, Father, this blue sky lauds You. The delicate green and orange flowers of the tulip poplar tree praise you. The distant blue hills praise you, together with the sweet-smelling air that is full of brilliant light. The bickering flycatchers praise you with the lowing cattle and the quails that whistle over there. I, too, Father praise you, with all these my brothers, and they give voice to my own heart and to my own silence. We are all one silence and a diversity of voices. . . . Here I am. In me the world is present and You are present. I am a link in the chain of light and of presence. . . .

The love for nature was never sentimental or romantically Wordsworthian. Merton saw the presence of God in nature; he did not divinize it. Indeed, he instinctively recoiled from such sentimentality. Walking among the trees after a November ice storm in 1958 he saw "the glass trees were brilliant and fragile in the sun and great halos of light whirled in the sycamores — the land was transformed like St. Seraphim of Sarov [the great Russian mystic; ed.], full of the Holy Ghost." Merton then adds quickly in a parenthesis: "Yet I remain suspicious of its coldness and its appeal to makers of Christmas cards."

It should not surprise us that he also loved art and architecture. In *No Man Is an Island* he argued that flashes of aesthetic intuition were a kind of insight into the nature of contemplation. His notebooks are full of allusions to the books of architecture and art which he enjoyed. He was a keen student of the writings of the Indian philosopher and art critic, Ananda Coomaraswamy, whose thesis that all great art developed out of a matrix of religious experience interested him deeply. His close friendship with the artist printer Victor Hammer and Hammer's wife Carolyn allowed him time to discuss art with him even though Hammer's severe understanding of acceptable art (Hammer had a horror of abstract art in general and abstract expressionism in particular) did not mesh with Merton's ideas totally. He treasured the opportunities he had to go to Lexington and spend time at the home of the Hammers, drinking tea (and good brandy!) and discussing art. Finally, from his student days at Columbia University he had developed a great love for the thomistic aesthetics of Jacques Maritain, especially as it was set out in Maritain's classic *Art and Scholasticism.*

Merton also kept up a correspondence with his old Columbia classmate Ad Reinhardt, who had already gained a certain reputation in New York art circles. He was naturally sympathetic to Reinhardt's convictions about simplicity and spareness in painting. Reinhardt had produced a body of minimalist painting that not only reduced color down to black on black or white on white, but in the process erased almost any hint of form in his work. At first glance, many of his mature works looked simply like canvas painted totally in black or white. In 1957 Reinhardt sent him one of his "black on black" paintings, a panel that looked as if there was only a black surface on the small painted surface but which, in fact, had a broad thick cross painted black on the black, visible only on close inspection. Merton loved the painting (it eventually went to his hermitage) because it was a spur for meditation. Reinhardt also sent Merton art papers, Chinese pens, inks, and other supplies to encourage the monk, who had been a cartoonist and illustrator while at Columbia, to exercise his artistic gifts. Merton's calligraphies and abstract drawings are a direct result of this encouragement.

All during this decade Merton struggled to put together a book under the working title *Art & Worship.* After many false starts the project was abandoned, partly because Merton himself could not work out to his own satisfaction a workable theory of religious aesthetics. His notebooks of the period are filled with frustrated paragraphs as he sought illustrations, rewrote texts, and discussed the project with publishers. While his own taste was eclectic enough (he loved Byzantine icons, Romanesque architecture, and the abstract art of painters like the Swiss artist Paul Klee as well as the art of the Aztecs and Asian art in general) he was unable to bring these disparate interests together in such a way as to articulate a coherent theory of religious art.

Critics have discussed this artistic impasse but it seems clear that there are a number of factors that kept Merton from being a theoretician of art even though he was a lover of art. Partially, it was the Cistercian emphasis — deriving in part from Saint Bernard of Clairvaux's criticism of the art of Cluny — on simplicity, spareness, and clarity, even though Gethsemani, judging from photographs, was cluttered with bad art when Merton entered. This desire for religiously minimal art coincided with his own penchant for imageless contemplation, which at a certain level clashed with the more sacramental imagination of the liturgy. Finally, and probably most importantly, cloistered monks, with their small opportunities to travel and look, just did not have enough visual experience to develop a theory or theology of art. Even though Merton had a good visual eye (as his drawings and, later, his photography would demonstrate) he, like his beloved Saint John of the Cross, was better at producing drawings — almost as an aside — than he was at talking about art.

In the busy decade of the 1950s, as we have seen, Merton developed a way of being for a contemplative monk that did justice to his own catholic concerns for the intellectual life of the modern world. We see him drawn into the world of ecumenism, cultural dialogue, and interreligious communication. He also underwent a personal conversion, epitomized by his famous epiphany in downtown Louisville, that provided him with the basis for what was coming: the social upheavals both in the United States and the world. Merton, from the fastness of his monastery, would have his place amid these tumultuous events.

Merton, in the fifties, could be classified as a member of the American Catholic "liberal" elite — that group identified with those who were passionate for social justice, liturgical reform, and a broader place in American culture. Their favored outlets were such organs as *The Catholic Worker* newspaper with its fiercely uncompromising pacifism and love for the poor and the avant-garde, the Benedictine sponsored *Worship* with its twin messages of liturgical reform and social justice, the intellectual quarterly *Thought* edited at Fordham University, the literary quarterly *Renascence,* the lay-edited journal of opinion *Commonweal,* and *Jubilee* magazine edited by his old Columbia classmate and friend, Ed Rice. Indeed, one could thumb through the back issues of *Jubilee* and find in its pages some of the then most creative and searching attempts to widen the worldview of American Catholicism. The magazine, now long defunct, provides, as it were, an optic nerve for the study of Catholicism in its optimistic vigor on the eve of the Council.

The aspirations of these groups and the outlets connected with their name would come full flower, in somewhat unexpected ways, with the surprise calling of the Second Vatican Council by Pope John XXIII shortly after his election as pope in 1958. The coming Council would bring with it changes that neither Merton nor most Catholics of the time could even imagine. The tone of Vatican II was set by the thinkers and theologians Merton most admired. The patient labors they undertook in what the French call *ressourcement* — the recuperation of the ancient tradition of Christian life in the areas of scripture, patristics, scholastic theology, and ecumenism — would provide the intellectual fuel for the reforms of the Council. Americans learned of most of those intellectual efforts from a small body of "advanced" thinkers, and among those, surely, was Thomas Merton. Most of the truly revolutionary elements of the Council would find genial agreement (and some anticipations) in the scattered writings of Merton even though they were never systematically explored in his work. In that sense, one must say that his thinking and writing was more intuitive and spontaneous, but at the same time it was deeply rooted in the ancient wisdom of the monastic, ascetic, and contemplative tradition of the church.

On the eve of the Second Vatican Council one could situate Merton as a person who, among a small coterie of like-minded people, exposed American Catholics to a vision of the church drawn from ancient sources of wisdom in an open fashion. He also served as a conduit for thinking that came from the new movements current on the continent. Finally, despite his relative isolation, he was already making contacts with the larger intellectual world of thinkers who, without necessarily professing an explicit religious faith, were nonetheless deeply involved in finding some spiritual underpinnings for a culture they saw as badly flawed. In all of these ways, Merton became a central part of the movement that gave legitimacy to the term "dialogue." That movement, of course, would take on a more central place in the life of the Catholic Church through the forces unleashed by the new attitudes developed through the deliberations of the Second Vatican Council.

3 Towards Mount Olivet

Who shall ascend the hill of the Lord?

Psalm 24:3

T HE EARLY MONTHS OF 1960 SAW A NUMBER OF SMALL
events whose full significance for the world would only become
clear in the next few years. In response to Viet Cong attacks on the
army bases of the South Vietnamese, the United States doubled its
number of military advisors. After a long search, Israeli intelligence
discovered the Nazi war criminal Adolf Eichmann in Argentina and
had him brought to Israel for trial (and eventual execution). The new
pope was in the midst of plans for the opening of the Second Vatican
Council. Lorenzo Barbato, a Venetian friend of Pope John, visited Merton at the monastery and delivered personal gifts from the pope, including a priestly stole.

In the summer of 1960 Merton read the galleys for a collection of
his essays which would come out that same year under the title *Disputed Questions*. The essays collected in that volume, despite Merton's
somewhat rhetorical introduction arguing for a thematic coherence,

seems to be a rag bag of pieces dealing with a number of rather disparate topics. In that sense, *Disputed Questions* very much followed the
Merton formula of publishing the work of the previous years in order
for them to gain a wider audience. Nonetheless, a few years later, Merton himself would say that this collection marked a turning point in
the kind of writing that he wished to do. The title, like so many that
Merton devised, had an edge to it. "Disputed Questions" referred to
the medieval academic practice of discussing philosophical and theological propositions that were the subject of controversy in the universities. The topics of disputed questions, as the phrase indicates, dealt
with those issues that were not settled (e.g., the doctrines found in the
creeds) but open to consideration and debate. Most of the medieval
scholastics, preeminently Saint Thomas Aquinas, contributed to the
literature called generically *Questiones Disputae* and frequently published them under that rubric.

Merton's title was somewhat ironic in that a few of the subjects to
which he turned his attention were either not talked about at all in
Catholic theological circles or were tangential to the life of contemplative monks. The issues, then, were not as much disputed as were the
topics to which he addressed himself — topics, in many cases, that
Merton thought should be discussed. In other words, it was the dispu-
tatious character of his subject matter that would lead to puzzlement
for those who had fixed ideas about what subjects monks should write
about.

In *Disputed Questions* there were three studies of varying length
which focused on Boris Pasternak, who had died earlier in 1960. Those
essays reflect Merton's preoccupation with the "Pasternak Affair."
There were a number of studies of monastic and eremitical figures
(John Climacus, John of the Cross, Saint Bernard of Clairvaux, etc.),
some short pieces on art, and two essays on Christian love. Many of
the works in this volume had seen previous publication, but as a
whole, represent some of the main themes of Merton's thinking in the
previous decade. The clusters of essays could also be seen as a kind of
work in progress, as Merton had an abiding interest in solitude and
struggled for a long time (unsuccessfully) to write a full-length study
on Christian art.

The collection of such essays into a single volume would be a
strategy Merton would use frequently over the next decade to gather

together his increasingly scattered contributions to journals and magazines both here and abroad. These published collections of essays were, so to speak, the published reflections of the intense discussion, exchanges, and occasional writing that derived from his extended "conversations" with so many different dialogue partners, real and imagined. The demand for such contributions from his pen was such that, as noted before, when asked by an Italian priest to contribute an essay for his journal, Merton said, somewhat testily in his private journal, people must think "I sweat articles." In that particular instance, Merton was being asked to identify himself and his reputation with an evangelizing scheme (the *Mondo Migliore* movement) then popular in Italy. The basic point, however, is this: publication of his collected essays, hitherto scattered in somewhat out-of-the-way places, was a strategy employed by Merton to move to a wider audience issues which, in the first instance, were available only to the few. Such collections also announced, albeit implicitly, that these were the issues of interest to the monk. They came from his preoccupations (art, literature, culture, monastic practice, contemplative values) and not from some external command.

The most substantial essay in *Disputed Questions* is "A Philosophy of Solitude" in which Merton attempted to sort out for his own satisfaction how one was to understand the meaning of solitude, what its human significance was, how it was to be distinguished from loneliness or alienation, and finally, how solitude relates to social reality. This essay was a reworking of a briefer one that he originally published some years earlier in a French journal under the title "Dans le desert de Dieu."

Merton considered this reworked essay as one of the most important that he had ever written. In a sense, it was an advancement beyond the more general remarks he had written in the preface to *Thoughts in Solitude*. He makes it quite clear, at the outset, that he avoided in this essay the word "solitary" as a simple synonym for "monk" or "monastic" because the kind of solitary he was interested in "may well be a layman, and of the sort most remote from cloistered life, like Thoreau or Emily Dickinson." In other words, he desired in this piece to write an apologia for solitude as a positive concept in general, and at the same time to clear up misunderstandings about the idea.

The earlier volume, *Thoughts in Solitude,* was the setting down of the thoughts and aspirations of a monastic solitary, but "Philosophy of Solitude" is a more structured attempt to justify the role of the solitary in human society and in the church. "Philosophy of Solitude," in short, was his attempt to set out a theoretical apology and the theoretical justification for such a life. The essay is also, although most would not have known this, an attempt to justify his own desire for a more solitary life to those in his own religious order, which was staunchly communal in its orientation. However, he appeals less to the monastic tradition to make that justification and more to the very religious concept of solitude more generally and more phenomenologically understood.

The solitary, Merton argues in "Philosophy of Solitude," reacts against the all too human love for what Pascal called *divertissement* just as the solitary avoids the temptation to succumb to the thinking of the group and the passion for conformity in society. Hence, the authentic solitary can take up, assuming purity of intention and clarity of purpose, the prophetic task of disagreeing completely "with those who imagine that the call to diversion and self-deception is the voice of truth and who can summon the full authority of their prejudices to prove it." One sees, in that argument, something that will emerge more clearly in his thinking, namely, that the solitude for which he looks is not only to enable the pure search for God, but the search itself has a prophetic character to it: a concern for the illusions and sins of the world.

By combining those two elements of contemplative solitude and the witness against the evils of the world he shows that the solitary life is not, as some imagine, an exercise in self-indulgence or mere flight from the "real" world. This prophetic edge becomes increasingly the way he understands the traditional notion of *contemptus mundi.* The essay's argument, then, is more easily understood when seen against the background of the worries about collectivism, bureaucratic power, and the rising power of the media that was a staple of social criticism of the time. Merton's argument, in short, must be read against both the collective impulse in totalitarian societies and the smothering effects of rampant consumerism in capitalist society.

Merton goes on to argue that the vocation to solitude carries its own dangers and deceptions, pitfalls amply discussed in ancient monastic literature. Hence, a solitary cannot be detached from others who might advise him or her and/or warn against excessive asceticism or disdain for the world. The solitary must never give in to the temptation to become a freelance spiritual person. It is only when the solitary learns the traditional monastic virtues of charity, hospitality, discretion, fidelity, and so on that such dangers are avoided. Such a person, seemingly apart from the world, is in fact deeply concerned with the world and with its fortunes.

Throughout "Philosophy of Solitude" Merton makes clear that he is not talking about mere physical isolation (although some physical self-separation at least for times seems extremely helpful) but that interior solitude which is a kind of forgetfulness of the self and its false layers of deception and masks. Without some of that interior solitude, Merton concludes, there can be no growth or maturity: "Unless one becomes empty and alone, he cannot give himself in love because he does not possess the deep self which is the only gift worthy of love." That deepest solitary "I" is the one that dwells beneath all human falsity and is, as Merton often loved to say, the dwelling of God's self dwelling within us as uncreated saving grace. It is also clear from these considerations that solitude is not a synonym for loneliness, individualism, or egocentricity. It is only when a person is alone in his or her solitude that he or she can reach out to the other in love and freedom.

The most interesting aspect of this particular essay is not so much the persuasiveness of its argument as its attempt to synthesize elements of Merton's thinking. One detects in the essay a balanced tension between solitude and social responsibility; between insight and illusion; between community and the solitary life. There is a prophetic theme in Merton's conviction that only the person who understands and values interior solitude finds the capacity to say "No" to the pretensions, ideologies, and slogans of the crowd. Too often Merton's critics box him off as a social activist or a spiritual writer, but in a study like "Philosophy of Solitude" one sees that his own desire was not to split such orientations but to find some way to combine them into a coherent whole.

The articulation of the sense of the authentic self, set forth in that essay, is more expansively treated in Merton's rewriting of *Seeds of Contemplation* which he was working on at the same time that he was reading galleys for *Disputed Questions*. When *New Seeds of Contemplation* was published in 1962, Merton opened the book with some chapters in which he argued that only when one stripped away personal evasions, illusions, and masks could a person become a true contemplative. He never defines the term "contemplation," but provides in his opening pages a number of descriptive phrases to explain what he meant by the term.

Contemplation is not simply "looking" or "gazing" in a heightened fashion. It is more deeply attitudinal. Contemplation is "spiritual wonder," "awareness of the reality of the Source," a kind of "spiritual vision," a more "profound depth of faith," "knowledge too deep for words," etc. Finally, he stipulates that contemplation reaches out to the knowledge and even to the experience of the transcendent and unknowable God. Negatively, contemplation is not a function of musing on the subject of the Cartesian ego nor is it simply the experience of prayer or ecstasy or prophecy. Contemplation is, above all, awareness. Authentic contemplation, further, is a bulwark against the pseudomysticisms of the age: the collective mystique of the Party or the Nation or the Crowd. One senses in these warnings Merton's close reading of Arthur Koestler and other social critics of his school, which he had done all through the latter half of the 1950s. It is precisely the contemplative life of the solitary that stands prophetically against the false mysticism of mass society.

The rest of *New Seeds of Contemplation*, after the first five chapters which attempt to describe contemplation both positively and negatively, consists of relatively brief chapters in which he meditates on a wide range of spiritual topics. These brief chapters represent an old method of Merton: to choose a word or phrase and then supply an extended meditation on those words. It was a practice begun with *Thoughts in Solitude* but inspired ultimately by Merton adopting this practice from Saint John of the Cross. Merton ends *New Seeds* with a wonderfully evocative chapter entitled "The General Dance." Picking up on one of his fundamental themes, namely, that the Word of God is entwined in the very act of creation as well as its maintenance, and that this Word of God — the Wisdom spoken of in Proverbs 8 — is also the Word made Flesh; and this Word is approachable by a contemplative outlook. Merton sees this Word as like a cosmic dance in which the presence of God echoes in creation and in persons. We can find that newness through contemplative awakening when, turning inside out all virtues, "the emptiness and the purity of vision that make them evident, provide a glimpse of the cosmic dance."

More than one Merton commentator has noted the radical shift in

Merton's thinking between the earlier version(s) of *Seeds* and the rewriting of *New Seeds*. By far, the most significant change is the philosophical shift by which he abandons the dry scholastic analysis of human life rooted in philosophy for a more person-centered personalism. He also begins to abandon his ferocious shunning of the world (don't read newspapers!) to a softer (don't read advertisements!) and more realistic line for people in the world who would read his book. In the preface to the new version of the book, the author confesses this shift quite openly. The first book was written in "isolation," and more to the point, when the author, in his words "had no experience in confronting the needs and problems of other men."

One can see in these and similar reflections Merton's struggles to integrate his own sense of the deep life of prayer and his analysis of the contemporary situation, where he detects impulses towards the transcendent amid looming façades of illusion and impulses to violence and manipulation. By insisting that people had a contemplative dimension in their lives, no matter how attenuated or latent their awareness of it, he made his entry point into dialogue with those who represented the best in the culture of his day. In other words, his contemplative life was not only for himself but for the world in which he lived, albeit at the margins.

Merton's use of the term "self" often hides the fact from unwary readers that it is a contemporary synonym Merton employs for the ancient Pauline metaphors of dying to the old and rising in the new, or putting off the "old" man and putting on the "new" man, with the change indicating a new way of being in the world, a new way of seeing things, and a new perspective on life. In a collection of essays published in the same year as *Disputed Questions* under the title *The New Man* (1961), it is telling that a number of the studies focus on the biblical notion of "image and likeness" as well as the concept of the second Adam and life in Christ. In fact, one could argue that the essays in *The New Man* constitute the most sustained series of studies that Merton ever did on purely theological and christological themes. There are nine essays in the volume, but the whole book is set out in consecutively numbered paragraphs much like the "century" works of the Christian East. *The New Man* is an understudied but crucial text for grasping Merton's essentially Christian theological vision.

The basic themes of this book run in the manner of a fugue

81

through the whole. The essay "Life in Christ" in *The New Man*, for example, argues a vision of Jesus Christ that is heavily in debt to the contemplative monastic tradition. Christ is not merely a teacher of the spiritual life. Christ creates the Christian life through the gift of his Spirit, which dwells in all of us. To discover the Spirit of Christ within us is to discover the true image and likeness of God described in the Book of Genesis. The contemplative life is nothing else but making present this image of God through us. The contemplative person is the one who is illuminated with "the face of Christ" (the phrase is borrowed from the Greek fathers). The whole of this essay is characterized by a high trinitarian doctrine borrowed largely from Merton's long meditation on the Russian tradition: Christ is the Way through the power of the Holy Spirit to the "unimaginable" Father.

It should not go unnoted that the "new man" of the title is an implicit rebuke to the Marxist claim to building a "new man" — the theoretical capstone of a classless society. Merton's "new man" is, in short, an alternative vision to the oft discussed "new Soviet man" of the Cold War era. From the fifties on Merton had carried on, even though it was not systematically done, an attempt to construct a Christian humanism as an alternative to the Marxist humanism he detected in the writers he was reading for intellectual nourishment.

All of the transformative themes in biblical thought have a bearing on Merton's understanding of the true self. After all, it was almost a commonplace in monastic literature to describe the monastic life as a kind of "therapy" in which the old person died and a new person was born in the light of God's saving grace. This "newness" is the gradual coming alive into awareness that God dwells intimately within the very heart of each person. The very act of taking a new monastic name and the ritual custom of lying prostrate and then rising at the time of monastic profession of vows is a "performance" of that ideal. As Paul says, anyone who is in Christ is a new creation.

It is also worthwhile to note in passing that Merton's concern with the true self not only reflects an old concern in ascetical and contemplative literature but also his awareness of the literature of the French existentialists, who wrote passionately about the search for authenticity and the authentic self while analyzing the "absurdity" of human existence. Attempts to describe the "meaning of man" were not restricted to the camp of the Marxists. Merton's reading in the early

writings of Jean-Paul Sartre as well as the writings of the phenomen-
ologist Maurice Merleau-Ponty was episodic, but he would eventually
make a careful study of both the fiction and nonfiction of Albert
Camus, who in the monk's estimation plumbed real issues in a profoundly satisfying manner. It is also worthwhile, again in passing, to
note that the popular literature of the time was centrally occupied with
analyses of the loss of the individual self in the face of mass culture
and the rise of large corporations. This was, after all, the time of popular works like *The Man in the Grey Flannel Suit* and David Riesman's influential *The Lonely Crowd* as well as a host of lesser critics of the culture, in which there were sharp distinctions made between the desire
for personal autonomy and the crushing pressures of mass society,
whether it was the consumer culture of the West or the bureaucratic
societies of the East.

The end of the fifties saw the Catholic Church energized with
new hope as Catholics reacted to the stunning announcement by Pope
John XXIII that he was convoking an Ecumenical Council, the first to
be convoked since the First Vatican Council abruptly ended its deliberations in 1870 as a result of the onset of the Franco-Prussian war. One
of the central themes that John XXIII wished the council to pursue was
the relationship of the Roman Catholic Church and other Christian
bodies. The papal call for such a dialogue would profoundly impact
the way the church in general related to the larger world of Christianity. The papal desire for greater Christian unity derived from both his
sense of the rising tide of atheism in the world and his sense that parts
of the world, emerging from colonialism, faced enormous challenges
in the sociopolitical arena. Nor was the pope indifferent to the weakness of the churches during the Nazi and Fascist periods less than two
decades earlier. Pope John was realist enough to know that organizational unity or even theological harmony among various Christians
was a long way off, but he did think that those who invoked the
name of Christ could do much together for the world in the name of
the gospel.

These first tentative steps of ecumenical openness were felt at the
Abbey of Gethsemani, encouraged by the abbot who saw such an attitude of ecumenical exchange as fulfilling the "mind of the Holy See."
The practical consequence of such an open attitude was that there
came a steady stream of Protestant visitors from nearby seminaries to

"discuss" church relationships, and from the part of the visitors, to have a sympathetic look at the workings of Christian monasticism. This work, so congenial to the traditional monastic service of hospitality, has continued to this day at the Abbey of Gethsemani. In any given month one will find both individuals and groups of non–Roman Catholic persons staying at the abbey on retreat or for time of prayer.

Merton's personal journals for this period regularly note visitations from groups from Asbury Seminary (Methodist) in Kentucky, from groups led by Glenn Hinson (later one of the founders of the International Thomas Merton Society) and his students from the Southern Seminary (Baptist) in Louisville, from the Presbyterian Seminary in the same city, by seminary students from Sewanee (Episcopal) in Tennessee, from Hebrew Union College and Seminary in Cincinnati, from the Presbyterian Seminary in Lexington, and from divinity school groups with their professors from Vanderbilt Divinity School in Nashville. On these occasions there were usually informal presentations from Merton, some questions and answers, and discussion as well as the first attempts at common prayer.

It is fairly clear to me, based on conversations with some of the participants, that these exchanges never had the character of technical theological exchanges, since by temperament and training that was hardly Merton's forte. The meetings had more of the quality of mutual exchange and common prayer in line with Merton's desire to further a dialogue of friendship. These encounters, in other words, were another mode of creating networks of persons who could meet together for serious spiritual discussion, intellectual exchange, and prayer.

These various groups came with such regularity that the abbot and the abbatial council of his senior advisors decided that it might be useful to build a separate meeting place for such encounters, both to afford a space for the guests and for the less noble reason of ridding the guest house (which was usually crowded with retreatants anyway) and the novitiate of the smell of cigarette smoke and too much noisy conversation. After much discussion, planning, and so on, the monks constructed a small building of three rooms with a limestone fireplace and a broad porch on a slight hill called Mount Olivet, about a short mile walk from the monastery. The plans had been made by the abbey's Brother Clement Dorsey, who had been a student of Frank Lloyd Wright before entering the monastery. The cottage sat on the crest of a small hill shaded in the back by a copse of trees, with a clear area in the front that looked like a small meadow as it dropped down from the porch of the building. When first constructed, the building had neither electricity nor plumbing. Its cinder-block plainness had little claim to aesthetic note, but it did possess the requisite Cistercian resistance to ornamentation while providing pleasure for those who favored the plain style.

Anyone who has looked at this slight building, especially when mentally abstracting from its later additions like the chapel built on the side of the building in 1968, would recognize immediately that it was not very well designed for conferences but would make a service-able cottage for one person — i.e., it would make a nice, if somewhat primitive, hermitage. Merton understood that fact. "Clearly it is a hermitage and not a conference center," he wrote in his journal. Evidently, his abbot saw this too, although both kept all this possible use as something only tacitly understood. The "conference" center might have been called Mount Olivet, but for Merton it was named Our Lady of Mount Carmel — a fitting patroness for a hermitage. Not only did Merton have a great devotion to the Madonna of Mount Carmel (he wrote a wonderful prayer in her honor) but he certainly had in the back of his mind the memory of those early hermits in the Middle Ages who lived on Mount Carmel in ancient Palestine near present day Haifa, the lineal ancestors of the Carmelite friars who maintain a friary there even to this day.

Abbot James Fox was quite aware of Merton's desire to go to a more primitive monastery or to make a foundation in Latin America. Despite Rome's no to this plan in 1959, Merton had not totally abandoned the dream. He was still importuned by Ernesto Cardenal (now out of Gethsemani and in Mexico studying for the priesthood), by Dom Gregorio Lemercier of the Benedictine monastery in Cuernavaca outside Mexico City (who had encouraged Merton in the first place), and by some of the monks at Gethsemani who desired a new start. Against this attitude for change was the combined judgment of his theological advisor, the Jesuit Jean Danielou in Paris and Cardinal Valerio Valeri of the Congregation of Religious in Rome as well as the adamantine Dom James, who had visited Rome personally (according to Merton) to tell Rome in no uncertain terms that Merton should not be granted a decree of exclaustration by the Vatican. In the long run it was probably providential that Merton did not go to the priory in Cuernavaca. Dom Gregorio, himself hardly a model of monastic stability, had the entire community psychoanalyzed in the late 1960s with the net result that most of the monks abandoned the priory along with Dom Gregorio, who himself left to marry.

The planned "conference center" was a way for the abbot to allow Merton some spiritual and physical space at Gethsemani while still keeping him at the monastery. In that sense, Mount Olivet was an enlargement upon the primitive plywood shack called Saint Anne which Merton had used in the previous decade. Dom James gets a bad press in some pages of Merton's journals and in some of the more tendentious Merton biographies, but without having ever known the man, it is clear that he was shrewd enough to see that Merton's impulsiveness, enthusiasm, and somewhat impractical side needed structure. At the same time, it was equally clear that Merton's energies and talents needed some lessening of the strictly confining discipline of the abbey.

Even though there had been some peripheral hermits in the early history of the Cistercians (Merton studied them assiduously!), the Order was fiercely community minded; Cistercians were a cenobitical Order and not an eremitical one. As Merton gained some daily time at the hermitage — first, a few hours when he was free, then full days — he was slowly setting a precedent that was quite new for the Trappists. His permanent move to the hermitage, to be discussed at its proper moment, would not come for a few years. The fact that Dom James himself entered a hermitage when he resigned as abbot after having used his own influential voice in the general chapter in Rome to argue the case for Cistercian hermits, and that at least two or three hermits live on the Gethsemani property today as well as those who live attached to other Cistercian monasteries, is largely due to the pioneering efforts of Merton. What had been a historical curiosity in early Cistercian history slowly became an option for some few monks who had proved themselves in the life of the community. Nonetheless, the hermit life is the exception rather than the norm in the Cistercian Order. For most of the monks the hermit experience consists of regular times when they can retreat from the community for a few days or weeks of solitude.

One can track, with the aid of his now published journals, the slow development by which Merton finally got his hermitage. In the early 1950s there were the few hours spent in the shed called Saint Anne's or a little space found in the loft of one of the barns. When the center on Mount Olivet was built in the beginning of the next decade, one sees Merton using the place for a few hours; then he got permission to sleep there on occasion. Next came electricity and soon afterwards some basic appliances like a stove and a refrigerator. Finally, in 1965, Merton made a permanent move to the hermitage. Each of these slow incremental steps are recorded by Merton in his journal either in passing or as the marking of a grand event.

Merton's struggle with the Order over his desired move to another monastery was not Merton's only conflict with church authority. All monastic writers had to submit their writings to the censors within the Order to receive clearance before they submitted their work to a publisher. Indeed, after the censors in the Order gave their approval the manuscripts were then submitted to a diocesan censor (typically, in the place where the book was to be published) for the bishop's *imprimatur*. Typically, this internal censorship was a way to guarantee that the monk was not publishing anything contrary to the Catholic faith.

In Merton's case, however, the dispute he had with the General of the Order (the Frenchman, Dom Gabriel Sortais) concerned not heresy but the topics that Merton addressed. The General, for instance, was irritated with some characterizations of the monastic life in *Disputed Questions*. He had vetoed the publication of D. T. Suzuki's introduction to Merton's translations of the sayings of the desert fathers, which would appear from New Directions in 1961 as *The Wisdom of the Desert*. It struck the Father General as unseemly that an "unbeliever" should interpret the sayings of the ancient desert fathers and mothers. That judgment, in itself, says something about the intellectual distance that existed between Merton and his older confreres.

Dom Gabriel was especially chary of Merton's writings on social issues in general and on the morality of atomic weaponry in particular. In the period 1960-1962 Merton wrote a number of letters, essays, and reviews about the then burning topics of atomic war, the ethics of building bomb shelters, the debate over limited atomic exchanges, atmospheric and underground testing of hydrogen and atomic weapons, and so on. These writings must be seen against the large debates going on at the time both in the United States and in Europe. It is fair to say that most American Catholics and the vast majority of the American hierarchy sided with the West in its Cold War struggle and found, as a consequence, no strong moral revulsion at a nuclear arsenal built as a deterrence to communist aggression. Those in the Catholic community who favored disarmament or, worse, pacifism, were very much a minority.

Merton's peace instincts were fueled both by his own personal debt to his long dead Quaker mother as well as his long-standing admiration for Mahatma Gandhi, but also to his friendship with Catholic activists in the peace movement like Dorothy Day and Jim Forest of the Catholic Workers and his Jesuit friend, Daniel Berrigan. He was also genuinely appalled that some moral theologians in the United States, some Catholic philosophers, and not a few members of the American Catholic hierarchy could develop a moral calculus that permitted an acceptable death toll in an atomic exchange with the Soviet Union in the name of victory over an enemy. Nor was he unaware of the fact that European Catholics were less enamored of atomic arsenals than were their American counterparts and coreligionists. He was equally horrified over theological discussions in some clerical journals about whether one could defend a personal bomb shelter with guns against others looking for shelter in case of atomic attack. As he wrote to his British friend Etta Gullick, "One could certainly wish that the Catholic position on nuclear war was half as strict as the Catholic position on birth control."

The Abbot General's attitude was that such writings were not the proper provenance of the monk, but Merton was convinced that the abbot — a true French patriot of aristocratic background who evidently favored France's independent nuclear *force de frappé* — wanted no monastic jeremiads against the possession and use of atomic weapons. When the Abbot General finally forbade Merton from writing on such topics, Merton, good monk that he was, obeyed but employed a somewhat circumspect ruse to avoid being reduced to total silence. Merton would write his thoughts on "dangerous topics" in the form of letters to friends or occasional correspondents. These reflections, often in the form of essays, began to circulate in mimeographed versions that recipients could or could not, as they saw fit, duplicate for the benefit of others.

This underground strategy, also employed in the 1950s by the Jesuit thinker Teilhard de Chardin who was silenced by church authorities and forbidden to write for publication, was a kind of Catholic *samizdat* — the strategy used in those same days by dissidents who wrote under the control of the totalitarian regimes of Eastern Europe. Merton, always brilliant in choosing ironical titles, called these missives *The Cold War Letters*. The "Cold War" referred not only to the contemporary struggles between East and West in the sociopolitical realm, but to Merton's own guerrilla skirmishes against what he saw as an unfair use of religious authority to silence him. This internal war was also "cold" because it had not broken out in acts of open defiance of church authority or, from the superior's point of view, disciplinary actions. Merton, whatever his faults, was an obedient (if crafty) monk. His struggles with ecclesiastical censorship were part and parcel of life in Catholic circles before the reforms of the Second Vatican Council.

It would be a mistake, however, to see this conflict between the monk and his superiors as a simple struggle between the forces of truth and the powers of obscurantism. Such a simplistic reading of the matter does not do justice to the issues then at stake. What resides under this tension between Merton and his abbot and the Order's authorities was a clash of religious worldviews and not only mere political disagreements. Merton struggled to get out from under a concept of monasticism that was seen only as otherworldly, penitential, and an agency of prayer and mortification framed in some ahistorical fashion. Such a view of monasticism is summed up in the old dictum *est monachi plangentis et non docentis officium* ("It is the monk's calling to weep and not to teach").

Merton valued all of the traditional strands of monastic life and he was quite prepared to weep (and had done so) but he attempted to understand them not in a somewhat rigid and abstract fashion but in terms of how the monk, in concrete terms, was to live vis-à-vis the world without falling into illusions of angelism or perfectionism. His whole monastic life, from the early 1950s on, was an attempt to come to grips with that problem. It would haunt him until his dying day.

Even sympathetic critics and friends felt that Merton at times was too judgmental and harsh in his cultural criticism and too rigid in the manner in which he separated the Good Guys and the Bad Guys. He seemed to be just too far in front of the pack on social issues. Since he wrote in relative isolation it is not surprising that some of his judgments were lopsided or too strenuous. The great monastic scholar Jean Leclercq, a longtime correspondent and admirer of Merton, made that precise critique in letters to him. Merton would listen to a wise monk like Leclercq and examine whether or not he was going off onto peripheral tangents in his writing and thinking. In his journal, after a visit of Dom Leclercq in the summer of 1961, Merton considered the criticism seriously but then added up a list of his works that he stood by. It would be the first of a number of times that he would take the pulse of his writing by way of a list:

> Most of the *Seven Storey Mtn*, and *Jonas* and anything on solitude, esp. the notes in *Disputed Questions*, a lot of the poems, *Seeds of Contemplation*, and *New Seeds* (I think), a good part of *The Silent Life*. Perhaps a few pages of *No Man Is an Island*, a good bit of *The Secular Journal*. And most of the recent work: *The Behavior of Titans* especially. And the thought on Herakleitos and the Chinese stuff? Maybe.

The Silent Life, published in 1957, was a primer on the monastic life divided into three parts: a section on monastic virtues and ideals; a second section on the cenobitic life of the Benedictines and Cistercians; and a third on the eremitical orders of Carthusians and Camaldolese. The earlier volume *No Man Is an Island* (published in 1955) is a collection of meditations and essays on themes dear to Merton's heart: silence, asceticism, mercy, pure intention in prayer, recollection, interior solitude. It was in that book, discussed in the previous chapter, that Merton, according to William Shannon, first began to formulate a strategy of asking radically difficult questions in the light of religious experience. It was also a book in which Merton began to think more of community and social reality and seemed less focused on individual spiritual perfection. *The Secular Journal* (published in 1959 after a comedy of errors involving his complete inability to keep up with his contractual obligations to publishers) was a much abridged version of the journal he kept in the years before Merton entered the monastery, with sections on his life in the Village, his trip to Cuba, and his time at Saint Bonaventure's College where he taught. That work is now of only historical value since we have the complete journal of that period in print.

The Behavior of Titans marks a turning point in the kind of book that Merton would find increasingly more to his taste. In content and style it is a most unlikely work coming from the pen of a monk. Using Prometheus, Atlas, and the "Fat Man" as his archetypes, Merton produced a meditation on the struggles of the two superpowers who engaged in a "promethean" battle of which the consequences could only be terrible. The "Fat Man" of course is the code name for the atomic bomb that had been dropped on Hiroshima in 1945. In the middle section of this oddly compelling work, he addresses the bystanders who see themselves as "innocent" while confessing his "crimes against the state." The book ends with an essay in homage to the ancient Greek philosopher Herakleitos, who stands, in the monk's mind, as a wisdom figure and an antagonist to purely linear and syllogistic reasoning. From the extant fragments of the old philosopher and mystic Merton intuited a man who was intoxicated by the search for the Logos that stood behind all the change and turmoil of temporal existence. He loved the cryptic and paradoxical way Herakleitos wrote. The Herakleitos essay is, in this author's estimation, one of the best sustained essays that Merton ever wrote.

The Behavior of Titans contains within it many of the hallmarks of the kind of writing that Merton would increasingly produce in the future. Adopting figures taken from the intellectual tradition of the West (and beyond!) Merton would "read" those figures against the background of his own monastic life and in the light of the current great social problems of the day, especially the problems of world peace, disarmament, and increasingly, the question of racial justice. As his journals make clear, it is this kind of work that Merton frequently sent to his secular or nonbelieving friends as well as to those intellectuals (like Czeslaw Milosz) who would see and be sympathetic to what he was attempting.

It was these kinds of work, however, that created puzzlement and confusion for his immediate and distant superiors. Such works would also brand him, among many, as a leftist for his unwillingness to stand firmly and explicitly with the Western view of things during the Cold War period. The more Merton wrote in such a vein, the more he became a *bête noire* among conservative Catholics, being chided both in the press and in a steady stream of letters to him, his superiors, and to Rome — letters that were often vituperative in character. By the 1960s the "pious" Thomas Merton as spiritual writer was receding in

91

the minds of many in favor of a Thomas Merton as central to the leftist wing of the American Catholic Church.

Typical of this new style of writing was a long poem entitled "Original Child Bomb" with the ominous subtitle "Points for meditation to be scratched on the wall of a cave." Originally published in the English pacifist journal *Pax*, it was published in 1962 as a limited-edition book by New Directions, with drawings by the noted illustrator and artist Emil Antonucci. The poem consisted of a series of excerpts from news accounts, articles, pilot diaries, news reports, etc. describing the dropping of the atomic bomb in the waning days of World War II. Reminiscent of the style popularized by the American novelist John Dos Passos in the thirties, Merton's desire was to highlight the horrors of manmade weapons of total destruction by a dispassionate account of the facts.

After a terse opening sentence ("In the year 1945 an Original Child was born. The name Original Child was given to it by the Japanese people, who recognized that it was the first of its kind."). There then follows forty numbered "points" about the dropping of the bomb. The use of the term "points" in the subtitle would have been immediately recognized by Catholics as the term used for the separate considerations made by someone meditating on the scriptures in the Ignatian tradition of mental prayer. As one meditated on the "points" one was expected to visualize them, to experience what Ignatius called "composition of place." The poet clearly wanted his readers to visualize the horrors he was describing by using the factual sources he could find. By using the term "points" Merton was in essence turning Christian meditation, traditionally understood and practiced, into a new form in order to de-abstract technological horrors into something that could be grasped and imagined.

The same theme of the horrors that could be generated by an amoral (immoral!) technology is a powerful poem with the long title "Chant to be used in procession around a site with furnaces," which Merton sent to his friend Dorothy Day to be published in the staunchly pacifist newspaper, *The Catholic Worker.* Published in August, 1961, it also found its way into the British Catholic journal *Blackfriars* the next year and into the little "beatnik" book published by Lawrence Ferlinghetti of City Lights Books in San Francisco, called the *Journal for the Protection of All Beings.* Had they known who they were, it is certain that the Cistercian authorities would have been aghast to see Merton published in the beatnik company of Allen Ginsberg, Gregory Corso, etc.

"Chant . . ." is a powerful evocation of Auschwitz told through the proud voice of the commandant (or, perhaps, Adolf Eichmann) who, with no sense of penance or sorrow, alludes to the "showers" of Auschwitz, saying, "I made cleaning arrangements and then I made the travelers sleep and after that I made soap." The poem immediately adds, "I was born into a Catholic family but as these people were not going to need a priest I did not become a priest I installed a perfectly good machine it gave satisfaction to many."

Again, the poem used factual data gleaned from books Merton read, but unlike "Child Bomb" this work does not speak in neutral "journalistic" tones; the voice drips with withering irony and open sarcasm. It is no wonder that the *noir* comedian Lenny Bruce, having most likely found the poem in the Ferlinghetti volume, recited it as part of his comedy routine using a mock German accent while giving a Hitler salute as he goose-stepped about a nightclub stage. Whether Merton knew that or even who Lenny Bruce was, is not clear.

William Shannon, in his biography of Thomas Merton (*The Silent Lamp*), singles out three works — the letter on Giants, the Child Bomb poem, and the Chant poem — all written in 1960-1961, as the sign of Merton's definitive entrance into the peace movement. To that observation I would only add that it was the style he developed in these works that would be the vehicle he would use for such writings: a style that was partially "historical" in its sources, mosaic in its composition, allusive in its message, and founded on a kind of holy rage at the antihuman and un-Christian foundation of certain technologies at the service of destruction and death. This style also employed figures from various non-Christian sources (e.g., note the figures taken from the Greek classics) as vehicles for his vision. The genre of the prose-poem was perfectly suited to the kind of writing Merton loved to do. It was a kind of writing that would increasingly occupy his energies until his death. These publications were pointers that led to his final works like *Cables to the Ace* and *The Geography of Lograire*.

His involvement with the peace and civil rights movement brought with it a whole new range of correspondents with whom he shared ideas, manifestos, poems, and books. He was in regular correspondence with Jean and Hildegard Goss-Mayr, European Christian peace activists who, at Merton's instigation, forwarded peace materials to the commission working on the Second Vatican Council. Merton also began a correspondence with Wilbur H. ("Ping") Ferry, who was vice-president at the Santa Barbara Center for Democratic Institutions. Merton began that correspondence at the suggestion of Jay Laughlin, his publisher at New Directions in New York, with the hope that some kind of link with the Center would enrich his own work with the many visitors who came to the abbey for discussion and reflection. Merton also hoped that he might inject a "contemplative dimension" into the discussion of war and peace. They would continue to write until Merton's death; in fact, he visited the Center just before he left for Asia on his fateful trip.

James Forest was another activist who entered Merton's orbit in 1961 through their mutual interest in peace. A conscientious objector who worked at the Catholic Worker house in New York City, Forest began to write to Thomas Merton through his contacts with Dorothy Day. They remained in contact from then on, especially when Forest became a founding member of the Catholic Peace Fellowship, which was a branch of the Fellowship of Reconciliation — an organization Merton knew and valued. Merton would regularly send materials to Forest for publication in *The Catholic Worker* and from Forest would receive materials produced by the peace movement. Forest was the recipient of a number of the "Cold War Letters," and he published a few essays by Merton without using the monk's name because of Merton's problems with the monastic censors. Years after Merton's death, Forest, who now lives in the Hague in the Netherlands and is a convert to Russian Orthodoxy, would write a well illustrated biography of his friend: *Thomas Merton: A Pictorial Biography* (1980) and name one of his sons for him.

This peace network, informally organized if "organized" is even the word for it, was very much a minority strain in the American Catholic Church. That is an important fact to keep in mind. The overwhelming majority of the Catholic hierarchy and most of the Catholic laity were either ardent or complacent cold warriors. There was much lurid preachment about the "Church of Silence" and a steady drumbeat of anti-communism. At the end of every Sunday Mass there were prayers for the "conversion of Russia" recited in every parish church in the country. Many parishes, shaped by immigrant mores, served as a source of resistance to regimes back in the homeland. In 1948 Italian parishes in the United States carried on a quite open campaign to keep their relatives in Italy from voting for the Italian Communist Party. Catholics of a certain age will remember the lurid books and articles about the persecuted church behind the Iron Curtain. Membership in the Communist Party brought with it the threat or reality of excommunication. In the period of Joseph McCarthy there was the common quip made that the period was characterized as the time when the graduates of Fordham investigated the graduates of Yale.

In the midst of these projects of social activism, Merton also developed some new networks of correspondents that would both enlarge the circle of his intellectual contacts and provide him opportunities for deeper interreligious dialogue. Merton had been in correspondence for some time with the noted Arabist, Louis Massignon. Massignon, a devout Christian (he would eventually be ordained an Eastern rite priest), and a chair holder at the Collège de France, introduced Merton to the world of Islamic mysticism which was Massignon's particular field of expertise. Merton also greatly admired Massignon's staunch resistance to those who favored violence in what was then French colonial Algeria, even though Massignon, a staunch French patriot, could not envision an independent Algeria.

Massignon was a natural soulmate for Merton. He was French, devoutly Catholic, a noted intellectual, and a passionate devotee of mysticism and comparative studies. Merton was not only sympathetic to Massignon's scholarly interests but strongly admired the French scholar's efforts at peacemaking during the French crisis over civil unrest in the French colony of Algeria, which was spilling over into terrorist incidents in Paris itself.

Through the suggestion of Massignon, Merton began a correspondence with a retired Pakistani civil servant named Abdul Aziz, who was also a member of a Sufi order of mystically inclined Muslims. It was Aziz who initiated the correspondence after receiving Merton's name from Massignon when Aziz asked him to recommend a genuine Christian mystic and contemplative.

The correspondence between Aziz and Merton began in 1960 and lasted until the year of Merton's death. They exchanged books and articles and discussed the mystical tradition in Islam and Christianity, with special emphasis on the great Islamic mystics, Rumi and Al Hallaj (Massignon wrote a massive work on the latter now considered a classic — *The Passion of Al Hallaj*), as well as their Christian counterparts, especially Saint John of the Cross. One sees Merton struggling to find analogues in Christian theology that would bridge the gap between the Islamic stress on the absolute unity of God and the trinitarian structures of Christian belief. He affirms his belief that every person who sincerely believes in God and acts according to his conscience will certainly be saved and come "to the vision of God."

Judging from only Merton's side of the correspondence, Aziz (who was not a scholar) must have been fairly conversant with Christian sources, since Merton mentions the *Philokalia* (an early modern compilation of Eastern Christian monastic and ascetic texts which has attained classic status in the Christian East), which Aziz had evidently studied. Merton promises Aziz that he would try to get him some writings of the Hesychast mystics from the Orthodox centers on Mount Athos, where he thinks Aziz would find a "point of contact between Christian mysticism and the Sufis."

For all of Merton's use of the "I" in his writing he was notoriously reticent about his own life of prayer and his own contemplative experiences. Merton was both self-revealing and self-concealing. It is for that reason that a letter Merton wrote to Abdul Aziz on January 2, 1966, is so extraordinary and now so famous. Aziz asked Merton about his daily life and his habits and experiences of prayer. Merton replied that he rarely wrote about such matters but as a sign of friendship and in confidence he would outline his daily life in the hermitage (we will discuss this in its proper place). He then went on to describe his prayer in terms that Aziz could understand. The passage is well known but it bears repeating in part:

> Strictly speaking I have a very simple way of prayer. It is centered entirely on attention to the presence of God and to His will and His love. . . . One might say that this gives my meditation the character described by the Prophet as "being before God as if you saw Him." Yet it does not mean imagining anything or conceiving a precise image of God, for to my mind this would be a kind of idolatry. . . . My prayer tends very much towards what you call *fana*. There is in my heart this great thirst to recognize totally the nothingness of all that

96

is not God. My prayer is then a kind of praise rising up out of the center of Nothing and Silence. . . . It is not "thinking about" anything, but a direct seeking of the Face of the Invisible, which cannot be found unless we become lost in Him who is invisible. . . .

It has often struck me that this letter, read in its entirety, is a hermeneutical key to understanding fully what Merton is driving at in his more discursive observations on contemplation, for example, in the opening chapters of *New Seeds of Contemplation*. It is also a text that permits an interested inquirer to grasp what kind of a contemplative Merton is. His emphasis on silence, lack of image, presence, and so on is characteristic of the dark mysticism that goes back to Saint Gregory of Nyssa, mediated through the writings of the Pseudo Dionysius and down to John of the Cross, and mediated again through the monastic and scholastic doctors of the Middle Ages. That kind of mysticism, it should be noted, would be amenable to the aesthetics and praxis of the Zen tradition with its emphasis on simplicity, spareness, and flight from the iconic. In other words, Merton's predilection for this kind of "imageless" mysticism explains, among other things, his interest in the Shaker aesthetic, his penchant for abstract art, his fascination with Chinese calligraphy, and his unswerving concern for Eastern mysticism.

It was also in 1961 that Merton began to write to an English lecturer, Etta Gullick, who taught at one of Oxford's theological colleges as a lecturer on prayer. Because of her interest in the seventeenth-century English spiritual director Benet of Canfield, whose *Rule of Perfection* she was editing, she wrote to Merton to ask if he would comment on her manuscript and perhaps write an introduction to her work. The introduction never did get written, but a close epistolary relationship developed. They exchanged books, articles, and suggestions for reading. They had a mutually instinctive love for the English mystics, for the writings of the German Dominican, Meister Eckhart, and for Orthodox spirituality. Gullick introduced Merton to the writings of English writers like the platonically inclined philosopher E. I. Watkin (with whom Merton corresponded) and the formidable Oxford philosopher Elizabeth Anscombe. Gullick also recommended journals like the Benedictine sponsored *Downside Review* and the Dominican edited journal *Blackfriars*. Interspersed with lengthy comments on spiritual literature, Merton's letters would also keep Gullick informed about his writings on peace, which he insisted derived from his passionate moral convictions about the evil of atomic weaponry. Merton's position was quite clear:

> What is worse about the Catholic silence on this subject (the Popes have certainly spoken out) is the idea that moral theology *obligates* one to take the lowest and most secularized position. . . . One would certainly hope that the Catholic position on nuclear war was half as strict as the Catholic position on birth control. . . . It is impossible not to be in some way involved but we must be very careful that we are not passively involved. . . .

One other "cluster" of correspondents who began to exchange letters with the monk were some Jewish rabbis who shared Merton's interest both in religious mysticism and social activism. The most conspicuous of these exchanges was the one between Rabbi Abraham Heschel and Merton, which began in 1960. In his journal, Merton said that he regarded Heschel as one of the most significant spiritual writers of his generation. He not only valued Heschel's writings but explained to him that he was using his now classic study of the prophets as a text for his novices. It was not until 1964 that Heschel visited Merton at Gethsemani, but their sympathetic exchanges did have one concrete result. When the debates on how the Council was to respond to Christianity's relationship to Judaism were in full discussion, Merton, at Heschel's request, wrote Cardinal Bea in Rome to ensure a satisfactory text on Judaism coming from the Council. That intervention (in 1964) led Merton to a further exchange of letters with Heschel, since both were afraid of a watered-down statement coming from the conciliar fathers. Worse still, an earlier draft called upon the conversion of the Jews; in response to that Merton wrote Heschel that he was appalled at such a crude suggestion: ". . . my latent ambition to be a true Jew under my Catholic skin will surely be realized if I continue to go through experiences like this. . . ."

The final document from the Council *(Nostra Aetate)* on the relationship of Christianity to non-Christian religions, while not exclusively dealing with Judaism, was a repudiation of any hint that anti-Semitism could be proclaimed in the name of the Catholic tradition. The exchange between Merton and Heschel hints, at least, how far the

dialogue between Catholics and Jews had to go and from where it began. The rabbi and the monk, of course, had a further tie in that both
were conspicuous voices against the war in Vietnam; Heschel by reason of his involvement with the interreligious group "Clergy Concerned" and Merton through his close contacts with the peace movement in general.

Along with his irregular correspondence with Abraham Heschel,
Merton was also in steady correspondence with Zalman Schachter,
who was an expert on Jewish mysticism and an ordained Hasidic
rabbi. Schachter supplied Merton with a number of important Hasidic
texts (Merton had first learned about this tradition from his reading of
Martin Buber) and, from the rabbinical seminary in Cincinnati, visited
the monastery on a number of occasions, sometimes bringing students
with him. The correspondence between the two men is an interesting
complement to the Merton/Heschel correspondence; one can find a
better sense of how Merton himself understood his Christianity in relationship to Judaism. What is clear is that he is not a crude "super-
sessionist," arguing as he does that the biblical tradition is a seamless
whole. In some of his private journal jottings he argues (to himself)
that if he cannot learn to read the psalms "as a Jew" he will never understand them.

It was from the suggestion of Zalman Schachter that Zwi Werblowsky visited Merton before he left the United States to take up a
chair at the Hebrew University in Israel. Their exchange at Gethsemani focused on Zen, but Werblowsky also became a conduit for
Jewish materials to Merton, especially works on mysticism. Although
Merton never studied this topic in any systematic fashion, it was a
mark of his catholic tastes in reading as well as his capacity for (epistolary) friendship that he sought to understand this tradition, not only to
help his own life but in order to practice the interior ecumenism that
had been a strategy with him since the middle 1950s.

In many ways the first years of the 1960s were a pivotal moment
in Merton's life. One sees in those years certain shifts taking place both
in his personal life and in the ways he was thinking and the directions
in which that thought was taking him.

In the first place, there is no doubt that the building of the "retreat" center in the hills behind the monastery was a portent for his
own future style of life. It would become a hermitage, but the precise

shape and the character of that eremitical life was still largely to be worked out. How much and how little contact he was to have with his own monastic community, and more importantly, with the larger world both religious and secular, was still to be determined. At this time there was no clear sense about what duties (if any) the community could expect of him should he take up the hermit's life. Since he was very much a pioneer, all of the details of the solitary life would, in a very real sense, have to be discovered and/or invented.

Second, the vexatious issues of church authority in general and censorship in particular not only reflected a certain way of "doing business" in the church but were symptomatic of changes to come. More crucially, they helped to shape a different understanding of how a contemplative was to live vis-à-vis the world and its problems. That this issue was new and path-breaking is evident from the fact that the commonplaces discussed about the relationship of social justice and contemplation, found everywhere in the literature and official documents today, were a rarity until a few figures like Thomas Merton raised them in an environment that was at best indifferent and generally hostile to such enterprises.

It is worth noting that in the modern period Merton was hardly alone in feeling the hand of church censorship. Some of the most preeminent names in modern Catholicism were silenced for "the good of the church." Teilhard de Chardin was never allowed to publish his spiritual writings in his lifetime and was forbidden to accept a chair at the Collège de France. Yves Congar, Jean-Marie Chenu, Jean Danielou, as well as a host of others who were identified with *la nouvelle théologie* were silenced or forbidden to teach. In the early 1960s the Jesuits dispatched Daniel Berrigan to Latin America to keep him from harm's way. Merton, in short, was in very good company.

Third, in a way that was already anticipated in the fifties, one sees in Merton's interests a widening grasp of how seemingly disparate areas of culture have, in fact, some connection. Merton did not think it odd to be interested in the Islamic Sufi mystical tradition while at the same time reading Jewish Hasidic masters. He did not, by such reading, espouse any simplistic syncretism or a vague Huxleyesque *philosophia perennis*. Merton was unapologetically but not triumphalistically a Christian mystic. He did very much accept, however, that the Spirit moves all over the world, and from quite disparate experiences by quite diverse people one learns to deepen the contemplative life. He came to adopt this point of view because he had already worked out, to his satisfaction, that the cosmic Christ was operative in all things.

It is important to note that while Merton rarely left the monastery he did not depend only on books to broaden his life. One sees "clusters" of correspondents who helped him deepen, support, and enhance his studies, while he in turn encouraged their work, wrote for their causes, and advised them when asked. Merton, in short, had wide networks of like-minded people with whom he had a common intellectual and spiritual life. This "networking" (to use a now hackneyed but fashionable phrase) was not an accident for Merton; he saw such exchanges as part and parcel of his vocation: to be a friend, confidante, and participant in a great conversation (or conversations!) about the crucial issues of the day, a conversation in which he would be the person who would speak for, and from, the contemplative perspective.

All of these activities were being done against the background of the preparations for, and the opening sessions of, the Second Vatican Council. The intellectual and spiritual ferment of those events would turn, in time, the Catholic Church towards a more incarnational understanding of the church in the world. The final document to come out of the Council, The Pastoral Constitution on the Church in the Modern World (*Gaudium et Spes* — 1965), for the first time in history, used a conciliar document to address all people of good will. The constitution also stipulated the church's conviction that it needed to search the "Signs of the Times" — a task that Merton had committed himself to, from his monastic perspective, in a full fashion.

Merton summed up his attitude about contemplation and the world very nicely in a letter to the Brazilian nun, Sister Emmanuel, who was his Portuguese translator. In a 1962 letter headed "Cold War Letter #22" he wrote:

> . . . I think at least some contemplatives must try to understand the providential events of the day. God works in history, therefore a contemplative who has no sense of history, no sense of historical responsibility . . . is not fully a Christian contemplative: he is gazing at God as a static essence, or as a nameless ground of being. But we are face

101

to face with the Lord of history and with Christ the King and savior, the light of the world who comes forth from the Father and returns to the Father. We must confront Him in the awful paradoxes of our day, in which we see that our society is being judged. . . . In a word we have to continue to be Christians in the full light of the Gospel.

It is a curious but true fact: the various clusters of interests and correspondents that Merton constructed in the late 1950s correspond to many of the fundamental themes that would find expression in the deliberations of the Second Vatican Council, especially in the areas of peace and war, ecumenical and interreligious relations, and the presence of grace outside the Christian community. Although the contemplative life gets only tangential attention in the conciliar deliberations, the themes that this contemplative monk had given his life to were basic in the larger deliberations of the Council. Merton never figured prominently in the work of the Council; that task largely was given over to the theological experts (the so-called *periti*) who were in Rome. Merton remained, like other prominent Catholic thinkers Romano Guardini and Hans Urs von Balthasar, on the periphery of the conciliar debates in Rome. All three, however, made their silent contributions but in radically different ways. Much of what concerned the Council had been central to Merton's concerns, albeit from the perspective of a cloistered monk.

4 Taking Up the Hermit Life

You expected a hermit to live in the wilderness
But he has a little house and a garden,
Surrounded by cheerful birch groves,
Ten minutes off the highway,
Just follow the signs.

"Hermitage," Wislawa Szymborska

I N TRADITIONAL PARLANCE THE MONASTIC LIFE IS KNOWN
as the *vita regularis*, which literally means life under a rule *(regula)*.
Such a life is also "regular" in the sense that it is governed by that rule
and, as a consequence, is a rather "surprise free" life. Monks pretty
much know what they are supposed to be doing at any given time of
the day. There is a time for rising, prayer, work, leisure, study, and so
on. That schedule follows a rather predictable horarium. To read Merton's journals for the years 1963-1965 is to see that life in some detail.
Even though, as we shall see, he would eventually go permanently to
the hermitage of Mount Olivet in the woods behind the monastery, he

still ordered his life according to the rounds of the monastic day and the liturgical calendar.

In various places, mainly in the letters and in the journals, Merton described his daily routine in the hermitage. It was a day that began with early rising long before dawn, regular prayer, periods of meditation, manual work, study, writing, and the celebration of the liturgy. It was a day, in short, that was very much a traditional monastic day even if, unlike most of the monks, his were frequently interrupted by visitors both announced and unbidden. Nonetheless, as he wrote in *A Vow of Conversation*, living alone in the hermitage allowed him to "live with the tempo of the sun and of the day, in complete harmony with all that is around me." The tempo of sun and day does capture the monastic routine; the daily schedule did admit of variation according to the season, and the yearly round was marked mainly by the liturgical calendar. Merton almost always dated his journal entries both by month and day as well as the saint's day or liturgical season being observed.

Merton was meticulous enough as a journal keeper that with a sense of the monastic horarium in mind as it changed during the year, and with a close reading of the journals, it would be easy enough to plot out where he was and what he was doing on most days in this period. That is not an unimportant fact, as Merton affords us the opportunity to remember that his writing wove itself into a regular life of prayer, community affairs, teaching, and work.

Yet the seeming regularity of that life must be seen against the background of momentous events that were taking place outside the monastery. The final sessions of the Second Vatican Council, which would come to an end in December of 1965, were taking place with their practical impact on the religious life of the monastery. One of the first documents approved by the Council was its reformation of the liturgy, and it was only natural for religious communities to discuss how and when and under what fashion the monastery should switch from Latin to a vernacular liturgy and how quickly. Such a change would mean not only translation but the more technical issue of the appropriate music, as much of the daily liturgy was sung in the ancient form of Gregorian chant.

There was enormous social unrest in the United States in the same period as the civil rights movement and all of its attendant tu-

mult of marches, demonstrations, and urban riots made daily head-
lines and the first place on the evening television (even though this
news came in bits and pieces; the monks neither read the daily papers,
subscribed to news magazines, possessed radios, nor watched the television). The war in Vietnam was escalating at a fierce rate as well as
the reaction against that war, which inevitably caused the antiwar
movement to become associated with the civil rights movement itself.
College and university campuses were in frequent turmoil. The seemingly placid quality of American Catholic life was shattered as confrontations between clergy and religious and bishops made the head-
lines and the changes coming from the Council upset hallowed ways
of doing things. The first stirring of the countercultural movement that
would become, in the parlance of the press, the "Flower Children" or
the Hippies was gaining ground. The somewhat regimented life on
Catholic college and university campuses would boil with change as
university personnel found themselves in tension with church authority, and students made their first attempts at resistance towards the
traditional discipline of their academic superiors.

The year 1963 alone saw a series of momentous events. Pope
John XXIII published his famous peace encyclical *Pacem in Terris.* There
was, alas, little peace on earth. Buddhist monks immolated themselves
in Saigon. Violence in Birmingham led to Martin Luther King's arrest
and the subsequent writing of the now famous "Letter from a Birmingham Jail." Pope John XXIII died and Paul VI was elected as his successor. In November of that year John Kennedy was assassinated in Dal-
las. On January 1st (1964) the new president, Lyndon Johnson,
committed the United States to a more active role in the fight against
North Vietnam, for all practical purposes taking over the active prose-
cution of the war. By the end of that year there would be nearly 250,000
American military personnel in that violence-torn country.

All of these events reverberate in the consciousness and in the
writings of Merton during this time, even though he frequently
learned of such events through the less-than-satisfactory means of
clippings mailed to him, letters from friends, conversations at the
monastery gatehouse, irregular access to weekly magazines or newspapers, or on infrequent visits to the city of Louisville where he would
haunt the public library. Even in the more liberal sixties Merton could
still wryly note how he hid a copy of *Newsweek* under his mattress

when the abbot made him a surprise visit! Radios and televisions were unknown in the house, and listening to recorded music was considered either a rare treat or part of instruction.

In fact, an argument could be made that these seemingly diverse forces of social and church change were of a piece in the sense that church reform and social activism had an intricate relationship, almost a symbiotic character — signified, perhaps simplistically, by the pictures found frequently in those days depicting the "two Johns" (John XXIII and John Kennedy). While the reform of monasticism was tied up with the reforms of the Council, the understanding of what it meant to be a monk became problematical in the face of the short-lived but symptomatic rise of the so-called "death of God" theologians and the concomitant debates about how the church could be relevant in a secular age. The byword "relevancy" meant, for church people, not only making their own practices relevant but also raised the further question about the church's relevancy vis-à-vis the larger world.

All of the impulses towards a church active in this world would almost inevitably force monastics to ask about their place in such a new religious reality. Relevancy (the word of the decade) then inevitably raised the issue of pacifism and social justice. This was the time, after all, of Harvey Cox's much read paean of praise for secularity in *The Secular City*, even though Merton was not impressed much with Cox's argument or the solidity of his theology. The English writer and Anglican bishop John Robinson had a best seller in his work *Honest to God*, which framed issues in a manner very similar to that of Cox. For Merton personally, there was also the added issue of both the civil rights movement and the peace movement, as he saw clearly that were he to understand his commitment to monasticism it could not be done detached from these great social struggles. He had already committed himself to living his contemplative life in the midst of history, and in the 1960s history was very chaotic.

The intertwining of these many social events and upheavals becomes clear when one looks at the volume of essays that Merton worked on in 1963 and finally published in 1964 under the title *Seeds of Destruction*. That rather hefty anthology of essays of over three hundred pages had three large sections. In part one there was a series of studies under the general title "The Black Revolution," with the monk's critique of the past history of racial segregation and the coming crisis in American race relations. Merton's argument was simplicity itself. The Civil Rights Act of 1964 marked not the end of the civil rights struggle but only its beginning. The reaction to that legislation was resistance and violence (Merton was thinking of the Kennedy assassination in 1963) and, as he noted in a prefatory note to "Letters to a White Liberal," where minds are full of hatred and imaginations seethe with cruelty, torment, and so on, violence and death will follow. Merton did not flinch from the implications of the new revolution brought about by the civil rights movement: there had to be a complete overhaul of the existing social system in America that would allow civil rights to come to authentic fruition. Inevitably, the overhaul of a long-established way of doing things brought pain and a totally new and alien way of being. Americans needed to face up to that fact despite its being an unpleasant (and in some ways unthinkable) reality.

Merton's view was so pessimistic about the race situation that Martin Marty, the noted religious commentator and professor of American religious history at the University of Chicago, would chide Merton in print for his dour sensationalism even though some years later in the decade he uttered a "mea culpa" in the pages of the liberal weekly newspaper *The National Catholic Reporter* indicating that Merton prophetically warned of coming unrest and urban riots.

The second large section of the book had two separate topics. The first was a series of brief studies on the question of war and peace, the role of the Christian peacemaker, and an extended appreciative commentary on the encyclical letter *Pacem in Terris* of Pope John XXIII. The second part of that section was a consideration of Christianity as existing in a diaspora situation. Inspired by a famous essay on the diaspora church by the German theologian Karl Rahner, Merton reflected on how the Christian was to live in the world when he or she was part of a minority in an increasingly secularized and indifferent world, especially the post-industrial world of the West.

If the diaspora situation (Rahner was thinking of the situation in Europe, with the East under Marxist constraints and the West increasingly secularized) was one that challenged every individual Christian, then how much more problematical was the situation of the contemplative monk? It is clear that Rahner's essay and Merton's response to it generated a topic close to Merton's heart: How does the monk live or how should the monk live in a situation where the traditional cultural props of Christianity were eroding? One source for his reflection was the situation of the first desert monks who fled to the desert as a protest against the decadence of the late Roman Empire; perhaps the modern monks had to be like the desert dwellers of old: living in a diaspora of their own making. He would return to this topic in the final months of his life as he attempted to puzzle out the future meaning of monasticism and Christianity itself. Merton would have probably been consoled had he read Rahner's famous remark that the Christian of the future would either be a mystic or would not be a Christian at all, but Merton's reading in Rahner was rather desultory and sporadic.

When a priest wrote to Merton charging him with giving in to pessimism by accepting Rahner's diagnosis of the future of Christianity, Merton responded with a long and thoughtful letter. He recognized that the priest dealt with large numbers of people in a parish setting, but Merton's point was that the good of the church did not depend on keeping alive large institutions. Christian optimism meant full and total acceptance of the mercy of God given to all men "in Christ." Grasping that concept was much more preferable than hoping for a medieval hegemony; it allowed for the real possibility that the Christian and the monk "are actually in a position of working out their own salvation and that of the world together with the non-Christian and the non-monk." Christian optimism, Merton concluded, was not to be equated with a "Rotarian cult of result and success" guided by the hands of "clerical Babbitts."

The third part of *Seeds of Destruction*, which included the letter cited above, was subtitled "Letters in a Time of Crisis." These letters were, of course, culled from the famous "Cold War Letters" that Merton had circulated in mimeographed form when he was under the strict censorship of the Order. In a somewhat more relaxed atmosphere (and with the encouragement of a more sympathetic censor at the Trappist monastery of the Holy Spirit in Conyers, Georgia), Merton was now able to permit these letters to reach a larger audience. The thirty-five that appear in this volume are addressed to a most heterogeneous collection of people. There are letters to old friends like Robert Lax and Mark Van Doren, to Latin American intellectuals, to an unnamed rabbi and to unnamed contemplative nuns, Spanish seminarians, scholars, teachers, lay missionaries, diplomats, and Muslims. There are letters to social activists like Dorothy Day and Catherine de Hueck Doherty (who was the foundress of Friendship House in Harlem where Merton worked in 1941 before entering the monastery) as well as to writers as diverse as the African American novelist James Baldwin and the old French philosopher Jacques Maritain. The very range of the recipients of those letters reflects nearly two decades of interests that would bring Merton into contact not only with his fellow Catholics but any number of secular intellectuals, Jews, Muslims, and other Christians who were not members of the church of Rome. In turn, their interests included social activism, publishing, poetry, religious faith, philosophy, public policy, literature, and always, the spiritual dimension of humanism. The "Cold War Letters" were almost a shorthand vision into Merton's wide circle of correspondents as well as a summary survey of his variegated interests.

While the topics addressed in these letters were diverse and their length varied, it is possible to detect in them some motifs that were, as it were, Mertonian constants: the need for self-appropriation as a way to God; the necessity of moral integrity at a time of moral confusion; the links between contemplative living and social justice; the need for a prophetic critique of both church and society. Tucked in the middle of this volume was a tribute to Mohandas Gandhi. Merton had been interested in Gandhi since his days as a high school student at Oakham, the public school he attended in the middle thirties in England. Gandhi represented many qualities with which Merton would have a natural sympathy. Gandhi was a man of prayer; he was an ascetic; he was an apostle of nonviolence; he had mastered the dialectic of withdrawal from the world and engagement with it. In addition, Gandhi, while remaining faithful to his own Indian tradition, found it fruitful to use Christian sources as part of his overall worldview. Gandhi, in short, knew how to live in a tradition while benefiting from the insights of other traditions.

This brief tribute to Gandhi in *Seeds of Destruction* would be enlarged by Merton into an anthology of Gandhian texts on nonviolence, which he would publish in 1965 under the title *Gandhi on Non-Violence*. Merton had copied this series of texts out of Gandhi's writings (especially his letters) on a stenographer's pad in the late 1950s. His work on Gandhi added to the general interest in the Indian sage by those —

like Martin Luther King, Jr. — who were committed to nonviolent protest. It takes only a moment's reflection to see how the monk would have been attracted to a person who was a truth seeker, who lived in community, who joined asceticism to nonviolence, and for whom the crossing of religious traditions was done in a respectful fashion. The fact that Merton and Gandhi are often linked today in pacifist literature shows how naturally the work and thought of the two connect; their pacifism derived from a deep religious core and not from some abstract philosophical framework.

Some of the themes that concerned Merton in the prose pieces in *Seeds of Destruction* found resonances in the collection of poetry he assembled and published in 1963 under the title *Emblems of a Season of Fury*. In that volume he collected his "Chant to be used in processions around a site with furnaces" but one also finds his moving lament over the death, by bombing, of the Negro children in Birmingham with the title "And the children of Birmingham." The volume also reprinted his apocalyptic prose poem "A Letter to Pablo Antonio Cuadra Concerning Giants" as well as a translation from the Spanish of ten poems by Cuadra. In addition he had translations of Latin American poets (Ernesto Cardenal, Jorge Andrade, Cesar Vallejo, and Alfonso Cortes) as well as versions of seven poems translated from the French of Raissa Maritain, the wife of his friend, the philosopher Jacques Maritain. He would in the next year pay a more sustained tribute to Raissa Maritain by writing an introductory essay for a translation of her book of meditations on the Lord's Prayer, which appeared in English in 1964.

Towards the end of September in 1963, after a day of recollection, Merton did, as he did frequently, a kind of self-assessment of his scholarly projects. He set, as his priorities, his work as a poet, translator of poetry, and contact with poets "especially in Latin America" as a high priority. He also listed as a high priority "monastic articles and essays" as well as "my own creative work, whatever that might be." To those areas of writing, he added a dual resolution to cut down on unnecessary contacts of "time consuming palaver" as well as a resolve to the "deepening of my grasp on spiritual reality." Ten months later (July 10, 1964) he expanded the list a bit but still consistent with what he had written earlier, along with a rationale for his eclectic areas of research:

Some conclusions: literature, contemplation, solitude, Latin America — Asia, Zen, Islam, etc. All these things *combine in my life*. It would be madness to make a "monasticism" by simply excluding them. I would be less a monk. Others have their own way, I have mine. [my emphasis]

During this same period between 1963 and 1965 Merton was also working on two other projects that would finally be published in time. *Seasons of Celebration* (1965) was a collection of essays, occasional pieces, and meditations that he had published in various places going back to 1950. The volume opens with a reflection on personalism (Merton was sympathetic to the ideas of the French personalist philosophers Gabriel Marcel and Emmanuel Mounier and the latter's journal *L'Esprit*, as well as the personalist philosophy espoused by the Catholic Worker communities which had been inspired by Mounier) and the liturgy, but it then has a wide variety of chapters that deal with aspects of the liturgical year, a study of some of the liturgical writings of Saint Bernard of Clairvaux, and reflections on various gospel topics. It ends with an essay on liturgical renewal — which he had written in 1964 during the debates and subsequent reforms of the liturgy stipulated at the Second Vatican Council. The volume, in short, was a bit of an omnium-gatherum for which Merton expressed little pride when he later calculated the worth of his writing. The Cistercian censor, it seems, agreed; according to Merton he granted the permission to publish but thought that Merton had "written himself out." *Seasons of Celebration*, except for some fine pages on personalism, consists of pieces dealing with liturgy but in a rather uninspired fashion; it was, as is often said, basically a "desk clearing" exercise by an author who could sell by the sheer power of his name.

He was also going over his notebooks from the previous decade and adding new material as he prepared a volume that would be a journal sequel to *The Sign of Jonas*. It appeared in 1966 under the title *Conjectures of a Guilty Bystander*, but reflects interests that go back to the middle 1950s. Unlike *The Sign of Jonas* this volume, which will be discussed a bit more thoroughly in its proper place, was less tied to the calendar. Reflecting his own shifting understanding of how to write and seeking a new, more experimental voice, it is more discursive, allusive, and wide ranging. *Conjectures* is less fervently pious and less conspicuously "monastic" in its tone, thus providing a good indicator of how Merton's outlook was changing over the years. In that sense, it stands as a fine counterpoint to the kinds of material he anthologized in *Seasons of Celebration*, which was a much more conventionally "Catholic" book.

So much of Merton's life — even in this book — deals with his writing that it is easy to forget that these publishing projects took up only a portion of his time. During the period 1963-1965 Merton was slowly weaning himself away from community life and his duties as novice master, orienting his life more to life in the hermitage. A careful reading of the journals for this period can mark the steps by which he eventually makes a permanent move to the small cottage of Mount Olivet, which he called Our Lady of Mount Carmel. All through the years 1963 and 1964 he was spending free days or parts of days in the hermitage. In October of 1964 he received permission to sleep in the hermitage and a bed was brought up for that purpose (even though there was yet no electricity or in-house plumbing). Within a month he had tested out some days in his cabin, with only a walk to the monastery for the celebration of Mass. "How full the days are," he wrote in his journal in November, "full of slow and quiet, ordered, occupied (sawing wood, sweeping, reading, taking notes, meditating, praying, tending the fire or just looking at the valley). Only here do I feel my life is authentically *human*" [Merton's emphasis]. A month later he wrote down the round of activities that filled up his day, describing everything from his household chores to his time for prayer, meditation, reading, walking, and writing.

One benefit for his readers is that since he had to make a daily walk to the monastery for Mass (until he got a chapel) and, further, since he had a porch looking out over the woods, Merton's keen poetic eye for nature comes alive in his journals and in his writings. He is alert for the shy deer that peer out from the brush; he is sensitive to the birds (which he could name with a practiced eye); he marvels at the change in weather and the etched treeline against the snow in winter. These closely observed moments would frequently show up in his poetry, albeit in transformed ways. At the same time, humorously, he is less than enamored with the king snake that had taken up residence in his hermitage's outhouse: "Hello, you bastard, are you in there?" is the salute that he records in his journal as he gingerly entered the outhouse. The king snake dialogue would continue until, a few years later, Merton got indoor plumbing in the hermitage.

One way in which Merton was able to focus more fully on the world of nature that he observed around his hermitage was with a camera he got from one of the monks. Typically enough, he would look for old tree stumps or wooded knots to photograph up close in an attempt to see these natural shapes in what his favorite poet, Gerard Manley Hopkins, would have called their "inscape." Merton had a natural photographic eye and his first tinkering with a camera would become more intense later in his life when he was given both a better instrument and encouragement from the writer, musicologist, and photographer John Howard Griffin, who was later designated as his official biographer even though Griffin's worsening health precluded his finishing the task.

Merton had some drawing skill (inherited from his painter father?) which he had put to use as a cartoonist and illustrator for campus magazines during his days at Columbia University. Thanks to the encouragement of his old Columbia classmate, Ad Reinhardt, who already had made a name for himself as a member of the New York School of abstract expressionists, Merton began to experiment with abstract calligraphies done on art papers (along with some Chinese brushes) that Reinhardt had sent him. These drawings basically consisted of gestural abstractions which, at times, looked as if they were modeled on Zen calligraphy, while others derived from his intuitive mastery of the Chinese ink brushes he had gotten from Reinhardt. A close study of these pieces shows that Merton was doing very little copying of Zen ideograms. His pieces were spontaneously controlled (the oxymoron is noted but is a Zen commonplace) exercises in pure abstraction, with the most aesthetically pleasing those that utilized the least number of strokes.

In time, Merton became confident enough of his gift that he framed some of his work and had it exhibited at both Spalding College (now Spalding University) and Bellarmine College in Louisville, with the proceeds of the sales going to his "charities," which in effect meant the work of social justice. He was pleasantly surprised to discover that his artwork sold at the exhibitions in Louisville. What had been a kind of hobby for him produced some art works that sold in their own day but are prized collectors' items today, commanding handsome prices.

Despite these joyful solitary days in the woods and his various "creative" works, Merton still entertained (or: suffered) streams of visitors who came to him with their various projects and because of mutual interest. He noted the arrival of the Anglican theologian from Oxford, Canon Donald Allchin, who would become a good friend and a steady correspondent. It was from this friendship that he came to appreciate the Anglican heritage that he had somewhat disparaged in *The Seven Storey Mountain.* Allchin's interest in spirituality and his close ties to Anglican monastic life would make him a fruitful dialogue partner as well as a source for bibliography and offprints. He enjoyed the company of the poet and literary critic Miguel Grinberg, who visited from Buenos Aires, as well as his more local friends, especially the Oxford-trained patristics scholar Glenn Hinson, from the Southern Baptist seminary in Louisville.

One of the more interesting of these meetings was a retreat organized for some people active in the pacifist Fellowship of Reconciliation. In November, 1964, the Berrigan brothers, Dan and Phil, as well as Wilbur "Ping" Ferry, John Howard Yoder, A. J. Muste, Jim Forest, and others gathered for two days of discussion both at the gatehouse and at the hermitage. A major theme of these discussions orbited around the work of the French Protestant social critic and professor of jurisprudence Jacques Ellul, whom Merton, thanks to the urging of Ping Ferry, had been reading with some care. Daniel Berrigan said Mass for the group using English and, as Merton noted, uncanonically gave communion to the Protestants. Merton saw this "retreat" as an important part of his life. The meeting was a concrete instance of the kind of perfect contemplative encounter Merton most often experienced only through the mails. He hoped for more such encounters. When Merton made his fateful trip to the East in 1968 he was making some preliminary plans to invite Martin Luther King, Jr., to the monastery for a similar retreat. His admiration for King was enormous because of King's unwavering commitment to nonviolence. He had used King's life and writings as a primary source for his "Letters to White Liberals" discussed earlier in this chapter.

In fact, the retreat of the peacemakers was a kind of model of the kind of dialogue for which Merton was inclined: small groups of likeminded persons who could speak on deep subjects from the integrity of their own positions. Merton was not an academically trained theologian, and his sympathies were not for the technical kind of theological exchange. There is every indication, for example, that Merton followed the theological debates of the period of the Council more as an observer than a keen participant except for those areas for which he had a deep existential interest. His instincts were for the deep interior dialogue of persons of good will who had common religious concerns.

The frenetic pace of the antiwar protests and the civil rights movement came to the attention of the monastery secondhand. As we have noted, the monks did not receive "secular" newspapers or magazines nor did they possess radios or televisions. Most of the outside news they got came from announcements from the abbot in their daily meeting in chapter or from materials read to them when they ate in the refectory. Such material reflected what the abbot thought useful (in the early 1960s, before the presidential assassination, Merton complained that every time John F. Kennedy sneezed, there was a report of the fact in the chapter room). Merton's involvement with the peace movement, as a consequence, was heavily dependent on what friends sent him in the mail and what he would intuit from his reading. He had little opportunity to experience the vividness of television coverage or actual participation in peace marches and demonstrations.

Merton's lack of firsthand awareness of the intensity of what was going on in the "secular" world became apparent when he learned (a day after the event) that a young Catholic Worker, Roger LaPorte, burned himself alive in front of the headquarters of the United Nations as a protest against the war. LaPorte had used a form of protest like that practiced by some Buddhist monks in Vietnam who had immolated themselves as a protest against the government in South Vietnam early in the decade. Merton sent a telegram (on November 11, 1965) withdrawing his name from the Catholic Peace Fellowship after this act of suicide even though he did not hold the CPF responsible for the affair. "What is happening?" "Is everybody nuts?" he scribbles into his journal. He received clarifications about the LaPorte suicide from people he trusted like Dorothy Day, Daniel Berrigan, and another Catholic Worker, the pacifist Tom Cornell. Once it was clear to him that the event was an aberration, that LaPorte was not a very stable person psychologically, and nothing that LaPorte had done derived from any spoken or unspoken policy of the peace movement generally he withdrew his resignation. However, the whole incident of Roger LaPorte's suicide does show, somewhat parenthetically, how separated Merton was from the frantic and nervous pace of historical events and the intensity of events outside the monastery. LaPorte's self-immolation had a profound impact on him nonetheless, because of his fears that some people were not disciplined enough to follow nonviolence fully. This fear, of course, was one that people like Martin Luther King, Jr., had to face in the civil rights movement.

It is one of the curious paradoxes (contradictions?) in Merton's life that he would agitate so persistently and write so longingly of solitude and withdrawal while, almost at the same time, complain so bitterly that the abbot, Dom James, would deny him permission to travel to meetings or conferences. Apart from business or medical excursions into Louisville or occasional trips to see his artist friends Victor and Carolyn Hammer in nearby Lexington, the abbot resisted Merton's desire to accept invitations to go to the Benedictine abbey in Collegeville (Minnesota) to attend meetings with the Benedictine monks there who were working on ecumenical matters, just as the abbot did not want Merton going to Europe to visit the editors (of which he was one) of the European Cistercian journal of monastic scholarship. Almost petulantly, Merton would complain of Dom James's frequent trips to visit monasteries or the abbot's goings to Rome on business or his permitting the young monks to travel in Europe while they studied in Rome while he would be denied the opportunity to do any travel at all.

One exception to this no-travel ban came in June of 1964 when the monk was permitted to leave Gethsemani to go to New York City to spend a few days with the aged (he was then in his nineties) Zen Buddhist scholar, D. T. Suzuki. Suzuki's secretary had written an invitation for Merton to visit Suzuki, who, because of the infirmities of age and his physical frailty, could not come to Kentucky. In accordance with the abbot's instructions, Merton was to make this a strictly limited visit with no seeing of friends or giving talks or arranging other meetings. The trip was to be a strictly private one. It was the first time Merton had been back to the city since he left for the monastery in 1941. Not surprisingly, he devoted an entire long section in his journal to the trip.

Merton stayed at Butler Hall on the campus of Columbia University, walked to Corpus Christi Church each day to celebrate Mass in the church where he had been received into the Catholic faith a generation ago. The brief stay in New York — he was there only two full days — was an exercise in nostalgia for Merton. His lodgings were close to Harlem where he thought about his days working with the Baroness de Hueck at Friendship House before he became a monk. He looked with some faint sense of the passing years at the young students who attended the university where he had studied as an undergraduate a quarter of a century ago. He took a taxicab to the Guggenheim Museum across the park to see a show of the paintings of Vincent Van Gogh, but expressed his disappointment at the absence of the works of the Swiss painter Paul Klee, an artist for whom he had immense respect. He had little patience for, or time at, the Metropolitan Museum, which he thought a bit of a relic. He ate alone and stayed apart, and except for his time with Suzuki, spoke only to a cab driver who told him of his marital woes as they traveled from the West Side through Central Park on the way to the Guggenheim Museum.

Suzuki and Merton had two long talks introduced by the drinking of green tea prepared by Suzuki's secretary, drunk with the ceremonial three and a half sips characteristic of Zen. Merton brought a new poem he had written inspired by the visit of some Hiroshima survivors (people known as the Hibakusha) and the little paper cranes they had folded as symbols of peace; the poem includes the sadly powerful lines: "The child's hand / Folding these wings / Wins no wars and ends them all." The poem represented both his deep feelings against violence and war as well as a tribute to the Japanese scholar whom he regarded as a real sage.

Merton also read some translations he had done from the poetry of the Brazilian writer, Fernando Pessoa. Suzuki, in turn, read some Zen stories from the so-called "Blue Cliff Collection." They spoke of Zen and of the Christian mystic Meister Eckhart, whom Suzuki liked very much. Merton was pleased that Suzuki approved of his recently published essay "The Zen Revival" and was surprised that Suzuki told him that the Zen people, who were predisposed to the writings of Saint John of the Cross, liked Merton's *The Ascent to Truth* more than the author himself did. Merton asked Suzuki to send him an example of the old Zen master's calligraphy which, when the scroll finally did arrive at the monastery in the fall, Merton hung in his hermitage. Suzuki's secretary gave Merton some autographed copies of the old man's books while Merton promised to send Suzuki more of his own work.

Reflecting on that visit in his later journals, Merton felt that the real sense of the meeting was to be found in the meeting of two minds that experienced a deep level of interior understanding. It was a kind of vindication of what Merton thought some contemplative monks ought to be doing: engaging in deep levels of dialogue with those who sought the truth even when their paths were quite disparate and their vocabularies different. Merton wrote later of this visit: "I had a renewed sense of being 'situated' in this world. This is a legitimate consolation."

In the course of their conversation, Suzuki told Merton how much he admired the writings of Chuang Tzu, the fourth-century master of Taoism, whom he regarded as representing the best philosophy in Asia. Merton had been reading Chuang Tzu in translation in the years before he met Suzuki in New York. His interest in the ancient Taoist writer was abetted by the encouragement of his friend and correspondent, the Seton Hall scholar John Wu, with whom he had been in correspondence since 1961. Aided by Wu's literal translation of some of Chuang Tzu's texts and his comparative study of several translations in English, French, and German, Merton worked on what he called "readings" of Chuang Tzu's texts. In 1965 he published *The Way of Chuang Tzu* (from New Directions) with a "note to the reader" and an introduction to his "translations." In the note to the reader he asks that no one think that he is "pulling the rabbit Christianity out of a Taoist hat." He simply read the ancient Taoist master, he noted, in the same spirit that Saint Augustine read Plotinus or Saint Thomas Aquinas read Aristotle.

The readings that Merton does supply in his text show how easy it would be for Merton to love these writings; they are very much like the "wisdom" stories that belong to the tradition of the desert writers whom he had published in *The Wisdom of the Desert*. It was that book which Merton had hoped would be prefaced by some lines Suzuki had written but which did not appear when the book was published. Within those stories, of course, is the basic assumption of both Taoist wisdom and Christian monasticism: to take up the contemplative search was to follow a Way of Life, which, in Chinese, is the *Tao*. In fact, it was Chuang Tzu who mediated the *Tao* (Way) to

the world by writing of the legendary Lao Tzu who was its pur-
ported founder.

It has often been alleged that Merton, in his mature years, became a religious syncretist who, through his concern with mystical experience, blurred the edges of Christian belief to accommodate his increasing fascination with Eastern religions. A close reading of his
journals and letters would give the lie to such a charge. First of all,
much of his study of these religious traditions was done from within
the context of his monastic life. Hence, even in the hermitage, Merton
faithfully followed the daily recitation of the psalms, meditated on his
scriptural reading (the traditional *lectio divina*), and spent time in silent
prayer. Furthermore, he frequently noted both in his published and
unpublished writing that his studies were designed to help him
deepen his own Christian monastic life. Finally, he was not unaware of
the possibility that charges of religious indifferentism could be leveled
against him by conservatives who lived within the straitjacketed scholasticism of the day. It is true that the charge of religious indifferentism
leveled against him in his own lifetime was a symptom of how far at
the edge Merton was as a Catholic thinker in his own day. His interests
were anything but typical.

In an interesting journal entry (June 25, 1965) Merton faces the issue of such charges of religious indifferentism in an unambiguous and
straightforward fashion:

> There is one thing more — I may be interested in Oriental religions,
> etc. — but there can be no obscuring the essential difference — this
> personal communion with Christ at the center and heart of all real-
> ity, as a source of grace and life. "God is love" may be clarified if one
> says that "God is Void" and if in the void one finds absolute
> indetermination and hence absolute freedom. . . . All that is "inter-
> esting" but none of it touches on the mystery of personality in God
> and His personal love for me. Again I am void too — and I have free-
> dom of *am* a kind of freedom, meaningless unless oriented to Him.
> [Merton's emphasis]

The key phrase in the above passage is "Christ at the center and
heart of all reality" since Merton's christology continued to be deeply
in debt to the cosmic christology reflected in Saint John's Gospel and

119

in such Pauline epistles as those to the Colossians, Ephesians, and Philippians. In the previous decade, under the influence of the Russian theologians whom he continued to read, and in his own profound meditation on Christ as Wisdom, Merton worked out what theologians call a "high" christology seen as the Logos through whom the world is created and sustained, and as the Wisdom undergirding all that is. That complex sophianic approach to theology was never better expressed than in his poem "Hagia Sophia," written in the late 1950s and reprinted in his volume *Emblems in a Season of Fury*. It was precisely that kind of christology that permitted him to see the hidden yearnings of the contemplatives of other traditions. It was also a christology very much in line with the tradition of monastic theology in general and the Cistercian writers in particular. Finally, it was the kind of christology that suffused the poetry of Gerard Manley Hopkins, whose work was a continuing inspiration for him. If there was anything "Eastern" about Merton's approach to religion it was the deep debt that he owed to Eastern Christian patristic writings and the contemplative theology of the monastic fathers.

It is also worthwhile pointing out that Merton saw the contemplative search as a way of life and not simply a doctrine to be embraced. Like those who seek the *Tao* or follow after the Stoic *Logos*, the Christian monk must be ready to integrate what he most deeply believes into a wholesome change of life so that discipline, asceticism, regularity, intellectual work, and the life of worship fuse into one way of being. As Pierre Hadot in his now classic work *Philosophy as a Way of Life* has argued, in antiquity to become a lover of wisdom (i.e., a philosopher) was to embrace a way of living. Hadot sees this perception of the ancient philosophers as embracing an alternative way of living in pursuit of wisdom as a link to the origins of monasticism. The Cappadocian Fathers of the fourth century called the contemplative life of the monk "the philosophical way of life." Merton extended that insight to study others in the East, like the ancient Taoists, Buddhists, and Hindus, who also championed the idea of the contemplative path as a way of life. After all, *Tao* means "Way" in Chinese, and to seek truth was to enter on to the Way. Merton could hardly have missed the fact that in the Acts of the Apostles, Christians were called "The followers of the Way."

During all of these years of intense activity Merton continued in his role as director of novices, a role that included, apart from giving individual spiritual direction, formal study in the sources of monasticism in general and the Cistercian way of monasticism in particular. The piles of mimeographed notes running to over a thousand pages and the huge number of audiotapes in the Merton archives testify to how seriously he took this task. In the late 1950s and spilling over into the early sixties Merton worked on two manuscripts, one of which would never become a book. The other would be published posthumously even though we know, from references in his journals and letters, that he was at work on it in the early sixties.

"The Inner Experience" was a reworking and enlargement of ideas only sketched out in his early pamphlet "What Is Contemplation?" which Saint Mary's College in Indiana published in 1948. Merton wanted to expand that early, rather immature, and very brief work into something more substantial, but despite his various tinkerings, he was never satisfied with the results. As a consequence he stipulated in his literary will that it was never to be published as a book. That stipulation has been honored even though the work has seen light as a series of essays in eight parts published, beginning in 1983, in the journal *Cistercian Studies* (now *Cistercian Studies Quarterly*). Even though it is easy to see that this work had never been fully worked out (the final sections are rather sketchy) it is a work not without interest as an attempt to break free from the more scholastic understandings of contemplation (with their somewhat byzantine discussions of epistemology and various theories of divine grace) to a deeper, fuller understanding of the experience of God in contemplative prayer.

Recent studies of "The Inner Experience" by scholars like Michael Casey, Anne Carr, and especially William H. Shannon's monograph-length work have shown that it was a mature work of contemplative theology, albeit not completely worked out to Merton's satisfaction. Its final chapters attempt to read the traditional theology of prayer against the background of recent developments in psychology. Those final chapters, however, follow on a detailed analysis of ascetical and mystical theology derived from Merton's careful and exhaustive study of that tradition. In that sense, the piles of mimeographed pages he wrote for his students (especially the long manuscript of over two hundred single-spaced pages on mystical theology composed in 1961 and never published) must be seen as the background for the eight chapters that make up "The Inner Experience."

A work more closely derived from Merton's constant study of the ancient monastic tradition (and his classes in this subject at the monastery) is a book that was not published until a year after his death. This work was a kind of satisfactory statement that Merton felt he had not made in the unfinished essays comprising "The Inner Experience." This work came out under two quite different titles from two different publishers. *The Climate of Monastic Prayer* was published by the rather new enterprise called Cistercian Publications (a publishing venture first housed at the Trappist monastery of Spencer, Massachusetts, which Merton strongly supported; the press is now housed at Western Michigan University in Kalamazoo) in 1969 and, characteristic of the new post–Vatican II atmosphere, had a moving preface written by Merton's friend and correspondent, the Quaker writer Douglas Steere. Then Herder & Herder Company (now Crossroad Publishing Company) published the same book with the same preface in the same year under the title *Contemplative Prayer,* which was thought to be a more commercially viable title for a general readership.

Contemplative Prayer is an interesting work for a number of reasons. Generally speaking, it is an elaboration of arguments Merton made in *New Seeds of Contemplation* but now written in a more explicitly monastic context. First, the work combines a deep knowledge of early monastic sources both of the West and the East, but these sources are read against the experience of twentieth-century people of prayer. There is, for example, a rather convincing rereading of the existentialist concept of "dread" (elaborated, for example, in the writings of Søren Kierkegaard) in the light of Saint John of the Cross's doctrine of the "night of the senses" and the "night of faith." Furthermore, Merton considers prayer as a way of finding true human authenticity (his reading of Sartre, Merleau-Ponty, and Camus shows up as intellectual background in this discussion) while analyzing the ways in which religious people can be inauthentic and false to themselves. The focus on "authenticity" is, as we have seen, a topic that runs like a thread in Merton's writings from *Seeds of Contemplation* through *Thoughts in Solitude* and in the seminal essay "A Philosophy of Solitude" in *Disputed Questions.*

Second, Merton argues that there is no contradiction or tension between participation in the liturgy and the search for God in imageless prayer. Indeed, he warns monks not to think that the mere attendance at liturgy makes one a contemplative. By a close reading of the early monastic writers he argues that the experience of God in contemplative prayer presupposes a life in the liturgy; indeed, the life of deep prayer is an extension of true participation in praying the liturgy. Merton emphasizes this connection in order to attack both a kind of liturgical routine and the ever present danger of quietism. For that reason, he is also quite wary of the term "meditation" and its various "schools," if by meditation one thinks only of mental activities separated from an integrated life or a kind of mechanical process of mental exercises. Merton did not want to over-intellectualize contemplative prayer. Such prayer was not "thinking about" God; it was a resting in the presence of God. The life of vocal prayer, refection, etc. were all steps towards that goal.

One might note in passing that Merton's insistence that contemplative prayer not be detached from the life of liturgy and devotion has the practical consequence of instructing people how to read "mystical" texts. Thus, to cite an obvious example, if one reads Saint John of the Cross or Saint Teresa of Avila without keeping in mind that they lived their lives in the context of liturgical prayer, the celebration of the Eucharist, and ordinary devotionalism, it would be easy to misread their writings. More than once, Merton himself had to warn people not to turn the reading of such writings into explorations of exotic experiences detached from the life of faith and praxis. By disposition and study Merton was highly suspicious of "do it yourself" mysticism cut loose from any community of practice and asceticism. Such individualism too often led to illusion and/or self-absorption.

Contemplative Prayer is, in fact, also an attempt to correct some deficiencies in the theology of prayer that had plagued much Catholic spiritual writing in the post-Reformation era. Merton argued that a purely intellectualized form of meditation — "thinking about God" — did not do honor to the most authentic strains of Christian prayer. Too much of Catholic writing on meditation in the period after the Reformation had lost contact with the older monastic principles of contemplative prayer. Such forms of pious rationalism had within them the seeds of illusion and the odor of a kind of Pelagian intellectual straining. Contemplative prayer was resting in the presence of God and not some form of mental gymnastics.

Throughout *Contemplative Prayer* Merton argues that this kind of contemplative prayer is, at its root, not anything esoteric or odd. It certainly could not be developed by the sheer dint of following some kind of "method" of prayer. For him, prayer derives from a basic stance of turning from what keeps us from God and nourishing what brings us to God, which in the monastic vocabulary, borrowing from the beatitudes of Jesus, is simply called "purity of heart." This purity of heart, a hallowed term in monasticism, does not mean "a kind of gnosticism which would elevate the contemplative above the ordinary Christian by initiating him into a realm of esoteric knowledge and experience, delivering him from the ordinary struggles and sufferings of human existence, and elevating him to a privileged state among the spiritually pure, as if he were almost an angel. . . ."

Finally, and almost implicitly, *Contemplative Prayer* carries within it a critique of what Merton sees as the failings of institutional monasticism as well as observations about what he thinks monasticism ought to be vis-à-vis the church and the larger world. Early in the work he contrasts two fictional figures from Dostoevsky's *The Brothers Karamazov*. Father Ferapont symbolizes the monk who is completely observant, meticulous for the monastic life, fierce in his orthodoxy, and unsullied in his virtue. Father Ferapont overcomes the world by "sheer effort," a form of crypto-Pelagianism; he then feels free to call down curses upon the world he has resisted. By contrast, the elder, Father Zosima, is the kind and compassionate man of prayer who identifies himself with the suffering and sinful world. He is less dependent on monastic structures but is ultimately nourished by them. Thus, Merton writes, the "Zosima type of monasticism can well flourish in offbeat situations, even in the midst of the world. Perhaps such 'monks' may have no overt monastic connections whatever."

Towards the end of *Contemplative Prayer* Merton insists that the monastic spirit of the desert, of the ascetic life, of self-denial and simplicity are not impulses that destroy the life of the senses or of artistic impulses or of culture more generally understood. Despite the obvious fact that even contemporary Cistercian life is ascetic by most standards Merton still felt it necessary to understand this asceticism in such a way as not to give comfort to the Jansenist deformations that had become lodged in much traditional ascetic writing. Such impulses, found in the monastic life, were in fact distortions of what these impulses ought to be. Indeed, he points out a commonplace, namely, that monasticism has always had a specific culture that encompassed the visual arts, literature, music, and learned writing. There is nothing meritorious in ignorance or a willful starvation of the whole person. Contemplative prayer, in fact, presupposes such a culture as a matrix from which authentic prayer derives.

In a footnote to his brief discussion of monastic culture, a term made popular by his friend the Benedictine Jean Leclercq, he adds a coda that reflected his own understanding of how monastic culture should look in the contemporary world. That note reflects both the spirit of the post-conciliar Catholic Church and Merton's own self-understanding as a monk:

> One could say, for example, that for a twentieth-century monk 'monastic culture' would imply not only an education in monastic theology, tradition, and literature, as well as art, architecture, poetry, etc. but also in other religious cultures. Hence a knowledge of Zen, of Sufism, of Hinduism can rightly claim a place in the monastic culture of the modern monk of the West.

These monastic issues were not simply Merton's own preoccupations. Anyone who reads through the letters from 1963 through 1965 gathered in *The School of Charity: The Letters of Thomas Merton on Religious Renewal and Spiritual Direction*, which his former secretary Brother Patrick Hart assembled, will see a vast correspondence coming from contemplative monks and nuns from the United States, Great Britain, Europe, and elsewhere, seeking Merton's advice on two quite different sets of issues. First, how should monasteries go about implementing the reforms permitted as a result of the Second Vatican Council? And in the light of these changes and upheavals, what is the meaning of monasticism in the contemporary world? It does not take much imagination to see that these questions are a microcosm of questions being asked in the larger Catholic world of the time. The fact that this correspondence involves everyone from simple nuns and monks to officials in the Vatican Curia indicates how deeply involved Merton was in these issues.

In the first place, Merton showed, surprisingly enough for some, some cautious and conservative instincts. He was not in favor of the full and immediate implementation of a totally new vernacular liturgy. In a letter to an English Benedictine nun at Stanbrook Abbey he begged her community not to jettison the Latin liturgy with the heedless speed that it seems to have been abandoned in American monasteries. He saw, presciently, that were Latin abandoned, the ancient tradition of liturgical chant could also be compromised. He did not see the virtue of jettisoning usages for the sheer sake of change. More to the point, he thought many of the suggested accidental changes, along with the interminable discussions about such changes, were a kind of evasion that did not get down to the real issues at hand. These changes in monastic style or restructuring of the liturgy or making adaptations of the daily horarium did nothing, in his estimation, to face up to deeper questions of the very nature and meaning of monasticism itself.

What were these deeper issues?

Quite bluntly, Merton raised this issue: Why did so many good young people enter the monastery full of hope and promise only to leave after a few years or, in some cases, after their final profession and even ordination to the priesthood? After a number of years in monastic formation as a novice director, he felt sure he had some answers to this question.

Part of the blame, in Merton's view, came from the fact that these younger people saw in the senior monks a kind of rigid observance of rules without any clear advance in the life of prayer and charity, or to put it more institutionally, they found monastic observance more geared towards success, to the maintenance of a certain style of life (with particular emphasis on the "strict" of the order's title "Cistercians of the Strict Obedience"), and to a kind of rigidity that suffocated individuals. Writing to a Dutch Trappist in 1966, Merton sums up his complaint about the loss of so many potentially good monks: "I felt that it seemed that men were being consistently sacrificed for the 'institution' and not even for the institution itself but sacrificed for a kind of abstract institutional image. . . ." It does not require a great imaginative leap to see that what Merton criticizes here in the life of the monk was also a critique being leveled by others at the church as a whole, namely, that too many people were sacrificed in the name of "good order" or "orthodoxy" or "fidelity to the Holy See."

That criticism written in 1966 was a repetition of one he wrote to Cardinal Paul Philippe in 1963, in which he warned that religious life was in a state of potential crisis because too many religious superiors and others thought that one could attract and hold members in religious communities if organizational changes were made. Such a notion, in Merton's estimation, was gravely misplaced. What was needed, in the monk's estimation, was an articulation of the deep root of the spiritual basis for religious commitment, not a rearrangement of institutional structures. Such structural change made sense only in the light of fostering spiritual maturity.

These criticisms may or may not have been justified, and Merton never imputed bad will to those who were his superiors even when he thought they exercised their authority in pursuit of an illusory form of life, but one thing is very clear: these problems were real issues. The criticisms were serious enough for Merton to devote his considerable energies to reforming the kind of education he gave his aspiring monks and to struggling, in his own fashion, to change usages and practices that in his estimation were illusory. He was very much concerned that monks not foster the illusion that by simply adhering to rules and practices one becomes a more perfect person. He called such monks, in a moment of exasperation, the "willpower boys." His writings argued for a kind of delicate balance in which a monastic culture with authentically deep foundations could be maintained while permitting a maximum degree of flexibility to allow for human growth and development.

It was only at the very end of his life, in some talks he gave on his way to Asia, that he put the matter in its starkest form: If all the usual monastic furniture and customs and usages were swept away, what kind of person would a monk be? It is clear, from books like *Contemplative Prayer* as well as his many essays and letters, that he constantly thought about that question both for himself and for the sake of monasticism itself. Furthermore, one of the reasons why Merton is still read by people outside the monastic world is that he posed questions whose applications are wider than the confines of the cloister. What Merton was asking, in brief, are questions like these: When does religion become illusory and manipulative? When do observances become mechanical and verge on the magical? How can religious authority be abused? How does one find a "home" in an institutionalized branch of Christianity without ending up serving the institution as an end in itself? How does one draw on that which is authentic in a tradition while bypassing that which is peripheral or only "remembered" as part of a thoughtless form of traditionalism? It does not require a great deal of imagination to transpose those questions from their monastic milieu to the more general arena of organized Christianity or even to religion in general.

On August 17, 1965, the Gethsemani monastic council voted favorably at its chapter meeting on the appointment of a new novice master, Father Baldwin, and at the same time affirmed Merton's right to retire to his hermitage full time by relieving him of those duties. In the few days after this decision Merton cleared out his novitiate office and went to the hermitage on August 20th. It was the feast of Saint Bernard of Clairvaux. Freed from his formal obligations as an "officer" of the monastery, and with a certain sadness as he thought of the community at prayer, he embarked on his new life — one that he had prayed and hoped for since his early days as a monk: a life of solitude and withdrawal.

On Christmas Eve (1965) he wrote a letter to a Franciscan sister, Elaine Banes, who was attempting to organize a contemplative group of sisters within her own congregation. He says that life in the hermitage is completely different from life in the monastery since in the hermitage one is completely on one's own; "you can't depend on anyone else to keep you going. Only God." Towards the end of that letter he says that "Of course there are trials. . . ." It would only become clear to him in the following year how burdensome those trials would be. For the present, however, as he wrote a few months earlier to Dom Jacques Winandy, himself a long-time proponent of the hermit life, that what he is discovering is "not eremitism or spirituality or contemplation but God. . . . It is much simpler just to be an ordinary Christian who is living alone. . . . I am grateful to God for every moment of it and will not spoil it by imagining that my life is in any way special, for that indeed poisons everything."

When Merton wrote that letter he had been in the monastery for nearly a quarter of a century. His long-time aspiration to lead a more solitary life, reiterated in many of his books and frequently in his journals, had been realized. He was now living on the edge of the monastic community of Gethsemani in a small cottage on a hill just north of the abbey. Would this radically change the life of this monk who was now in his fiftieth year?

5 Solitude and Love

The monk is a stranger in a foreign land; let him not occupy himself with anything and he will find rest.

Abba Arsenius

O N NEW YEAR'S EVE OF 1965 MERTON TOOK STOCK OF THE past year as he sat in his hermitage on a stormy evening. He noted his gratitude for the vote of the monastery's chapter allowing him to take up life in his hermitage, in which he had been living full time since the previous August. He was content with having finished his book on Chuang Tzu; in fact, he was very pleased with it since it was the kind of work that provided him with the most intellectual and spiritual satisfaction. He thought that the end of the Vatican Council with all that it had accomplished was a blessing, as was Pope Paul VI's visit to the United Nations, where the pope cried out "No more war!" He could not help but think that the papal cry vindicated the efforts of his fellow peacemakers and his own efforts for peace done from the fastness of his monastic home.

He thanked God for the better health of his friend, the artist Victor Hammer.

At the same time he reflected back on his own bouts of bad health during the year, including the stomach problems, which eventually he found out were caused by the polluted spring water near his hermitage, as well as the recurrent problems with the bursitis in his back, neck, and arm. The disturbing events during the racially troubled march in Selma, Alabama, and the worsening conditions in Vietnam as the American role in that war escalated were a source of alarm and sadness. He reflected on the difficulties he had with the Catholic Peace Fellowship after the self-immolation of one of its members, which he had finally settled by reconciliation after making a strong point about violence in the name of peace.

He then asked himself what the immediate future would bring. More illness? An escalation of the Asian war? By the end of that month, in an essay in the Catholic lay-edited journal of opinion *Commonweal* he would issue his first public statement on the war in Vietnam and his own opposition to it. [Before the year was over, 200,000 American military would be deployed to Vietnam.] Would he find fulfillment of his desire for more prayer and meditation? Would he finish his projected books, especially *Conjectures of a Guilty Bystander* and the collection of essays he had titled *Mystics and Zen Masters*?

As a coda to those New Year's musings, he added: "But I have no real plans, except to live and free the reality of my life and be ready when it ends and I am called to God. Whenever that may be!"

The early months in the hermitage triggered pages of reflections about the new way of living that derived from his experience of solitude. Merton found a new clarity in simple actions as his day unfolded: "I love the night silence, the early meditation, and the moon, the reading and the breakfast coffee (or good tea!), sawing wood after sunrise, washing up, tired, as the sun begins to grow warm . . . office in the late afternoon, quiet supper, reading, walking, looking at the hills, the silence, the moon, the does, darkness, prayer, bed." One sees in these descriptions his debt both to the Christian doctrine of living in the awareness of God's presence, but more directly, his own love for the Zen concept of "mindfulness." Both the Christian and Zen traditions emphasized the value to be accrued by doing even the most ordinary tasks with a sense of awareness or, as Christian writers would say, "under the gaze of

God." He would also reflect that the great blessing of solitude rested not only in the closeness to nature but "resides in the wakening and the attuning of the inmost heart to the voice of God — to the inexplicable, quiet, definite inner certitude of one's call to obey Him, to hear Him, to worship Him here, now, today and in silence and alone."

These personal jottings in his journals would eventually crystallize into two fascinating essays which he wrote for widely different audiences but which afforded him the chance to use his hermit life as a vehicle to express some of his deepest convictions about who he was, what he was doing, and what his life might mean. "Rain and the Rhinoceros" first saw light as an article Merton wrote for the then popular but now defunct *Holiday* magazine; it was published in 1965. It is a poetic meditation in which Merton reflects on his life in the hermitage during a rainstorm, with the rain standing symbolically for the rhythms of the natural world "cherished by this wonderful, unintelligible perfectly innocent speech." He speaks of reading the Syrian mystic and hermit Philoxenos by the light of a Coleman lantern, noting that the lantern came in a box in which it is advertised as something that "stretches days to give more hours of fun" — a sentiment that brought forth a whimsical snort from the hermit.

To this simple contemplative exercise of listening to the rain, meditating in silence on a spiritual author, he contrasts the rhinoceros (he had been reading the French text of Eugène Ionesco's absurdist play of the same name) which for Merton, as it did for Ionesco, stood for the person or institution that has become dehumanized and bestial. The contrast, then, is between the beneficent blessing of rain which falls naturally and the figure of the brute rhino as a symbol of the deformation of nature, especially human nature.

In the course of this rather bucolic picture Merton turns to something he notes frequently in his writing: the planes from nearby Fort Knox (he thinks) which are part of the Strategic Air Command flights with their bellies full of atomic bombs. It is the presence of these planes overhead that prevents him from allowing his solitude to become an evasion from the world. He describes their presence in a wonderful short paragraph full of ominous sarcasm:

> . . . at three thirty a.m. the SAC plane goes over, red light winking low under the clouds, skimming the wooded summits on the South

131

side of the valley, loaded with strong medicine. Very strong. Strong enough to burn up all these woods and stretch our hours of fun into eternities.

The contemplative life, in short, must be an advance into solitude and the desert, "a confrontation with poverty and the void, a renunciation of the empirical self, in the presence of death and nothingness." His vision of the atomic weapons within the SAC bombers may seem quaint now but at the time he surely knew of those, like the late General Curtis LeMay, who openly suggested bombing Vietnam "back to the Stone Age." That is the message of the silence heard in the rain and, in the rain's aftermath, in the "quail's sweet whistling in the wet bushes." He sees the silence afforded by being in the rain as analogous to being sheathed in the presence of God. This sound of the rain and of the silence after the rain, Merton saw, was the sound of the present moment but not one free from the burdens of actual history; as he concludes, "Yet even here the earth shakes. Over at Fort Knox the Rhinoceros is having fun."

It is not out of place to compare "Rain and the Rhinoceros" to the epilogue of The Sign of Jonas written more than a decade earlier. "The Fire Watch," described in an earlier chapter of this book, was a meditation on life in the monastery while "Rain and the Rhinoceros" was a reflection on life in the hermitage. The contrast in tone between the two essays, written more than a decade apart, is a sign of where Merton had been spiritually and where he was later. The piety is less overt in the later essay and the sociopolitical sense is much more apparent. Whereas Merton earlier saw nature as a sacramental sign of God's presence, he now sees nature in the same way but interspersed with the exigent intrusion of human activity, which can be a source of help (the Coleman lantern) or of ominous challenge (the SAC bombers from Fort Knox). "The Fire Watch" was purely "monastic," but "Rain and the Rhinoceros" was monastic in the way Merton understood monasticism after a quarter of a century of having lived the life in the midst of tumultuous changes in both church and society.

"Rain and the Rhinoceros" might also be profitably read in tandem with an essay called "Day of a Stranger," which was first published in the much more "highbrow" literary journal, The Hudson Review, in 1967 but which had been written in one draft or another a few years earlier. The word "stranger" in the title alludes to Camus's novel *L'Etranger*, which had been popularly translated as "The Stranger." In fact, the term "stranger" had a polyvalent significance: Benedict in the *Rule* saw monks as strangers in the world and Merton, de facto, was somewhat of a stranger to the monastery that existed a mile south of his hermitage.

The essay for *The Hudson Review* is a much more whimsical, almost fey, description of life in the hermitage, directed towards an audience who would have little knowledge of, or perhaps even sympathy for, the eremitical life but whose cultural background would be strongly literary. Merton again begins his essay with a reflection on the planes flying overhead; first of people probably flying from Miami to Chicago "with timeless cocktails" unaware of the monk-hermit rooted on the ground in his cottage on a hill. The contrast he seeks in this essay is between the mobility of the culture and the stability of the hermit. Then again, he notes the SAC plane with "the closed bay of a metal bird with a scientific egg at its breast. A womb easily and mechanically opened!" Merton will frequently use these avian images, contrasting them with the lazy hawks that circle over the "knobs" (as the Kentucky hills were known). It is also possible that he had in the back of his mind the contrasting image of the windhover in the poem by Hopkins of that name, or more ominously, the frequent use of hawks in the fierce nature poetry of the California poet, resident at Big Sur, Robinson Jeffers, who was one of Merton's favorite writers.

In contrasting his new life as a hermit with life in the world or even in the monastery he uses some language from pop sociology, especially taken from the then popular writer Marshall McLuhan. The hermit life is "cool" (the language here, of course, is Marshall McLuhan's description of various forms of media) while monastic life is "hot," with its hot words of "must" and "ought" and "should." The contrast between "cool" and "hot" was simply a way for Merton to describe the distinction he always kept in mind, i.e., the difference between monasticism as a "way of life" and monasticism understood as an "institution."

The hermit life has its own "mental ecology" so that there is room for the voices of poets of many languages, for Chuang Tzu's silences, for hermits like the sixth-century Syrian hermit Philoxenos, for the Algerian cenobite Albert Camus, for the clanging prose of Tertullian and the "dry catarrh of Sartre." To these macho voices are counterpoised the feminine voices of Flannery O'Connor, the mystical Angela of Foligno, the solitary Dame Julian of Norwich, Teresa of Avila, and "more personally, Raissa Maritain." The whole list of his imaginary community is too long to reproduce here but the point is clear. Merton sees his life as one in which, in the silence of the hermitage, he can carry on a contemplative dialogue with persons of various languages, poets of different temperaments, writers of different genders, and Christians of quite diverse historical traditions. This idea is as old as his determination, in the middle 1950s, to create an interior dialogue in order to reconcile differing and sometimes antagonistic versions of faith or culture. It is not insignificant that Merton reproduces those thoughts from the previous decade in *Conjectures of a Guilty Bystander*, which he was then preparing for publication.

Merton goes on to describe the daily rituals of work, cleaning up, eating, praying, watching the world of nature. These descriptions are punctuated with self-mocking dialogues with an imaginative visitor-interlocutor who represents, by turns, the inquiring journalist and the secular skeptic:

> Why live in the woods?
> Well, you have to live somewhere.
> Do you get lonely?
> Yes, sometimes.
> Are you mad at people?
> No.
> Are you mad at the monastery?
> No.
> What do you think of the future of monasticism?
> Nothing. I don't think about it.
> Is it true that your bad back is due to yoga?
> No.
> Is it true that you are practicing Zen in secret?
> Pardon me, I don't speak English.

Again, and typically, Merton juxtaposes his hermit life and the ominous life of his warring country. He has his supper, says his psalms, sits on a cool mat considering the Byzantine icon of the Nativity above his bed where he will sleep alone: "Meanwhile the metal cherub of the apocalypse passes over me in the clouds, treasuring its egg and its message."

If Merton had Camus's stranger in mind when he titled that essay he more than likely understood the title to stand for himself. He was, according to another title, a "bystander" — one who was at the margins of monastic life as well as at the periphery of the life enjoyed by those who subscribed to *The Hudson Review*. Nor was he unaware that the Christian in general and the monk in particular was a pilgrim and wanderer — a stranger *(peregrinus)* in the business of the secular world.

In a sense, Merton's reflections on his newly acquired hermit life are an interweaving of three distinct but interconnected elements: the life of study and prayer; the concern for making connections between this life and the life of society; and finally, all of this done within the framework of a regular round of living close to nature in silence and solitude. His desired goal, of course, was full human integration, with the consequence that his written description of life in the hermitage had about it an idealization that did not fully correspond to the work, restlessness, fits of illness, and personal struggles that were part and parcel of ordinary living. Nor was his solitude anything like absolute. Visitors, some welcome and others tolerated, regularly came to the monastery and some spent the day with him at the hermitage. Sometimes, an adventurous visitor to the monastery would discover the path to the hermitage (and, in the process, violate monastic enclosure) and just "stop by" for a mostly unwelcome visit. There was, in addition, one of the locals wandering around with a gun in order to hunt on the monastery property as well as the near constant whining of the chainsaw coming from one of his farming neighbors.

In 1965 Merton gathered up a number of his scattered prose pieces (including "Rain and the Rhinoceros"), and had them published in 1966 in a volume entitled *Raids on the Unspeakable*. Again, attention should be paid to the title. To raid is not necessarily to conquer. To raid (with the dual meaning of attack and rummage) the unspeakable is to try and make sense of the unspeakable violence abroad in the world. Although the anthology does not have a coherent thread to it, nonetheless, one recurring theme is the appalling violence of contemporary life.

The collection as a whole was, again, very much a potpourri. There was a brief tribute to Flannery O'Connor, the southern fiction writer whom he greatly admired and who had died in 1964. He thought her fierce early novella *Wise Blood* (1952) had something almost Sophoclean in its moral intensity and its unblinking use of violence. He also had a powerful essay on Adolf Eichmann (inspired by the monk's reading of the work of Hannah Arendt, who had followed the Eichmann trial in Jerusalem and wrote a highly contested essay and book about the event) followed by some prose poems dealing with peace and war.

Towards the end of the book was an interesting "Message to Poets," which Merton wrote for a congress of Latin American poets meeting in Mexico City, to which he had been invited by his friend, the Argentinian critic Miguel Grinberg but which he had been unable to attend. "Message to Poets" was part apologia for the life of poetry, an argument for the relevance of the irrelevant life, and a manifesto in favor of the power of language. His argument for the "relevance of the irrelevant" was, of course, a send-up of those who passionately but uncritically made "relevance" a battle cry in religious circles during the 1960s.

The last piece in the volume, an occasional one, consisted of reflections and some notes Merton wrote to accompany the exhibitions of his calligraphies and drawings, which now began to "travel" outside the area of Louisville. For the American edition of *Raids* he used some of these "summonses to awareness," as he called these abstract gestural calligraphies, both for the cover of the book and to separate out its various parts. As for the calligraphies themselves, Merton said they were as simple gestures, "unidentified vestiges" and "signatures of someone who was not around." Perhaps, he wrote, they might "awaken possibilities" and "dimly help to alter one's perceptions." That purpose and their evident oriental character was another way in which he made his crossing over to the Zen tradition in particular. Those brief notes do help a bit for those who have seen his drawings and come away mystified by them.

"Readings from Ibn Abbad" in the same volume is a not untypical Mertonian exercise. He had studied some French translations of the fourteenth-century Muslim mystic Ibn Abbad (some think his writings may have influenced Saint John of the Cross) done by a Lebanese Je-

136

suit. Merton responded to these texts by writing what he called "meditative and poetic notations" on what he had read. They are in fact rather loose paraphrases of the writings of Ibn Abbad. His purpose in doing so was to demonstrate how one might come to appreciate the personality and mysticism of this Moroccan holy man.

The very brief "A Devout Meditation in Memory of Adolf Eichmann" was inspired by the psychiatric report issued at the time of Eichmann's trial and recollected in Arendt's book on that trial (*Eichmann in Jerusalem*), which declared Eichmann to be "perfectly sane." Merton said that because someone was "sane" did not mean that they were in their "right mind." He argued that a purely rational calculation, apart from any deep sense of what a human is or what the meaning of a human might be, was a dangerous state to be in. What is sanity if it excludes love, care, response to need, compassion, and sympathy for the other? The ominous moral he draws from the Eichmann report is that if an atomic war were started, those that pushed the trigger would be eminently "sane" in that they had done their calculations and decided, based on a "sane" report, that *x* number of millions were expendable. The "sanity" of moderns was about as useful as the muscles of the dinosaur, he ended. His ironic description of "rationality" was simply a variation of his frequent observation (made most explicitly in the opening chapters of *New Seeds of Contemplation*) that to make the mistake of identifying the Cartesian "ego" with the true self was a fatal error of judgment. Merton's argument on this point was quite similar to the famous observation of Gilbert Keith Chesterton that the mad man was one who had lost everything except his mind, i.e., the capacity for wonder at serendipity, play, joy, human friendship, etc.

Merton was much pleased with *Raids* because the contents of the prose essays and prose poems reflected the kind of intellectual and spiritual work that he wanted to do. In a rather whimsical prologue to the volume written in the fall of 1965 he addresses his book directly, saying that his earlier books had been better mannered, more pious, and "seminary trained." "I love the whole lot of you," he says. "But, in some ways, *Raids*, I think I love you more than the rest." And why such love? Merton provides the motive power of his writings in his charge to *Raids*: ". . . to be human in this most inhuman of ages, to guard the image of man for it is the image of God." He then tells the book to go "with my blessing" but do not expect to make many friends.

In the spring of 1966 Merton went through a most unlikely experience for a Trappist monk turned hermit. During a hospital stay in Louisville while being treated for a recurrent back ailment he fell in love with a student nurse, a young woman (always referred to in the biographical literature as "M" to protect her privacy) nearly thirty years his junior. This incident in his life has been thoroughly discussed by Merton's biographers, with an especially fine treatment by Michael Mott in his authorized biographical work *The Seven Mountains of Thomas Merton*. We also now possess the journals for this period (*Learning to Love: The Journals of Thomas Merton*, vol. VI) so that we have a fuller understanding of the love affair at least from Merton's somewhat overwrought perspective. The young woman in question, to my knowledge, has never discussed this issue in public although she did speak with the Merton biographers.

The facts are easy enough to state even if the emotional undercurrents behind the events are hard to identify with satisfaction. While in the hospital for back surgery in March of that year, Merton was tended by a student nurse. There was a mutual attraction between them. Over the next months there was a series of clandestine meetings, some rather passionate, in various restaurants, parks, etc. in Louisville, as well as a flurry of letters, notes, and phone calls. Before the year was out it was clear that the love they may have felt for each other was, in practical fact, an intractable dilemma that could only be solved by separation. Since the student nurse had moved from Kentucky to Ohio after completing her training there was the temporary solution of physical distance. After this move there were still some calls, but they trailed off as time went by.

The cold hard fact was that no happy resolution was going to come from a situation in which a famous middle-aged monk writer would find happiness with a young student nurse outside the glare of publicity and notoriety. Furthermore, it is clear that Merton, even in his most love-besotted moments, could not envision leaving the monastic life despite the pages of agonizing schemes and hypothetical "solutions" to the problem in his journals, where he constructed fictive escapes, alternate modes of existence, and life-changing alternatives. As with many crises in his life, Merton worked out these putative alternatives on the safe pages of his journal along with agonizing pages of self-examination and long discussions with, among others, Ping Ferry and his psychiatrist friend from Louisville, Jim Wygal.

There is something almost serio-comic about this whole episode in Merton's life. There was the passionate scheming for the two to meet in various places (a psychiatrist friend's office; the airport; a public park; a local restaurant, etc.) and Merton's surreptitious telephone calls from the business offices of the monastery, as phones were in short supply in the abbey. When the abbot found out about the relationship, after Merton was reported by a brother who listened in on a conversation between the two at the gatehouse, there were the various ruses to get mail to each other despite Abbot Fox's stern and hardly unexpected admonition that Merton should break off the relationship immediately and totally.

All of this complex maneuvering was taking place while Merton was still in residence in the hermitage, reading books about mysticism and the drug LSD (then a fashionable topic, although Merton deplored the whole notion of mysticism developed through LSD or any other chemical agency for that matter) and listening to the music of Joan Baez (who would later that year visit Merton at the monastery and, in the process, urge him to leave Gethsemani for the larger world of peace activism) and Bob Dylan, whom he had learned about from various friends. In other words, there was a kind of crazy sixties freneticism about the whole scene familiar to anyone who lived through that period in American life, when the whole culture seemed on the verge of a collective nervous breakdown. One has visions of Merton in his hermitage listening to "Blowin' in the Wind" while writing of his love for M in his notebooks, interspersed with readings from the Psalter and the study of texts dealing with drugs.

Despite the somewhat surreal aura about this entire episode there are a number of points that are worth noting. First, Merton never hid this event by destroying his notes or journals; indeed, he kept a separate journal about his own reflections on it (the "Midsummer Journal," which he meant for M to have and is now published in the journals of this period) and wrote eighteen somewhat mawkish poems (later published in a limited edition) in response to his experience. Second, Merton was amazed that he was capable of deep human love, which was crucial for a person who had essentially been brought up as an orphan and whose experiences with women earlier in his life were, by and large according to his own admission, not those of love but — again in his words — "adulterous." Third, despite the agonies of passion and despite the moral ambiguity of some of his actions, he knew that his situation in fact and for the future as far as this young woman was concerned was an impossible one.

He knew, in brief, that while his love was genuine, his commitment to the religious life was irrevocable and his desire for the solitary life unwavering. If there was one continuous theme in his poems written about the love he had for this young woman, it was how to understand human love in all of its fleshly reality in relationship to the love of God — a theme hardly absent from many writers in the Christian mystical tradition. There was, however, one overriding obstacle in the face of this love: he was a monk vowed to the celibate life. It was precisely the stark reality of that conundrum which saturates the pages of his journal.

In July he wrote in his journal that the issue of his leaving Gethsemani for a "life in the world" with M was not "even a credible one" even though he felt a deep love for her and felt drawn to her "with almost agonizing desire." One reads these pages with a sense that two Mertons were writing: the one was a person who was experiencing deep human love with all the erotic allure that comes with it, and the other was the seasoned ascetic who, while not denying the love, could not bring it to a conclusion that would mean leaving the monastic life. Hovering in the background of this whole struggle was the issue, real enough for the monk, of the sinful character of any sexual relationship between a monk vowed to chastity and any woman, although just how sexual the relationship was is not for me to say based solely on the evidence at hand.

It took Merton some time to act on his religious convictions in a balanced fashion, i.e., choosing to remain in the monastic life; but his behavior until he made the break was not always as praiseworthy as it should have been. Once cannot but feel, at the same time, that too much has been made about the agonies of the monk (whose side of this episode we know only from his writings) to the detriment of the young woman (who later went on to marry and have a family) whose own voice is silent and whose story we know only from one side which was not hers. During this period of his life Merton was not al-

140

ways at his best, but it is a salutary experience to read the material from this period, especially for those who would like to turn Merton into a plaster saint. It may well be that he left a record of that experience precisely to fill out his portrait as a deeply human and flawed person.

Merton's decision not to destroy his journals (knowing that some time after his death they would be published), even though he burned the correspondence between himself and M, did result, almost accidentally, in one important gain. As far as we know, as a monk from Gethsemani once said to me, we do not possess in monastic literature (or Catholic spiritual literature in general, we might add) as complete a set of reflections on the struggle of an ascetic with the joys and demands of human love as we do in these writings. Underneath the somewhat obsessive tone of the journals there surely rests a substratum of genuine tension between the ideals of religious chastity and the natural human desire to love and be loved in a full and complete fashion. We know that Merton spoke to various friends about this whole matter, including his friend and psychiatrist, the late James Wygal; but it appears that, like so many episodes in his life, Merton worked this out mainly through reflections committed to his journals. Still and all, there is something faintly voyeuristic about reading these journals, if only because one frames a picture of the events solely through the eyes and pen of the monk.

After Merton's death there was an exchange of letters between Jay Laughlin (Merton's friend and publisher of New Directions) and M in which she had evidently lamented that Merton never understood how much he had meant to her. In sending her a copy of the eighteen poems (a limited edition of poems written for her by Merton) that Merton had composed separately from his regular journal, Laughlin replied in a manner that was surely truly the case:

> You were as close to him as any mortal person can be. He always spoke to me of you with the deepest affection and gratitude for what you brought to his life. But you know, in one way Tom didn't belong to this world in which you and I live in, that is something we have to understand, accept, and just be grateful and feel blessed that God privileged us to be his friend and have as much of him as he could give to us.

It is striking that during this entire romantic episode in his life — it lasted less than a year — Merton continued with many of his regular practices and duties. The title of the journal might allude to Shakespeare: the whole thing was a dream. He continued to read voraciously. He worked on his writing. He had moments of satisfaction with his life of meditation. He could still note with careful attention his observations of the world of nature. He took careful notes and crafted sections for his long experimental poem which would eventually be called "Cables to the Ace." He followed the work of the then fashionable "Death of God" theologians, finding some of them too facile and zestful in their enthusiasms while others (notably Thomas Altizer) attracted him with their eschatological and apocalyptic urgency. Altizer's work had the further attraction of being much inspired by the poetry of William Blake. In the midst of all of these frantic activities he was also suffering from various ailments that required visits to doctors; he continually needed medicine for his allergies and for the pain coming from his bursitis. There were also persistent dermatological problems with his hands, which caused outbreaks and eruptions bad enough to make his hands bleed when he wrote.

Oddly enough, despite the fact that he still agonized over his love for M and contacted her on occasion by phone and letter after she had already left Louisville, he decided to make a final commitment to the hermit life by a formal act on September 8th (the feast of the Nativity of Mary) in 1966. He prepared for this event by making a retreat which he spent, in part, by going over his journal and thinking through the events of the spring and summer. In a series of entries written before his commitment day, Merton argued (to himself) that it was a gift to have loved this woman even though he would of necessity have to sacrifice erotic and sexual love in order to be faithful to his vocation. He also saw himself as unstable, evasive, and not honest in terms of the interior portrait he had of himself (these lines may be profitably read against Merton's writings on the true and illusory self in *New Seeds!*). He further admitted that the intervention of the abbot was probably providential given that in the late spring and early summer he was behaving in an erratic and immature fashion. As he finished these reflections he had a sentence fragment: "Too much analyzing." Most readers who have read the journals and poems from this period — even, one suspects, the most sympathetic — would agree.

During this tumultuous summer for Thomas Merton, events in the United States were seething. While President Johnson promised an expansion of the programs of the Great Society there was relentless unrest across the country. This was the year of the infamous Watts riots in southern California and similar civil disturbances in Chicago, events that took place against the backdrop of continuous fighting in Southeast Asia.

During the fall of 1966 Merton occupied himself with an intense study of the writings of Albert Camus, from which study he would craft a series of essays which, after publication in various places, would find their way into the posthumous collected *Literary Essays of Thomas Merton*. There are a number of obvious reasons why Merton would be attracted to the Algerian-born writer, who in the 1960s was widely read and then honored as a Nobel laureate. Merton had a natural sympathy for the French intellectual life in general and in particular for the very French idea that an intellectual ought to be an engaged intellectual. He resonated with the fact that Camus came from Algeria and hence, in Merton's view, belonged to the same North African desert tradition that had produced tough-minded Christian writers like Tertullian and Saint Augustine (Camus had written his thesis on the bishop of Hippo — as did, curiously enough, Hannah Arendt).

Even though Camus was not a religious believer, he took deep religious issues very seriously, posing them (under the influence of Dostoevsky) as the terrible problem of the tension between belief in the transcendent as a possibility, and a world of suffering and seemingly capricious evil. Furthermore, since the problem of God's existence and the reality of evil made belief in God problematical, one could reasonably ask how it was possible to lead an authentic life in the face of the absurd fact of evil and suffering. After all, one could not appeal to some transcendent ground that would balance good and evil in the end. In his great trilogy of novels (*The Stranger; The Plague; The Fall*) and in his nonfiction works, Camus posed these issues with — and here is a favorite Camusian word that Merton loved — lucidity. The fact that Camus at least took Christianity with seriousness made him a favorite nonbeliever for the writers of the Christian Left in the sixties.

What attracted Merton most intensely to Camus was the novelist's demand that people not shirk the moral responsibility to struggle against evil even when that struggle seemed a Sisyphean task of frustration (recall Camus's famous essay "The Myth of Sisyphus"). A human person must accept the world as it is and struggle against that which is evil and death dealing. Merton saw Doctor Rieux, the hero of *The Plague,* as more religiously authentic than the pessimistic Father Paneloux, who succumbed, in Merton's estimation, to a kind of fatalism under the guise of "accepting God's will." Camus's heroes, in short, were moral ascetics who maintained their integrity when, humanly speaking, their fidelity seemed absurd.

Nor is it insignificant that Camus's heroes were solitary figures (the French word *L'Etranger* used as the title of his first great novel is only minimally satisfactory when translated as "The Stranger" — it is more like "Outsider" or "Marginalized" in the sense that Camus desired to convey). In that sense, all of the heroes of the trilogy of novels acted on the margins and from various perspectives provided, either explicitly or implicitly, a critique of the society within which they found themselves. They were all loners, and with the possible exception of the hero of the early novel *L'Etranger,* articulated what they saw as the fundamental problems of human existence. Merton found this to be as true of Clemence, the central figure in *The Fall,* as he did of Doctor Rieux in *The Plague.* It is interesting that the first essay Merton wrote on Camus in 1967 (but which was not published until 1968) had in its subtitle two of Camus's favorite words, which were also talismanic for Merton: "lucidity" and "absurd."

Merton hastened to note that, contrary to popular belief, Camus did not preach the "absurd" — he only wanted people to recognize it. In the final analysis, Merton wrote, the work of Camus reflected a humanism rooted in the author's convictions about the authentic value of human life. This humanism preached human solidarity against the absurd. The humanism of Camus has a "certain purity because it is based on the renunciation of all illusions, all misleading ideals, all deceptive and hypocritical social forms." Tellingly, Merton dedicated his commentary on *The Plague* to the Jesuit poet, priest, and peace activist, Daniel Berrigan. Merton would go on to write six other essays on Camus which would be published in various journals in various forms.

In a small spiral notebook found among Merton's papers there is a checklist of what he had finished or hoped to have finished (he was writing this list in January as almost a New Year's resolution) in 1966. Despite the turmoil in his private life, it was an impressive litany of writing projects. He was to write the text for a new picture book on Gethsemani; a series of articles on monastic history for various religious journals here and abroad; a list of seven words about which he hoped to write essays (he did two of them on "Purity" and on "Death"); some prefaces for the writings of his friend Ernesto Cardenal, who was living in Nicaragua attempting to start an alternative monastic community; prefaces for books by his Chinese collaborator John Wu and the Irish Jesuit scholar of Zen, resident in Japan, William Johnston; and an introduction to the Japanese translation of *Thoughts in Solitude*. Finally, he hoped to write up his notes from his study and close reading of the German poet Rainer Maria Rilke, whom he had been reading in German steadily for well over a year.

Doubleday published *Conjectures of a Guilty Bystander* in 1966. The case could be made that one could learn a great deal from reading Merton's autobiographical writings, beginning chronologically with *The Secular Journal* and ending with *Asian Journal*, even though he never regarded them as sequels. Even though all of those published works were refinements of materials he had jotted down in his private journals, the published works expressed what Merton finally wanted to say in a public fashion. Merton exegetes can compare the private journals (now all published) with the books he published in his own lifetime to see how he nuances and changes his perceptions, but the published books are invaluable for understanding the public face of the monk.

Those books also illustrate a progression in his thinking, his interests, and his style. There is a world of difference, for example, between *The Sign of Jonas*, with its explicit monastic orientation, and *Conjectures*, which is far more wide ranging, less centered on monastic existence as such, and concerned with a more experimental prose style.

The title of the volume is interesting in its own right. Merton frequently chose nouns (e.g., "raids" or "emblems" or "conjectures") which hinted that what he was doing was a work in progress or a thrust or a probe or something produced on the sidelines or at the margins. That Merton describes himself in the third person as a "bystander" reflects the frequent advice (some of it unrequested) that he

145

leave the cloister and become more actively involved in the great struggles for peace, social justice, and racial harmony. This radical change was urged upon him by, for example, Joan Baez when she visited him with her friend, Ira Sandperl, and by the theologian Rosemary Ruether in an exchange of letters in which the latter subjected the whole monastic enterprise to a searching critique. Indeed, the exchange of letters between these two is an excellent window into at least one aspect of the theological debates of the sixties. Ruether, who had been a Benedictine lay oblate when she was a young woman living in California, made a sharp critique of the monastic enterprise, with Merton offering rejoinders in the light of his own experience as — if the term is not too paradoxical — a "contemplative activist." However much they may have sparred through their letters, they could speak on more or less equal terms. Ruether was trained as a patristic scholar. Her book on Gregory of Nazianzus was to come out while they were writing each other; they both had a keen interest in religious subcultures. She arranged for a showing of some of Merton's art, the proceeds of which were to be used for projects of social justice with which she was involved.

Even though Merton had his own moments of doubt about staying at Gethsemani he never seriously contemplated leaving the monastic life altogether, however much he may have dreamed (and schemed!) about living his life elsewhere. What these external urgings, coming from a variety of sources, did do, however, was to help him clarify his own attitude towards the kind of life that he had embraced. It brought to the fore his long-standing meditation on the role of the contemplative. As a "bystander" (which is to say, someone who was not on the picket line or living in the inner city) he felt he had his own contribution to make from where he was and according to the fashion in which he shaped his own life. This is precisely the argument he made to Rosemary Ruether as a response to her somewhat strident demand that he get into the active life of the struggle for social justice. As a "bystander" Merton was able to describe himself in terms not unlike those of Paul Tillich, the Protestant theologian, who thought of Christians as those living on "the boundary" or "at the edges."

Merton made the case for his life as a monk as a "contemplative activist" most compellingly in a preface he wrote for the Japanese translation of *The Seven Storey Mountain*. In that preface he argued that a life can serve — to use the now fashionable term — as a "text" to say what one wishes the world to know. Such a life adds dimension and authenticity to what one might write. He wrote:

> To adopt a life that is essentially non-assertive, non-violent, a life of humility and peace is in itself a statement of one's position. . . . By my monastic life and vows I am saying NO to all the concentration camps, the aerial bombardments, the staged political trials, the judicial murders, the racial injustices, the economic tyrannies, and the whole socioeconomic apparatus. . . . I make monastic silence a protest against the lies of politicians, propagandists, and agitators, and when I speak it is to deny that my faith and my Church can ever seriously be aligned with these forces and injustices. . . .

The "guilty" of Merton's *Conjectures* must be understood at a number of levels. He probably felt a certain guilt in being cosseted in the safe confines of the monastery while so many who looked up to him were on the front lines of activism. Such a feeling would be natural enough. He also frequently used the term "guilt" to bring into the open the tacit (or even the explicit) complicity of the church in tolerating race segregation or displaying an unusual enthusiasm for war in the name of a crusade against "godless communism." This second sense of guilt is probably what the title is most concerned with expressing. In the same preface alluded to above, Merton says that he writes against those within his own church who had an overly sunny view of the church and its deeds. What such people needed, he felt, was the arrival of a moment when these ideological constructs would be severely judged, a moment that could bring about a liberation from the "servitude to and involvement in the structures of the secular world." To make one's guilt explicit is to judge prophetically that one has committed a life to the institution rather than to the core message the institution — whether it be church or monastery — is meant to proclaim.

Conjectures is not easy to summarize or categorize. Merton himself, in the preface, says that it contains material from his notebooks which go back to 1956, but it is not to be construed as a "spiritual journal." He describes the book as a "series of sketches and meditations" fitted together so that the parts act on each other. Even though, he continues, Protestant theologians like Dietrich Bonhoeffer and Karl Barth get much attention in his volume (including the wonderful essay under the title "Barth's Dream of Mozart," which makes up the first part of *Conjectures*), he is not writing "ecumenical theology." Merton then makes a very important point: he wanted this book to show how a monk might read a Protestant theologian or those from other religious traditions in order to illustrate how a Catholic can share the Protestant experience. This observation is crucial for Merton; as he says repeatedly in *Conjectures,* what he desires is to establish a kind of "interior dialogue" in which a person, true to his or her own tradition, can enterinto the religious life of another in a sympathetic fashion. This form of interior dialogue had been a leitmotif of his thinking for nearly two decades.

Since the Second Vatican Council opened a dialogue (Merton wrote this preface just as the Council ended) with the world's religions "it becomes necessary for at least a few contemplatives and monastic theologians to contribute something of their own to the discussion." Merton says that in *Conjectures* he wishes to do that in a singular, existential, poetic fashion, which — he concludes — is "proper to this monastic view." His form of dialogue, in short, was not to be construed as an exchange, however irenic, of technical theological materials. He was neither equipped or by temperament prone to that kind of labor, however necessary it was.

Conjectures is divided into five parts with each having a Mertonian subtitle — the fifth, for example, is "The Madman Runs to the East" — but, like the Zen saying from which it comes, there is no clear thematic thread that distinguishes that section from the preceding four. It is clear, however, that a constant refrain in this volume is a desire to get sympathetically into the heads of various figures to learn what they say and to experience what they experience.

He states baldly that one can not understand the Bible without becoming a Jew — a "spiritual Semite" to use Pope Pius XI's fine phrase. He argues that only by reading Orthodox theologians seriously can one enter into a real exchange between East and West. He loves the writings of Barth, but he sees him as deficient in his sacramental imagination; despite that hesitation he feels it crucial to study the Swiss theologian (curiously, both Merton and Barth died on the same day in 1968) with seriousness. His attempts to understand the then intellectual fascination with Marx is tempered by both his distrust of the Soviet political system and the Western temptation to demonize everything that smacks of "communism."

However more progressive his thinking and his concerns might be in this book, flashes of the deep spiritual intuitions break through in many places. He can note the rising of the sun over the pine trees, a "great golden basilica of fire and water . . . crows making a racket in the West, yet over all, the majestic peace of Sunday." He concludes with a line that might have been written by his poetic hero, Gerard Manley Hopkins: "This is the great truth: Christ has indeed conquered the world and it does belong to him alone." The Feast of Pentecost brings forth a great prayer praising the green spring. An antiphon from the office compels him to try to create a poem in English praising the cross.

It is always instructive to pay careful attention to Merton's sensitivity to the created world; we are reminded that for all of his bookishness he reveled in the lush world of his Kentucky home. In noting the distant treelines of the pastures — the knobs, as the Kentuckians call the hills of their area — with their rising fog, or in evoking the sunrises that come like a promise after the long night vigils of the monks, his writing in *Conjectures* and elsewhere compels us to praise God for creation. In fact, it struck me, rereading this journal, how frequently he invokes the rising of the sun over the quiet world as a clarion call for a life of adoration and praise. If there was one thing that was intensified in his life in the hermitage it was his increasing sensitivity to the times of the day and the turning of the seasons, as his entries in *Conjectures* amply attest.

One other visitor to Gethsemani in the late spring of 1966 became a very important friend and dialogue partner for Thomas Merton. Thich Nhat Hanh was a Vietnamese Buddhist monk and a published poet. Due to his peace activities and the resistance to those activities he was living in exile from his native Vietnam. As Merton's biographer Michael Mott points out, the two men had a number of things in common: they both had years of experience in monasteries; they were both poets who had written of their own brothers' death in war; both were deeply involved in peace work; and, finally, both were deeply contemplative. In addition, of course, Nhat Hanh was a Buddhist who could help Merton deepen his understanding of that tradition. Mott notes that Nhat Hanh's well regarded talk to the Gethsemani community erased any notion that

149

Buddhism was a world-denying or world-despising religion. On the contrary, Nhat Hanh's worldview had something almost Franciscan about it. It was for that reason, among others, that Merton gave a series of Sunday afternoon talks to the monks on the poetry of this gentle Buddhist monk. Nhat Hanh is still active at his monastic center, Plum village, in France, preaching, like Merton, on the contemplative virtues and their connection to peacemaking. His most recent book *Living Buddha/Living Christ* is as good and sympathetic a meditation on the meaning of the mysteries of Christianity as has ever been written by a non-Christian. One can only speculate what Merton would have made of it had he lived long enough to read it.

Merton's homage to this Buddhist monk ("Nhat Hanh Is My Brother") was published in the progressive Catholic magazine *Jubilee*, which was then edited by his old friend and former classmate, Ed Rice. His tribute to the monk, published in 1966, would be reprinted a number of times in anthologies and be translated into a number of languages, including German and Polish. Nhat Hanh's continuing dialogue with Christianity (notably in his recent moving book *Living Buddha/Living Christ* mentioned above) derives, at least in part, from his exchanges with the monk of Gethsemani. His regular teaching on the Buddhist concept of "mindfulness" strikes many resonances in the minds of those who know the Christian monastic vocabulary of "purity of heart."

On the last day of December in 1966 Merton drove into Louisville to see his doctor. It was a bitterly cold, frost-laden morning as he left the monastery for town. Later in his journal he wrote that Louisville would always mean M for him even though she was no longer in the city (and was soon to depart for Hawaii). He confessed that he had an interior struggle between his desire and his knowledge that "it *all* has to end" [his emphasis]. Still, he could not resist from calling her twice in what seemed to have been unsatisfactory conversations.

The next day, the first day of 1967, his entry for the new year was uncharacteristically short. He punctuated his entry with short but determined resolutions. He had to get back into "right order" and must make his "meditations what they ought to be." He confesses his foolishness, his exaggerations, his impulsiveness, as the probable cause of more harm than he understood. He concludes that his experience with M was something that was credible and acceptable but "in the past tense," and is only present in a friendship that has less "passion" and "perhaps, free of complications."

1966, in retrospect, had been an oddly unsettling year. Firmly settled in his hermitage where there should have been peace and detachment, he had in fact experienced a year of enormous internal personal turmoil and upheaval. It is true that he published two rather substantial books *(Raids on the Unspeakable* and *Conjectures of a Guilty Bystander)* as well as a celebratory book on Gethsemani itself, where he supplied the text for a series of photographs taken by three photographers, including two monks of the abbey *(Gethsemani: A Life of Praise)*, as well as a number of essays, reviews, and poems.

Amid the worthy monastic occupations, however, intruded the turmoil of the country over U.S. involvement in the war in Vietnam and Merton's place, however distant from actual events, as a figure in the peace movement. At the beginning of the year President Johnson had said in his state of the union address that the United States would stay in Vietnam until an equitable peace was established. Peace activists were discouraged by escalation. It is in this light that Merton's letter to the Catholic activist, Jim Forest, was crucial. The monk argued that it was not the result that was fundamental but the constant affirmation that working for peace was a value in itself, because (here the influence of Merton's hero, Gandhi, was patent) there was truth in the work of peace itself.

Parallel to the struggle for peace was the continuing racial struggle in the United States, which erupted in riots, demonstrations, confrontations, and violence. It was the year of the famous White House conference on civil rights in June and the Chicago riots of July. In fact, on New Year's Day (1967), as soon as he finished reflecting on his "state of soul" Merton passed on to his reading of literature from the southern freedom riders of the Student Nonviolent Coordinating Committee (SNCC). Again, from his hermitage, Merton continued his passionate writing in the name of racial justice.

1966, of course, is also the *annus mirabilis,* in which Merton fell deeply in love with M, with all the happiness and anguish it would imply. When one sees this experience in the light of everything else that was happening, it is only natural to ask whether it is at least partially explicable in terms of the deep human need for love and companionship in a time of crisis. Merton, after all, was not only in the midst of the social unrest experienced by all thinking people at the time, but also was hardly insensitive to the rapid change in his own monastic community as the monks tried to implement the enormous and rapid changes that resulted from the reforms of the Second Vatican Council. Anyone who reads the literature, popular or scholarly, on the religious life of the 1960s sees reflected in that writing increasing uncertainty as well as radical change, as a certain paradigm of religious life gave way to another understanding of what it meant to be a community of vowed persons. One offshoot of these intense debates was a large exodus of vowed religious, many of whom made their departures precisely in order to marry. Merton's own anguished "schemes" and "dreams" about living with M become explicable only against the background of this larger reality.

Merton was a central player among those who wrote and thought about the monastic life in the wake of Vatican II. After his death a collection of his essays on this topic was published under the title *Contemplation in a World of Action,* which contained some essays focused on this theme. One essay in particular had the telling title, "Is the Contemplative Life Finished?" It was not unlike another, briefer posthumous "note" published a year after his death in *Cistercian Studies,* a piece titled "Is the Contemplative Life an Evasion?"

In the next chapter we will deal with these issues more fully, but here it is worthwhile, at the risk of repetition, to note that the whole idea of the meaning of monasticism had been a central concern of Merton's since the mid 1950s. What had changed in the middle sixties is that the issue was no longer an internal concern of the Cistercians in particular or monks in general but had become a church-wide question: How do the church in general and religious orders in particular confront the realities of the contemporary world? This was an issue when Merton struggled with it and it is one that has not been completely resolved in our time. The struggles that Merton recorded in his published and unpublished writings were only a harbinger of a discussion that goes on today within Roman Catholic circles and religious circles more generally.

In a letter written in December of 1966 he responded to a Benedictine monk who complained that the monastic life was "useless," by saying that it *was* useless, at least in the sense that monasticism was never meant to serve some practical purpose. The monk, he wrote, should have the courage to "keep his life going as a sign of freedom and peace. . . ." Better still the monk should find ways of sharing with the larger world what many of them seek, namely, a "little silence and peace" in order to give themselves some perspective. He urged the unnamed monk not to get on the bandwagon of those who fought for more activity and "commitment." That approach, he said, was just silly.

That letter, apparently written in some haste, succinctly sums up something he deeply believed and about which he was willing to bet his life. The unnamed monk who wrote Merton, of course, expressed anxieties that Merton, after a quarter of a century in monastic life, knew all too well.

6 The Final Years: 1967-1968

In my end is my beginning.

T. S. Eliot

THE LAST TWO YEARS OF MERTON'S LIFE WERE SPENT IN frenetic activity punctuated, in his journals, with determined resolutions to cut down on his reading of extraneous materials, to limit his writing projects, to thin out his list of correspondents, and to limit more strictly the number of visitors who came to see him at the hermitage. He observed these resolutions with varying degrees of fidelity, but his capacity to observe them fully cut against the grain of his intellectually curious mind, his gregariousness (not a particularly helpful trait in a hermit), his restlessness, and his sense that his life was somehow bound up with the social turmoil of both the United States and the world at large. Furthermore, as we shall see, in 1968, his twenty-seventh year in the monastery, Merton got the opportunity to travel and he did so at such a pace that were we simply to map out his various comings and goings in the United States and Asia it would require a chapter in its own right.

155

One sign of his continuing interest in (and remote preparation for his Asian trip) Eastern religious thought was his collection of essays published as *Zen and the Birds of Appetite* (1968), which he finished editing in 1967. Part one of that volume contained a series of studies of Zen with an interesting separate section making up part two — a report on his dialogue with Zen master D. T. Suzuki, whom he had met in New York the previous year. Although *Zen and the Birds of Appetite* does not form a coherent whole as a book (there were studies on everything, from biographical essays to an article on Zen and art), its spirit of openness and his sympathetic reading of the Zen tradition has made it a highly popular and much read work. As a pioneering work on inter-religious dialogue by an American Catholic, it caught the imagination of many who were not even necessarily sympathetic to Catholic Christianity. In less than a decade it had been reissued in Great Britain under the title *Thomas Merton on Zen* and translated into Dutch, French, German, Italian, Japanese, Portuguese, and Spanish. It continues to be widely read even today.

Many see the approach to the religious traditions in Merton's *Zen* as a kind of model for those who would like to engage in interreligious dialogue at a contemplative level; the various studies in that volume demonstrate how one might "read" a different tradition while firmly rooted in one's own. As he wrote in his "Author's Note" to the volume, if there is a lot of fuss about "spirituality," "enlightenment," or just "turning on," it is often because "there are buzzards hovering around a corpse." He wanted no part of that kind of facile syncretism nor could he, since in Zen no one is enriched and there is no corpse. When the buzzards leave there is "no-body" and that is where Zen is. Merton, most certainly, did not want to be numbered among all of those folks in the sixties who were turning to the East for instant wisdom. In fact, Merton consistently critiqued the facile idea that one could become a "mystic" or "enlightened" via some easy route. What he loved about Zen was that it gave no comfort to the followers of the latest guru imported from India or the ersatz mysticism of the drug culture espoused by Timothy Leary ("turn on, tune in, drop out" was his catchword) or the rather vulgar theological posturings of a Harvey Cox, who in this period had abandoned the secular city and turned to festivity, play, and the siren call of Eastern thought.

There is little technical discussion, in this work, of Zen terms and their Christian theological analogues. Rather, Merton's approach to Zen was an honest attempt to understand the position of the Other as clearly as he could manage while showing where he felt affinities might be. He was most anxious to learn from his encounter in order to aid his own understanding as a contemplative monk. What he wanted to discover, as he says in this book, is whether Zen wisdom might help him embrace more fully the wisdom Paul speaks of in the opening of his first letter to the church at Corinth, a wisdom that stands against rationality and in favor of the folly and stumbling block of Christ. This search for authentic wisdom (a major theme of Paul's letter) was a theme that harkened back to his thinking in the 1950s, as he attempted to work out a way of being faithful to his own deeply felt Christianity while not appearing as an aggrandizer or covert apologist. He wanted to be a seeker and a learner along the path of wisdom.

Merton tried to find correlates between Zen vocabulary and Christian usages, but he never thought that it was possible (or even intellectually honest) to simply juxtapose Christian and Buddhist thought as if they were a priori similar. In an introduction to a book on Zen written by his friend John Wu (reprinted in *Zen and the Birds of Appetite* as "A Christian Looks at Zen") he says to make such facile parallels is like comparing a book on mathematics to a book on tennis. Worse still, in Merton's estimation, would be to approach a different religious system with the prior conviction that what one studies is a competing system of thought. Such an approach would lead one to tag doctrines, formulations, and ideas as wrong, heretical, ideological, or what have you. One must begin simply by listening and trying to understand. One must also bracket the Western penchant for doctrinal formulations by reminding oneself that before all else, Christianity is a living experience of unity in Christ.

One other project that engaged the monk's energies in this period was the final composition of two long, experimental, and highly complex poems which were both published by his friend Jay Laughlin of New Directions in 1968, the year of his death, as separate works under the titles: *Cables to the Ace* and *The Geography of Lograire*. Both works have received a good deal of critical attention (they are the sort of works that attract academic critics since there are a plethora of sources to track down, wordplay to be uncovered, patterns to be traced, allusions to be detected, meanings to be articulated, etc.). Despite judg-

157

ments to the contrary, Laughlin himself thought that these highly complex poetic works would be part of the long-term legacy of Merton the writer.

Cables consists of eighty-eight stanzas ranging in length from a line or two to some stanzas that run for a couple of pages (one of the longest is in French) with a prologue and an epilogue. The subtitle of the work speaks of "familiar liturgies of misunderstanding" — a description filled with ironic wryness. The poem is liturgical only in the sense that it is a public act in which the poet attempts to say some critically important things in an unfamiliar and destabilizing fashion. The poem is dedicated to his close friend, the poet Robert Lax, which in itself is a clue; the poem, in places, uses the punning familiarity and the arcane references the two friends habitually used when writing to one another. The posthumous publication of their correspondence under the title of *A Catch of Anti-Letters* reveals a constant stream of Joycean wordplay, neologisms, and stream of consciousness writing. Lax, further, was sometimes referred to as "Ace" in their exchange of letters. Hence, the poem may well mean something like: messages to Bob Lax. The use of the word "cables" in the title might also hint at urgency; typically the two friends corresponded with each other by mail while Lax lived as an expatriate on the Greek island of Patmos. "Cables" also alluded to the passage of electric charges or telegraphic messages (Eliot uses the image in *Four Quartets*) that reinforce the notion of urgency. In other words, as with many of Merton's book titles, there was a complex meaning system to be detected in the title if one were only patient and alert enough to detect it. In passing, it should be said that Merton settled on the final title after suggesting and rejecting other possibilities in his correspondence with Jay Laughlin. For a while he considered "The Ace of Freedoms" and even (inspired by a photograph he had taken of a tree root with a little hole in it) "Freedom's Little Eye."

Even casual readers of *Cables to the Ace* will catch the echoes of T. S. Eliot, Ezra Pound, and the lesser masters of literary modernism in this somewhat opaque work. Apart from an attempt to use the machinery of anti-poetry (Merton had a near fatal weakness for this kind of writing; he was a great reader of Charles Bukowsky) and literary pastiche to describe the condition of modernity, one is also struck by the cunning manner, towards the end of the poem, in stanza #80, where Christ appears in an almost wraithlike fashion to provide a counterpoint to the mosaic (a word Merton used to describe these poems) of modernity: "Slowly, slowly / Comes Christ through the garden. . . . Slowly, slowly / Comes Christ through the ruins. . . . Slowly, slowly / Christ rises on the cornfields."

The next seven stanzas are a heavily christianized verbal collage with allusions to *Four Quartets*, Meister Eckhart, John Ruusbroec, and Merton's own spiritual perceptions from his vantage point as a hermit. In a parenthesis at the very end of the poem Merton writes, in French, "to be continued." That promise underscores Merton's desire to do a lot more of this kind of experimental writing — and he would do so in *The Geography of Lograire*, which he saw also as a work in progress. In fact, there is some evidence that Merton, upon discovering this kind of writing, decided to make it a long-term vehicle for a certain kind of poetic communication.

Unlike many friendly Merton critics, I would say that apart from a few lovely patches, *Cables to the Ace* is an imperfect and somewhat self-indulgent piece of work. It has swaths of prosiness, too much inside jokiness, and irritating moments of pseudo-hip and sarcasm. While it is an interesting experiment in a new kind of writing (for Merton) it seems to be a kind of derivative exercise attempting to reach the kind of poetic vision found, say, in Hart Crane's *The Bridge*, Ezra Pound's *Pisan Cantos*, or William Carlos Williams's *Paterson*; but Merton lacked the time and discipline to see the work through to such a level of maturation. Like many of Merton's works it was a composition done in great haste. Merton never did assimilate the friendly advice, given to him when he was a young monk by both Evelyn Waugh and T. S. Eliot, that he write slowly and with great care and publish less.

Whether one can construct such a complex poetic work in such an abbreviated period is open to question. What seems to have motivated Merton was a desire to utilize a new kind of writing mode to express the many urgencies he sensed as he looked at the world from what he once described in a letter to Lax as his "hermit hatch." If the poem lacks full coherence, it certainly did not lack industry or urgency. The poem also allowed Merton to give full play to his penchant for "play" in literary composition. His notebooks, going all the way back to those written before he became a monk, were studded with poetic fragments, nonsense dialogues, verbal pastiches, lists of odd words, fragments culled from his omnivorous reading, and so on. Merton now began to use these exercises, once kept solely for himself in his journals, in a more fully realized fashion.

Merton himself was so taken with this kind of poetic mosaic that he wrote another long work, also published in 1968, under the title *The Geography of Lograire*. In June of that year Merton composed an "Author's Note" to the work in which he made a number of clarifications. First, he claimed that this work was simply the "first draft of a longer work in progress" which he described as a "beginning of patterns." He further confessed that this "wide angle mosaic of poems and dreams" was composed of his own experiences mixed with his readings of anthropological research done on the famous Oceanic "cargo cults," the clash between native and Hispanic cultures in Central and Latin America, and the Native American "Ghost Dance" in late nineteenth-century America. Finally, the nightmarish patches of the poem set in the United States come from those common areas to which "we are all vulnerable (advertising, news, etc.)." Finally, in the end of this introduction, Merton averred that these poems (note the plural) are "never explicitly theological or even metaphysical." He described the tactic in writing "on the whole that of an urbane structuralism," alluding perhaps to his then current reading in the works of Claude Lévi-Strauss, Roland Barthes, and Gaston Bachelard. "Draft" and "Pattern" and "Mosaic" are important clues (not unlike his description of his calligraphies as "gestures") for those who wish to approach the poem with any sense of understanding but, let it be said, that such understanding will never come from any attempt to read the whole work as a linear statement.

The Geography of Lograire, in typescript, was 160 pages long. Like Eliot's *The Wasteland* it has some pages of source notes that Merton had only partially finished before his death. In the published version, Jay Laughlin of New Directions confesses to an inability to track down all the sources Merton employed in constructing the poem. The work itself is divided into four long sections organized under the titles of the compass points: North, South, East, and West.

It is not difficult to understand why Merton would have been attracted to the cargo cults of Oceania or the North American Ghost Dance phenomena among the American Indians of the late nineteenth century or the lost cultures of the Incas and other Meso-American cultures. These religious manifestations, one in Melanesia and the others in Central America or the United States, as they were understood by anthropologists and religionists who wrote on the phenomena, were extreme reactions of native peoples against modernity as traditional cultures were put under threat of extinction by the forces of technology, science, and Western aggressiveness. All of these anthropological catastrophes were clearly reactions inspired by a deep sense of anomie experienced by native peoples in the face of modern assaults they could not comprehend. In that sense, at least as far as Merton was concerned, there was a correlation between the triumph of what Jacques Ellul called *techne* over the humanizing instincts of people in contemporary society with what happened, *in extremis*, to nonmodern peoples. In a 1967 letter to Rosemary Ruether he described his readings in anthropology as an attempt to get a grip on the clash of developed cultures with more "primitive" ones and the trauma such clashes produced. He saw movements like the cargo cults and the Ghost Dance phenomena as eschatological manifestations.

The critic of Merton's poetry, George Kilcourse, shrewdly notes that if *Cables* was a poem about communication ("cables") and its failures, *Geography* was a chronicle of the historically widespread ("geography") degradation of peoples and the "resilient hopes of the weak, the abused and the damaged of the earth whom we have come to call Third World People." As such, then, the poems are Merton's somewhat idiosyncratic take on some of the themes of the yet unborn critique of the liberation theologians. In that sense, at least, the poem is consistent with Merton's long-standing concerns about Latin America. These peoples are rendered specific in a precise geographical location so that the South section describes the plight of African Americans and the peoples of Central and South America, while North relates the struggles of the seventeenth-century English dissidents against Calvinist hegemony, while the East cantos speak of the cargo cults and the West of the American Ghost Dance outbreak. Undergirding all of these injustices is the recurrent image of the primordial murder of Abel by his brother Cain described in the Book of Genesis.

There is some evidence that Merton conceived of "Lograire" for the title of his second work as the name of an imaginary country based on the similarity of the real surname of the French poet Villon ("des loges"). The French *loges* meant huts used by foresters and other forest dwellers. If such is the case, Merton's title might well mean something like this: this is how the world's geography looks from the imaginary world of a forest dweller who is not a hermit but who once was the monastery's forester. That arcane wordplay (if accurate) does give a clue as to the broad intention of Merton in working on these compositions.

Whatever will be said of the poetic value of either of these works over time, one thing is very clear. Merton had discovered a manner — the poem mosaic — of synthesizing his vastly promiscuous reading towards a finality: the juxtaposition of social and personal sin and injustice against a vision of the true self and the yearning for the transcendent vocation of humans. In that sense, despite the difficulty of the genre and the novelty of his subject matter, Merton was mining an area that had been part of his vision since the late 1950s when he decided that his deep desire for the contemplative life also had to accommodate his desire for social and racial harmony, peace, and equity as well as his self-understanding as a poet. It took him the better part of a decade to discover the instrument to express this accommodation but, as already indicated, he felt he was on the right path once he had published *Raids on the Unspeakable*. His late poems were the natural descendants of those prose poems published in the late 1950s and very early 1960s even though in style and content the works were becoming more hermetic and complex.

Whatever these two long poetic works might mean, they are clear demonstrations of how Merton struggled to meld into one his sense of being a poet, a reader of the "Signs of the Times" (an obligation made more urgent by the pronouncements of the Second Vatican Council, which canonized this phrase in the pastoral constitution on the church in the modern world — *Gaudium et Spes*), and his adamantine conviction that a contemplative had an obligation to speak to his or her age. In other words, these poems represented the new genre for him. It should not surprise us that in one of his periodic judgments on his own writing, Merton judged these two poetic works as his "best" and — in his estimation — the only worthwhile work that he had done. One takes that judgment a bit gingerly; his instinct was to overpraise his more recent work at the expense of his earlier publications. Nonetheless, he knew that both works were very idiosyncratic. When he sent a manuscript of *Cables* to the censor he confessed that it was "experimental, hence, far out . . ." and that he knew it would never have gotten passed by the previous censor who had, Merton writes, "gone to his reward."

It is hard to say with any degree of certainty but it is possible that Merton had a long-range project in mind in which he would continue to produce literary works of this kind in order to express his sense of the spiritual condition of himself and the age. In the previous years he had come to a deeper sense of the power of literature to carry spiritual truth. That awareness explains his careful study of Rilke, his continuing interest in James Joyce, and a newfound interest in the novelist William Faulkner. We still possess some tapes of Merton's talks, given at the community, on the power of Faulkner's prose. As Michael Mott has noted, Faulkner also had an added attraction: he was a native of the Deep South who had powerful things to say about race relations. Faulkner's fiction, like that of Joyce, freely experimented with the description of events in differing patterns of time, had an intense concentrated power in its dense description, and was redolent of passion and humanism. He was a natural for the interests of Merton, especially because Faulkner was a favorite of Albert Camus in particular and the French existentialists generally.

It may well be that these experiments by Merton emerged out of his perception that much of traditional religious language had become debased by overuse and by ideological shadings. He possessed a keen eye for religious cant as it appeared in popular culture and in the more official halls of the church, whether it came from monasteries or Vatican pronunciamentos. His experiments, in short, may have been just that: an attempt to construct a new way of speaking about matters of religious and cultural urgency.

One "spin off" from his labors on *Cables* and *Geography* was a series of short essay reviews on Native American topics, published separately in various places but collected together only after his death in a short work titled *Ishi Means Man* (1976). "Ishi" was the name of the last member of a California tribe who died in 1911. The Berkeley anthropologist who cared for this lone survivor and recorded his native language noted that his name "Ishi" meant in his tongue, simply, "man." Merton felt the poignancy of that fact as this lone survivor of Western depredation died, bringing total extinction to his people. Could he not also be touched by the fact that *ish* is one of the Hebrew words for "man" used in the accounts of creation in the Book of Genesis? Who knows? One thing is clear, however: these essays on the Native Americans (Merton saw them as bearers of wisdom, as he made clear in the introduction to *The Wisdom of the Desert*) gave him the platform to say once again that there is an irreducible human dignity in each person which is always threatened by the incursion of large forces deriving from modern culture.

Two of the essays in *Ishi Means Man* deal with Native Americans in North America; the other two study specific events in Meso-America. Underlying all of these studies is a combination of sadness and rage at the destruction of native cultures and Merton's conviction that this destruction derived from an aggressive modern culture of exploitation. He makes the point that the attempt to turn the Shoshonean people into "modern" people by reservation education, erasure of native language and culture, and so on created a false identity for the Native American — a mask imposed by others which was illusory and destructive. These Native Americans were forced to become inauthentic persons, and were psychologically destroyed in the process. These ideas, gleaned from his reading, mainly of anthropologists, fit very nicely into his own central concerns about living authentically and openly by understanding the nature of the true self.

The essays in *Ishi Means Man* should be seen in tandem with *The Geography of Lograire* in that both works focus on the destruction of cultures by the untrammeled power of technology. That Merton used the examples of native peoples in North America, the destruction of cultures in Central and South America, and the peoples of Melanesia (the latter he learned of from his former novice Matthew Kelty, who had lived as a missionary in New Guinea before entering the monastery in 1960) was simply another way of talking about issues that had burdened him since the 1950s.

Ever since Merton became interested in the issue of peace and the struggle against the spread of nuclear weapons, he framed his own discussion in terms of the hubris of modern technology, the "rationality" of the makers of war, and the unwillingness to face up to the consequences of technology let loose on culture without any forethought. In his writings in the late fifties Merton argued those issues in terms of the West, but now he was interested in exemplary parallels in other

164

cultures. That he focused on native peoples is also easy to understand since he felt that their primitive style of life, close to nature and poor in possessions, bore a certain resemblance to the old desert ascetics of early monasticism.

In the period 1967-1968 Merton also bent his energies to one other literary project — the editing of, by design, a short-lived "little" magazine he called *Monks Pond*. In 1967 the abbey had purchased an offset press for its own in-house needs, like reproducing liturgical texts for use as the monastery switched to a vernacular liturgy or printing business materials for the running of Gethsemani Farms, but Merton thought that the press should be used for something besides what he called "cheese ads." Aided, after he began the enterprise, by a young Jesuit scholastic, Phil Stark, Merton saw four issues of *Monks Pond* through to publication before he left for his trip to Asia. Thumbing through these now hard-to-obtain magazines (the University of Kentucky Press published a facsimile edition of all four issues in one volume in 1989) reveals a roster of figures, some famous and some less so, from the world of Thomas Merton — figures he knew either personally or through correspondence. His own plan (inspired perhaps by the then flourishing "underground press" of the counterculture, which he learned about through his correspondence with a West Coast teenager and self-described hippie who edited such a magazine at her high school!) was to charge no money for the magazine, circulate it informally, and, as he wrote to his friend, the Kentucky poet Wendell Berry, let it flash out in the air after four issues or at most five if he were inordinately rich.

The table of contents in the first issue gives a sense of the whole. It includes photographs and calligraphies by Merton as well as a portion of *The Geography of Lograire* from the "North" section. There is an artistic manifesto by his friend, the abstract painter and former Columbia classmate Ad Reinhardt, who had died in the late summer of 1967. Merton's Asian interests are represented by a translation of some of the dialogues of the eighth-century Zen master Shen-Hui and an essay by the Chinese scholar John Wu, who had been a frequent collaborator of Merton. Merton's friend, the American expatriate Margaret Randall, who edited the bilingual literary magazine *El Corno Emplumado* in Mexico City, contributed a poem as did a number of other of Merton's friends.

Subsequent issues included, among others, a range of fine poets like Hayden Carruth, Mark Van Doren, Czeslaw Milosz, and Wendell Berry, as well as Latin American writers like Margaret Randall and Nicanor Parra. There were prose pieces like an anthology of Yoruba (African) proverbs, paraphrases of early humorous Zen dialogues, and drawings and photographs by Thomas Merton (now seriously engaged in the work of photography because of the encouragement of John Howard Griffin) and other photographs by the Kentuckian Eugene Meatyard, an optician in Lexington, Kentucky, who in time would be recognized as a self-taught master of photography. Meatyard himself visited Merton at Gethsemani and made some powerful and a few playful photographs of the monk.

At the head of the fourth issue, Merton explains, as a farewell to the magazine, that being editor was hell — with its incidents of lost correspondence, typographical errors, rejection of some good material, etc. — but the experience had also been a "good one." He noted that the first issue was out of print but that some of the remaining issues were still available, like the final one, "upon request." Like an artistic "happening," *Monks Pond* came to light, ran its life span, and then died. It is now remembered mostly as a much-sought-after but difficult-to-locate collector's item.

It is hard to understand why Merton decided to edit his little magazine in the midst of so many other time-consuming enterprises. Part of the explanation might be found in his fondness for small networks of readers, correspondents, and exchanges that had a more or less subversive hue about them. *Monks Pond* was, in a way, simply a variation of the "Cold War Letters" but with a different audience in mind. In that sense, *Monks Pond* was in continuity with Merton's epistolary conversations with various clusters of like-minded friends, his love for small visits of persons who were deeply interested in the spiritual life, his ecumenical gatherings in the early sixties, and his trust that beneath the differences of opinions, philosophies, and religious belief, there was something truly "monastic" about true seekers after truth and justice. *Monks Pond* was simply another vehicle for advancing that "good" project, and it did so on a scale that seemed appropriate for what Merton wanted to do with his energies. *Monks Pond* was, in short, a continuation by yet another means, of that wide but loose network of friends and fellow seekers whom Merton had cultivated all of his adult life. Finally, the journal allowed Merton to put the offset press at the abbey to a "good use" instead of allowing it to be only another element in the monastery's "business."

In the midst of these literary activities (done, it must be remembered, in the midst of his regular monastic observance) rather important changes were taking place in the monastery itself, changes that would directly impact Merton's future. The retirement of Abbot James Fox was certainly the most important of these changes; it would mean a new monastic administration with the inevitable changes that would bring and, more importantly for Merton, the possibility of a loosening of the reins that tied him so closely to the grounds of the abbey.

After some anxiously worrying pages in his private journal in which Merton fretted about who the new abbot might be, after some tentative counting of potential votes, and some modest monastic politicking for his own candidate (he resolutely resisted any idea of his election; in fact, many years earlier, in 1952, he had signed a document affirming a private vow before Abbot James never to aspire to or assume the abbatial office), he noted in his entry for January 15, 1968, with enormous satisfaction, that Flavian Burns, then living as a hermit on the monastery grounds, had been elected abbot to replace Dom James Fox, who would leave the community to take up the eremitical life nearby.

Father Flavian had been a student under Merton's tutelage and was then living on Gethsemani's grounds in a recently built hermitage. In due course, Abbot Flavian's election was ratified by the appropriate superiors in Rome. Merton's pleasure at the election of the new abbot derived, at least in part, from his conviction that the new superior would steer the community through the difficult period of renewal in the wake of the Council. Flavian Burns was not a member of the more traditional old guard in the monastery, and further, he would be more sympathetic to Merton's desire to travel on occasion. In addition, he did not see himself as an abbot for life. He accepted the post because it was his duty; he would accept similar posts both in Virginia and Missouri, but always with the intention of going back into a life of solitude. Dom Flavian's instincts were for solitude and not for a life of administration. Currently, he serves as a chaplain to a small monastery of Cistercian nuns in Virginia, having transferred his stability to the monastery in Berrysville, Virginia, where he served for a time as abbot.

Merton's continuing preoccupation with authentic monasticism had not diminished in this period. One sign of that continuing concern was two retreats he gave in 1967 and 1968 to some contemplative sisters who had come together at Gethsemani from a number of different communities to reflect on their lives as cloistered nuns or to seek, within their "active" orders, some space for contemplative communities within their congregations. Many of the women who came to this retreat had been in correspondence with Merton on matters concerning the renewal of religious life. Although these retreats marked a first for Merton they were a natural outgrowth of his huge correspondence with a variety of women religious who sought his counsel on religious issues. There is a whole roster of religious women who were long-time friends, such as Sister Therese Lentfoehr (who did not attend the retreat but did visit Merton once), who had written to him for decades and was a keeper of many of his manuscripts. Merton frequently spoke with Mother Angela Collins at the Carmel in Louisville on his visits to the city and was a regular correspondent with a Carmelite nun in Cleveland who was a sister of one of his closest monastic friends.

Merton did not write out his conference notes for this retreat, but a subsequent transcription of the taped conferences has been edited and published under the title *The Springs of Contemplation*. Many pages in that book consist of answers to specific questions the sisters asked Merton in the course of their time together. The questions reflect the time (the impact of the Youth Revolution and its then fashionable jargon can be found on practically every page) but the theme Merton underlined and insisted upon was the need to emphasize essentials. "Renewal," he said, "consists, above all, in recovering the truth. Everything else is accidental. Once we get on to this, everything else takes care of itself."

This "truth" of which Merton spoke consisted in grasping that God is closer to us, in the words of Augustine's *Confessions*, than we are to ourselves, and understanding this is to realize that God unifies everyone through the divine presence within us. When that is understood and lived then it becomes possible for the contemplative to aid others in seeing the same thing. Undergirding these conferences is Merton's conviction that the "apostolic" task of the contemplative is not to preach or work in inner cities, even though contemplatives may well be preachers or workers for social justice, but to be as authentic a contemplative as possible in one's place in life in order to share those gifts with other people. The second "truth," which follows upon the first, is the necessity to get beyond observance for the sake of observance to a bedrock understanding of what it means to be chaste, obedient, silent, and so on. If these observances are done merely from habit or for the good order of the monastery or convent they then become instruments of oppression rather than opportunities to live the life of freedom in God's grace. Superiors ought to have enough common sense, in the words of Saint Benedict in the Rule, to challenge the adept but not in such a way that the beginner gets crushed. The basic themes of the retreat were, first, that contemplatives need to be faithful to their vocation and, second, that the rules and order of the community ought to serve the life and not thwart it in the name of "edification" or "obedience" or "tradition."

The Springs of Contemplation must be read as very much a period piece, with its discussions alluding to the heyday of the Beatles, science fiction, and the other cultural detritus of the period while also understanding that under the ephemera alluded to in the transcriptions there were crucially important insights into the life that Merton and his audience of religious sisters enjoyed in common. As Merton noted in his journal in May (1968), there was much that was antiquated and even harmful in some religious observances, and if the natural tendency to resist change by a rigid adherence to custom was to win out, the inevitable outcome would be extinction of those communities. The task, as he understood it, was to encourage change and adaptation not for the sake of change but in order to get to the authentic insights the contemplative orders possessed.

The Springs of Contemplation must further be read against the background of the rapid and radical changes occurring in religious life in the American church in the wake of the Second Vatican Council. Religious sisters were in a tumultuous period, debating everything from the viability of religious habits to more basic questions about the purpose and ends of the active religious orders. There were open struggles of nuns and bishops over the question of appropriate changes in religious life. In the early part of the century, religious orders were a way of career mobility. Religious women could get advanced degrees, administer colleges, run hospitals, and so on. In the postwar period, however, women fought for and gained new opportunities. This new range of opportunities lessened the appeal of the religious orders. In fact, soon after the Council there was a vast exodus of religious women who left the cloister for other ways of life. The matter of meaning in religious life was even more acute for contemplatives, as the period was characterized by a cry for relevance and social activism. It is against this background that Merton's insistence that contemplatives understand fundamentally what the enclosed life is, became all the more powerful.

The message Merton conveyed to the sisters who came together for the Gethsemani retreat was the same message that appeared in the essays posthumously published under the title *Contemplation in a World of Action*, referred to earlier. One essay written in this period derived from a personal request of Pope Paul VI and deserves some special mention. The pope wanted to publish a message "for the world" from the contemplatives of the church, a set of reflections on the place of the contemplative in the life of the church in light of the recent world synod of bishops that had met to think about the work of the Council. Pope Paul wanted various "messages" sent out as part of the church's openness to the world.

Merton was somewhat dubious about this enterprise, arguing in a letter to an Italian Trappist confrere that contemplatives had little to say to (or about) the modern world since they were not even clear about their own vocation. Nonetheless, in deference to the papal wishes (Pope Paul VI had been both appreciative about and supportive of Merton's work) he worked on the "Message of Contemplatives" in late 1967 while resolutely resisting any approach that would advertise their own virtues by talking about long hours of prayer or the strictness of their lives. He did not want his letter to be any puff piece touting the monastic life or an advertisement that bragged about how tough and austere monastic life was. Merton always resisted (at least after the first flush of his early writings) any tendency to romanticize the monastic life.

The final draft of the "Message of Contemplatives" was the joint work of Merton, the French Cistercian André Louf, and the Carthusian, Jean-Baptiste Porion. All three had known each other through correspondence and exchanges of their published work. Indeed, Merton had corresponded with Dom Porion since the late 1940s. Louf was an outstanding Cistercian scholar and monastic theologian. The basic focus of the article was to argue their conviction that it was possible to enter into dialogue with God at an experiential level despite the obstacles put up by modern culture (recalling that this was the period of the secularization debate, the heyday of French existentialism, and the tail end of the "Death of God" theology fad). The contemplative authors asserted that like others they were explorers of that conviction. The tenor of this statement is better grasped when it is known that the same message, in an emended version, was also published as "The Contemplative and the Atheist," a title that sums up its essential concern: it was written with the unbeliever in mind.

The focus of Merton's efforts in his part of the "Message of Contemplatives" was simply a variation of his own persistent effort to link the contemplative life to a wider dialogue. Hence, the standard Merton bibliography records in this same period short essays under these rather typical titles: "Contemplation and Dialogue" (1965); "Contemplation and Ecumenism" (1965); "Contemplation and the Dialogue Between Religions" (1965); "Contemplation in a World of Action" (1968); "Contemplation and the Crisis of Faith" (1967); "Dialogue and Renewal in the Contemplative Life" (1968); etc. Many of these essays were attempts to reach down to the bedrock of contemplative experience in order to make the case that such experience could be a bridge to the deepest yearnings of the modern mind. It was this level of human experience that he was most anxious to address.

After the election of the new abbot it became possible for Merton to travel, first to other monastic and religious sites, and then finally to Asia to attend a conference in Bangkok, which was planned, at least in part, as an encounter between Christian and Buddhist monks. Dom Flavian, unlike Dom James, thought it beneficial for Merton to do some travel, not so much as a "reward" for faithful service but as an enhancement of the work he was doing as a spokesperson of, and contributor to, the enrichment of the monastic life.

The invitation to go to Asia came to Merton from the noted European scholar of monasticism, Dom Jean Leclercq, himself a Benedictine monk and the premier scholar of monasticism in his day. Merton saw this invitation as an opportunity to see Asia while, en route, he could visit monasteries of his own order — including those in Indonesia, perhaps those in Japan, and the monastery on the island of Lantao near Hong Kong, which housed many monks exiled from the main-

land after the communist takeover in 1948. Such a trip would be a natural extension of the labors with which he had been engaged for
nearly two decades.

In early 1968 Merton made a number of short trips (keeping,
characteristically, notebooks of observations, thoughts, reading anno-
tations, etc.) in the United States which were, as it were, preliminary
skirmishes before his great last trip to Asia. These excursions may be
summarized briefly. In May Merton flew to California to give some
conferences to the Cistercian nuns at Our Lady of the Redwoods in
Northern California while taking the opportunity to scout out some
possible hermitage sites along the Northern California coast. The Redwoods community had been founded by Belgian Cistercian women
under the charismatic leadership of Miriam Dardenne, who was herself attracted to the intellectual life. He then flew to Albuquerque to
visit the primitive Benedictine monastery of Christ in the Desert (then
a struggling foundation with only two monks and a hermit monk but
now a flourishing monastery) north of Santa Fe. In September he returned to New Mexico for a second visit to that monastery, with side
trips to see the painter Georgia O'Keeffe at her Ghost Ranch home near
Taos and to visit an Apache settlement. From there he flew back to
Chicago and then on to Alaska where he gave a series of retreats and
lectures, looking for but not finding a suitable hermitage. Evidently,
Merton had in mind an isolated place where he could go (or others
could go) for extended periods of retreat away from the mother monastery. It is quite likely that he had in mind such Buddhist practices as
the monastic forest retreats where the monks lived in complete solitude for a part of each year during the rainy season.

This trip to Alaska was the first stage of his Asian journey; he
would then fly to California and from San Francisco to Asia. These two
relatively brief trips in the United States are described by Merton himself in journals that were posthumously published: *Woods, Shore, and
Desert* on his impressions of California and New Mexico and similarly,
Merton in Alaska. Neither journal has any substantively intellectual
value beyond the lessons they might offer those who would like to see
things through the keen eye of an observant poet monk. Like everything Merton wrote on an *ad hoc* basis, there are momentary enthusiasms, jottings from books, curious conversations overheard (an exchange, for instance, between two stewardesses working in the galley

near his seat on a plane), graffiti observed, reactions to the world of nature, whimsical advertisements spotted along the way, sober accounts of meetings and persons, etc.

The late summer (1968) personal journals are filled with notes about inoculations, passports, purchase of luggage, packing, airline tickets, and so on, as Merton readied himself for the Asian journey. While he was clear about where he was going and what his end point was (the conference in Bangkok) he was not quite as clear about what was to happen afterwards. At one point in his journal he opined that he would not be back to Gethsemani before February or March. He wanted to spend Christmas in a monastery, so his choices were limited to either Hong Kong or Indonesia. Indonesia seemed like a desirable destination. He had taken the trouble to visit their embassy in Washington on a quick trip in August, and he had spent five hours talking with the ambassador about Indonesian culture, religion, and mysticism. His somewhat fluid plans, however, give the lie to those who have said that he intended to leave the monastic life totally or even find a new monastic home. What does seem to be the case is that he thought of looking for some place isolated enough for him to spend some time in solitude without severing his basic stability at his monastery home in Kentucky.

His last days in California in the first weeks of October were a flurry of activity. He gave another conference to the nuns at the Redwoods monastery, and he visited with his friend Wilbur "Ping" Ferry, who was then a fellow at the Center for Democratic Institutions at Santa Barbara. At the Santa Barbara Center Merton gave a seminar and met some French students who were active in the revolutionary events taking place in Paris. He had a visit with his old friend and correspondent Czeslaw Milosz (then teaching at Berkeley), met the teenage correspondent who was editor of a high school underground newspaper, and, on his last night in San Francisco, enjoyed the hospitality of the Beat poet and publisher Lawrence Ferlinghetti, who arranged for him to stay at the apartment owned by the famous City Lights bookstore. On October 15th "with Christian mantras and a great sense of destiny," as he wrote in his journal, he left the United States to travel East.

After an intermediate stop and change of planes in Tokyo Merton arrived in Bangkok, where he spent two days visiting Buddhist temples and discussing with local residents the predominantly monastic

Theravada Buddhist tradition that was part and parcel of Thai culture. He had an extended conversation on Theravada Buddhism, with its emphasis on the concept of mindfulness, courtesy of an English convert monk named Kantipolo. On October 18th he arrived in Calcutta, and as with most Westerners who first visit the city, he was overwhelmed by its poverty, noise, dirt, and crowds — a "subculture of poverty and overpopulation" that made him feel, in the words of his official biographer, a monk with a vow of poverty turned into a "rich daddy from the West, the tourist with a showy camera and a suitcase heavy with books and extra clothing."

It was in Calcutta that he attended a spiritual summit meeting sponsored by the Temple of Understanding — a meeting that was to have representatives from ten different religions who would spend four days pondering the relevance of religion in the modern world. Merton, in an informal talk to this group, positioned the monks in the world as "marginal persons" who stood at the edges of modernity, people who by their choice of life were deliberately "irrelevant" to the aspirations of the world. Only those who remember the cry for "relevancy" in the postconciliar rhetoric of reforming Catholicism in the late 1960s can capture the paradoxical nature of that observation! Merton nonetheless made one extremely important observation — which says something about his own instinctive sense of tradition and monastic rootedness. He told his audience that the upheaval in the circles of Western monasticism (the point could have been extended to the church at large) ran the risk of marginalizing authentic monastic observances and matters of enduring value. He was fearful that much change and "updating" derived more from enthusiasm than from considered thoughtfulness. He admitted that he did not know the situation in the East, but he said that their time "was coming" for such upheavals. He issued a warning that they not allow themselves to enter a frenzy of ill-considered change for the sake of change. He ended his informal talk (the formal paper he wrote was not delivered orally, but its text is reproduced in the appendices of the *Asian Journal*) with the plea that genuine dialogue must end, not in communication, but in communion — in a joining of hearts even while each person remains faithful to his or her own religious search.

At the end of the conference Merton composed and offered a prayer, now justly famous, that expressed this concept of communion succinctly and beautifully, with its affirmation that "in accepting one another wholeheartedly, we accept You and we adore You and we love You with our whole being. . . ."

While readying to leave Calcutta for New Delhi Merton received word that the Dalai Lama would receive him in early November. From New Delhi Merton left by train and then drove, with an English friend and student of Buddhism, to Dharamasala, where many of the exiled Tibetans had made their homes since their expulsion by the Chinese. The Tibetan community, with its air of deep religiousness and public acts of devotion, made a deep impression on him. He took the time to discuss Tibetan religious traditions and meditative practices with various people. On November 3rd, he had his first meeting with the Dalai Lama, which turned out so well that the Tibetan spiritual leader decided they had to meet at least two more times. In their subsequent meetings they discussed, among other things, meditative practices, the issue of Marxism, the character of *sunyata* ("emptiness"), the place of the contemplative in the modern world, and the Western monastic concept of religious vows, a subject that fascinated the Dalai Lama. Merton proudly notes in his journal that the Dalai Lama called him a Catholic *geshe* which, Merton's English friend told him, was high praise — like getting an honorary doctorate.

Returning to Calcutta via New Delhi Merton then went into the hill country of Darjeeling and then, by jeep, to a tea estate where he was to spend some days in a kind of retreat. He had the opportunity to have an extended conversation with a highly regarded Tibetan monk-hermit and meditation master named Chatral Rimpoche. Merton summarized his impression of that two-hour talk in this fashion: ". . . the half spoken message of the talk was our complete understanding of each other as people who were somehow *on the edge* of great realization and knew it and were trying somehow or other to go out and get lost in it — and that it was a grace for us to meet one another" [Merton's emphasis].

Nursing a bad head cold, Merton took the opportunity while resting at the Min tea estate to reflect a bit in his journal about his trip. He was delighted that he and the Dalai Lama were able to communicate with one another and share an essentially "spiritual experience of 'Buddhism' which is also somehow in harmony with Christianity." He thought about the hints of the Jesuits in Darjeeling that there was a need for real contemplatives in Asia but thought he did not have a call to live permanently there. He loved his hermitage at the monastery but thought it too susceptible to external and internal confusions. Should he go to Alaska or the California Redwoods? He could not see any way of severing his ties with Gethsemani: "I suppose," he wrote, "I ought eventually to end my days there." It would be, in his estimation, his official residence — which meant, in monastic parlance, where he would keep his "stability." Monastic stability, after all, did not mean that one always remained in one physical place. It meant, rather, that should a monk reside in some place other than his monastery, he would still regard the place where he made his stability to be his real home. Gethsemani was clearly his home, the only one he had known for the better part of his adult life.

He spent his remaining days at the tea estate reading, jotting down impressions of the daily life of the Bhutanese and Tibetan communities, saying Mass for the various Catholic communities, visiting other Tibetan holy men, writing descriptions, taking pictures, and thinking about the looming Himalayan mountain peak of Kanchenjunga visible on the opposite horizon from the tea estate, noting that anyone who thought they saw the same mountain each day, changed as it was by clouds and fogs and lesser and greater clarity of the air, was gripped by delusion. Speaking of the mountain range, he reflected that "the landslides are ironic and silent comments on the apparent permanence, the 'eternal snows' of solid Kanchenjunga."

After returning to Calcutta and a very brief visit to Madras, Merton flew to Ceylon (present-day Sri Lanka) on November 29th. He went on to Kandy where he had a conference with a German-born Buddhist *bhikku* who maintained a hermitage in the jungle while carrying on editorial work for Buddhists in Europe. He also interviewed a young Anglican priest who had opened a Christian ashram, adapting architecture, liturgy, discipline, and diet to an Eastern model after the manner of similar experiments in India by Catholics like Bede Griffiths and Henri LeSaux. These pioneers of monastic adaptation had lived in India as Catholic ascetics and monks while adapting their lives to the disciplines of the East: wearing saffron robes, praying in Sanskrit, observing a vegetarian diet, reflecting on the nexus between the scriptures and the Vedas. Merton had followed their work with interest for years.

Undoubtedly, the high point of his Ceylonese trip was a visit to the great recumbent sculptures of the Buddha at Polonnaruwa. Merton was accompanied reluctantly by the vicar general of the Catholic diocese, who thought the whole scene indecorously pagan and left his American monk visitor to explore the statues on his own while he stayed behind reading a guidebook to the place. Merton described the scene in a justly famous passage in the *Asian Journal*. Approaching the figures barefoot through the wet grass and noting their "great smiles," the "silence of the extraordinary faces," Merton said that he "was knocked over with a rush of relief and thankfulness of the *obvious* clarity of the figures . . ." [Merton's emphasis]. Merton then concludes:

> I was suddenly, almost forcibly, jerked clean out of the habitual, half tied vision of things, and an inner clearness, clarity, as if exploding from the rocks themselves, became evident and obvious . . . everything is emptiness and everything is compassion. I don't know when in my life I have ever had such a sense of beauty and spiritual validity running together in one aesthetic illumination. Surely, with Mahabilipuram and Polonnaruwa my Asian pilgrimage has become clear and purified itself.

This passage has been the subject of much comment. Did Merton imply that he experienced Buddhist *satori?* Was this a mystical experience? Did it say something about his "conversion" to a kind of Buddhist/Christian form of enlightenment as has been not infrequently alleged? How seriously and strictly are we to take these words, given Merton's not rare bouts of verbal enthusiasm?

It has always struck the careful reader that the key word in the above passage is "aesthetic." Merton was fully conversant with the language of religious experience in general and the language of mysticism in particular. He knew that generations of Catholic theologians distinguished aesthetic experiences — which may have overtones of the mystical about them — from authentically mystical ones, which come as an unearned grace from God. In fact, more recent theologians, sensitive to a too great fissure between nature and grace, might well be disinclined to distinguish too radically authentic from aesthetic mystical experience. What the Polonnaruwa passage seems to indicate is something like this: in the aesthetic experience of standing before the great recumbent Buddha figures I got a deep insight into what I have sought to understand and experience in my pilgrimage to the East: emptiness and compassion, that is, the contemplative capacity to transcend the world of sense but without losing a sense of being responsible for that world. What argues for that reading are his final words in this section of the journal: "This is Asia in its purity, not covered over with garbage, Asian or European or American, and it is clear, pure, complete." The experience, then, was one that can best be described as overwhelming, integrative, deep, and ineffable. It was a heightened moment of profound and fundamental insight. In that sense, at least, it was a kind of mystical moment of clarity.

Merton flew on to Singapore ("the city of transistors, tape recorders, cameras, perfumes, silk shirts, fine liquors . . .") on December 5th and left the city the next day for Bangkok again, where he spent two days sightseeing, taking care of correspondence, and planning further flights, etc. He was much impressed by the seeming nonchalance with which the citizens of Bangkok blended their daily activities with gestures and rituals of piety.

On December 8th he left Bangkok to go to the Red Cross Center outside the city, where the meeting of the Asian monastic superiors was to take place. On the morning of December 10th Merton delivered his paper on monasticism and Marxist perspectives. On that occasion he was, for the first and only time in his life, videotaped by a Dutch television crew. The basic thrust of that paper was to argue that there were certain monastic values in Marxism rightly understood, but those perspectives did not mean that there was a fundamental compatibility between a materialist culture and that of the transcendental search. When he finished his remarks, he noted that the questions and responses to that paper would take place, according to plan, in the afternoon. The meeting broke up for lunch and rest.

Evidently, Merton took a shower around 1:30 in the afternoon and, in an attempt to move a large fan, was electrocuted with 220 volts of direct current. That he was barefooted and the floor was damp added to the shock. When he was discovered, a fully shod monk received a slight jolt while attempting to remove the fan from Merton's body. He was declared dead by one of the Korean nuns present who was also a medical doctor. Despite persistent rumors that he had been assassinated by the CIA or by others who were unsympathetic to his prominence as a spokesperson for peace, the facts seem more straight-forward: he died either from electrocution directly or from a heart attack precipitated by the shock he received or he had a heart attack and fell over the fan. Those who first entered his room wrote of a smell of burning flesh and, further, that one of them received a shock while trying to remove the fan from Merton's body. Due to governmental red tape, his body was never autopsied; but the above scenario seems the most plausible one as the events were reconstructed by those who were there, including the nun who was also a medical doctor.

His death, on December 10th, was the twenty-seventh anniversary of his coming to the guest house of the monastery. He was just over a month shy of his fifty-fourth birthday. On that same day the newspapers also recorded the death of the great Swiss theologian, Karl Barth. Only a month before, President Johnson had called a halt to bombings in North Vietnam. While Merton had been in retreat in the Himalayas, Richard M. Nixon had been elected the 37th President of the United States of America.

Due to international complications, it took nearly a week for Merton's body to be returned to the United States. Abbot Flavian wanted an autopsy performed in Thailand but discovered that under Thai law the body would then have to be buried there. Local authorities allowed the body to come back to the United States undisturbed because it was argued that this was required for religious reasons, but the release of the body under those conditions precluded an autopsy in Thailand. Ironically, his body was flown back to this country on a U.S. military plane that also bore the remains of some American soldiers who had died in Vietnam. On December 17th the casket arrived at Gethsemani, where the funeral liturgy was celebrated that same day. Because of complications with paper work, the actual funeral was almost delayed to such a degree that Dom Flavian once remarked that Merton was almost late for his own funeral.

Merton, known as Father Louis in the monastery, was buried on the flank of the abbey church; his grave was marked with the same white cross as all the other monks. Abbot James Fox, who died some years later, is buried beside him where, as some of the monks jest, they can argue with each other for all eternity. By a curious coincidence, Merton died on the retired abbot's birthday. At the funeral Abbot Flavian, in the traditionally short homily given at a Trappist funeral, spoke of how Father Louis made the monastic life flourish; he spoke too of his assurance that Father Louis would continue to aid the monastic life by his writings and his example even though death had taken him.

On the day after his death the Trappist delegation at the conference, made up of monks from Australia, New Zealand, Hong Kong, Japan, India, and Indonesia, wrote a letter to Gethsemani's abbot, Dom Flavian Burns, outlining the events leading up to Merton's death. In that letter they also said this:

> He was known to us through his writings and by his reputation, but now that we have had the privilege to meet and live with him we know how truly great a monk he was. He endeared himself to everyone by his simplicity, his openness to all, his eagerness to give of all that he had, and above all by the fact that he was a true monk.

It was that affirmation of him as a "great monk" and a "true monk" that seems to have gotten to the heart of things. One of the monks at Merton's abbey once told this author an anecdote that underscored the point so elegantly made by the Trappist delegation writing from Bangkok. Gethsemani had another well-known monk writer who was Merton's contemporary. Father Raymond Flanagan was, at one time, a well-regarded spiritual writer and religious biographer. A former Jesuit, Father Raymond was a polar opposite in personality and intellect from Merton. He was a fierce traditionalist, a political conservative and admirer of Senator Joseph McCarthy, a lover of the old Trappist penitential discipline, an outspoken critic of most of Merton's views, and a person of adamantine opinions. When my monk friend saw Father Raymond in the cloister and told him that Father Louis had died in Thailand, Merton's old antagonist looked at the bearer of the news, and with eyes welling up, said simply "Father Louis was a damned good monk" and spun on his heels to walk away.

Merton's final talk in Bangkok was, as was his custom, not read but given somewhat extemporaneously from notes that he prepared. It was not a fully coherent work, with its snippets culled from his reading of Erich Fromm and Herbert Marcuse bolstering some less than compellingly analyzed parallels between Marxist and monastic thought. The latter part of the talk reported on Merton's impressions of his meetings with Hindu and Buddhist contemplatives and what could be learned from such contacts. At the conclusion of that talk he argued that openness to these traditions provided a wonderful opportunity to learn more about the potentiality of our own traditions. Those final reflections were among the most crucial points he made, even though this may not have been fully appreciated at the time.

This latter point only repeated what Merton had said for decades, namely, that authentic monasticism — indeed, authentic Christianity in general — had to be a learner as well as a teacher; this was simply an extension of the old theological tag of the *ecclesia docens et discens* — the teaching and learning church. While that seems to be a truism it was a somewhat novel idea for a church that was only then, in the wake of the Second Vatican Council, shedding its somewhat triumphalistic pretensions. It was for that reason that in his notes for his Calcutta speech Merton would affirm that he had come to Asia not as a "research scholar" or even as an "author," but as a "pilgrim who is anxious to obtain not just information, not just 'facts' about other monastic traditions, but to drink from ancient sources of monastic vision and experience."

In those same notes he made some glancing remarks about how such dialogues must take place — remarks that could easily be expanded into a program for ecumenical and interreligious dialogue. The first ingredient would be to utilize the "Asian" conditions of not hurrying and of patient waiting as a counterbalance to the Western passion for immediate visible results. There was the further necessity of finding mature persons who could remain perfectly faithful to their own religious traditions while learning in depth about the discipline and experience of other traditions. What Merton said in outline has been spelled out in some detail by theologian John Dunne, with his concept of "crossing over" to other traditions, experiences, disciplines, and then "coming home" to one's own tradition doubly enriched.

In 1959 the artist, architect, and liturgical designer Robert Rambusch sent Merton a set of the *Philokalia* — an anthology of ascetical writings which are considered classics of the Orthodox monastic tradition. Merton, whose knowledge of Greek was imperfect, plugged

181

away at those writings. Among his possessions returned to the monastery after his death, inserted in his breviary, was a card with a passage written out in Greek which Merton had copied from the *Philokalia*. The brief passage that caught Merton's eye, from the writings of one of the early ascetics, John Carpathios, could stand as a capsule statement for all that Merton ever strove for in his life:

> If we wish to please the true God and to be friends with the most blessed of friendships, let us present our spirit naked to God. Let us not draw into anything of this present world — no art, no thought, no reasoning, no self-justification — even though we should possess all the wisdom of the world.

7 Summing Up a Life

I seek to speak to you, in some way, to your own self. Who can tell what this means? I myself do not know.

Thomas Merton

IN AN EARLY POEM ENTITLED "THE QUICKENING OF ST. John the Baptist" (published in *The Tears of the Blind Lion* [1949]) Merton described the unborn John in his mother Elizabeth's womb leaping for joy when Mary, pregnant with the Christ Child, comes to visit. John the Baptist becomes a symbol of the contemplative monk: "Sing in your cell, small anchorite / How did you see her in the eyeless dark? / What secret syllable / Woke your young faith to the mad truth? . . ." The poetic conceit was an apt one, for what is the monk but one who waits in hope for the coming of the illuminating Word which is Christ? Was it not also how Merton saw his own vocation? The monk, as he describes him, was an expectant watcher who made himself hospitable for the experience of God's dwelling in his true self. His life was to be a hidden one like Jonah in the belly of the sea monster, praying in an enclosure far from the world of human activity.

183

Thomas Merton has been dead for well over three decades. In the period since his death there has been a steady trickle of his own works being posthumously published, as his occasional essays and his letters have turned up. The twenty-five-year restriction on his private journals, stipulated by him in his literary will, has now passed, and all of the notebooks and journals are in print. Writings about him in a spectrum of languages pour out at a steady rate. Membership in the International Thomas Merton Society continues to increase, with meetings held both in the United States and Canada as well as abroad. In 1996 the first Russian chapter of the Thomas Merton Society met in Moscow. At such meetings both here and abroad hundreds will come, including academics, contemplatives, artists, seekers, and some who are simply "fans" of his writing. His writings are now being translated into the languages of Eastern Europe, with regular volumes coming out both in Polish and Russian. A Dutch chapter of the Merton Society has encouraged more of his writings to be translated into the Dutch language. It is difficult to keep up with the monographs, theses, doctoral dissertations, scholarly essays, and popular articles written about him and his work. Courses on Thomas Merton and his writings are a staple in the curricula of many colleges and universities. A whole network of collectors of Mertoniana has driven up the price of occasional publications (like those limited editions and broadsheets printed by his friend, Victor Hammer) or autographed works or his art work to rather breathtaking levels.

A comprehensive bibliography of writings by and about Merton published in 1986 is over seven hundred pages long. That bibliography listed over twelve hundred entries alone for his essays and reviews. What size it would be today is anyone's guess, but we can fairly judge from the entries in the ongoing bibliography of *The Merton Seasonal*, published quarterly at the Thomas Merton Studies Center at Bellarmine College in Louisville, Kentucky. That center was designated by Thomas Merton himself as the official repository of his work and is now located in new quarters in the college library.

Hardly a day goes by, as the gatekeeper at the monastery of Gethsemani will testify, without someone coming to the monastery to speak to monks who knew him or simply to visit his grave. There is no sign of diminishing interest in Merton conferences, retreats, study days, and even web sites. Catholic Worker houses, shelters for the

184

homeless, centers for retreats, reading rooms at colleges, and other such places are named in his honor. Recently, it has been reported that someone is attempting to have a process of canonization started. Although he was a most saintly person, a visceral reaction tells us that the canonical process would not go far; Merton seems very unlike the pious persons who glide easily through Rome's canonical process.

One must ask what it is about Merton and his writings that has so caught the imagination of so many people of so many different backgrounds, religious allegiances, and cultural makeups. Why is it that one constantly meets or corresponds with people who say that their vocation to the religious life or their religious conversion or their inspiration to devote their lives to the service of others was due to an encounter with Merton and his writings? How is it that Catholics of a certain age remember clearly the impact that *The Seven Story Mountain* had on their imagination when they were young?

The answer to that question and others like it seems all the more intractable because people fall under the influence of quite different Mertons. There are admirers of Merton the social activist, Merton the contemplative, Merton the poet, or Merton the teacher of religious dialogue across denominations, creeds, and world traditions; or of Merton the "outsider," who refuses being catalogued by a single rubric. Single books, theses, and monographs have been written on each of those Mertons. Allen Ginsberg's now published diaries are full of references to Merton's books, which the Beat poet read for his own reasons, while memoirs of Catholics from the 1950s and 1960s invoke Merton's name as being almost talismanic for quite different motivations.

Histories of American Catholicism tend to place him either among the famous "converts" of the first half of the century or as a "social" activist. Little has been written in the standard histories to plumb the depth of his readership in the United States or to reflect on how little direct contact he had with American culture. For a few years in New York before his entrance into the monastery he experienced America outside the cloister (this was enough to give him a lifelong love for jazz, a respect for Black culture, and for some American writers), but for most of his adult life he knew America only through the lens of cloistered life. He was always a person of the Left because of his instinctive pacifism, his hatred of large-scale capitalism, his distrust of government, his deep suspicion of technological progress, and his am-

185

bivalence about naive American patriotism. About much of what went on in the American Catholic Church he had a jaundiced eye, especially anything that smacked of self-congratulations or emphasis on the material success of the church in its expansive building explosion after the Second World War.

A careful study of Merton's life in relation to American Catholicism does give the lie to a persistent stereotype about the Catholic Church in the United States. According to this caricature, the American church, at least before the Second Vatican Council, was a monolithic reality with a compliant laity and an authoritarian episcopacy. In this paradigm, the pope gave orders to the bishops, the bishops handed on the orders to the priests, the local pastor said "march," and everyone else — curates, nuns, religious brothers, and lay people — began to move. A popular management study done in the late fifties reported that the organizational structure of the Catholic Church was far more efficient than that of United States Steel; orders from "the top" got implemented with greater alacrity and efficiency in the Catholic Church. Many Catholics, especially bishops, took this study to be a compliment.

The reality was that within the broad unity of the church there were many catholicisms in the American church. The educated readership of those who subscribed to *Commonweal* were not cut from the same cloth as the membership of the many urban parishes that dotted the city landscapes of the industrial belt in the Midwest. The conservative Catholics who founded and wrote for *The National Review* were not the same Catholics who were nurtured by the liturgically minded and social-justice-oriented Catholics who identified with the Benedictine monks of Collegeville, Minnesota. It did not even occur to most Catholics that there had been a vibrant Catholic community in the Southwest long before the American Revolution. The Hispanic church was an invisible church to many, as were those African American Catholics who existed in conspicuous numbers along the Gulf Coast of Mississippi and Louisiana. The American church kept under its shelter both labor priests and bishops who would break strikes undertaken by their own gravediggers.

A shorthand way of noting these strata of cultural differences in American Catholicism would be to remember that Senator Joseph McCarthy of Wisconsin and Eugene McCarthy of Minnesota were both practicing members of the Catholic Church. Thomas Merton, during his lifetime, appealed to a certain Catholic sensibility while for others he was either a puzzle or an idiosyncratic convert or, once he began to speak on issues of peace, race, and nuclear disarmament, a dangerous Leftist. For over a decade a notoriously reactionary Catholic lecturer has circulated a videotape of her lecture, in which the main argument seems to be that Merton was poisoned by his interest in Freud, and further, that in many of his positions he was simply a heretic.

My own reflections on the issue of Merton's popularity and influence go back at least twenty years or more, when I wrote my first essays, in response to the tenth anniversary of his death, on him and his work. It was the first time I did a sustained study of Merton after my youthful encounter with *The Seven Storey Mountain* and *The Sign of Jonas* — the latter given to me as a high school graduation gift. Looking back over those reflections brings me to at least two firm convictions.

First, part of the allure of Merton is that he wrote everything out of a deeply centered life of faith expressed in prayer. Indeed, he wrote more compellingly on prayer than any other writer of his generation. Whether he wrote of art or social justice or monastic history or composed poems or occasional essays on a plethora of topics, he did so out of a deep center of the experience of God — not an "idea" of God but an experience of God — and, further, such experiences shine through in his writing. When, for example, he wrote of the Shakers who had once built a community (Pleasant Hill; now a museum) near the monastery, it was Merton's intuition that the very work they did as craftspeople testified to the presence of God — both the work of their hands and the integrity of their lives. He further saw in their spare aesthetic a kinship with Cistercian simplicity. He had an intuitive sympathy for their celibacy. How could a monk living in a monastery that had to pay its own way not love the Shaker dictum of "hands to work; hearts to God"? Finally, he loved their oddly idiosyncratic view of the world and their love, like that of monks, for the coming eschatological age of which they saw themselves the forerunners.

The "shining through" that is characteristic of so much of his writing does not have the air of conventional piety or devotion, even though he was a devout and pious person who composed some devotional and pious material, but it does have the air of religious authenticity. Precisely because it does not have the typical patina of pious effusion his writing is available to those who have a connatural distaste for such effusions. It is a kind of writing that seamlessly blends intelligence with deep experience.

Writing out of a deep experience of the reality of God gave Merton a kind of instinct for the presence of grace in the world. That instinct made him less rigidly sectarian than most of his Catholic compatriots. Not only could he read Protestant and Jewish thinkers with sympathy, but he was intuitively sensitive to what non-Christians and nonbelievers had to say. Even an irreligious writer like Henry Miller gained a nod from Merton because of his powerful integrity. This is not to say that Merton grew mawkish before all religious sentiment. He had a notoriously short fuse in the face of religious sentimentality, ideological evasions, and attempts to use doctrine as a club to beat down opponents real and imagined. In that sense, as Walter Conn has argued, Merton was a spiritually integrated person, at home in his own tradition but not a prisoner of it.

In a very profound way, Merton is a "theologian" in the oldest sense of the term — not as a professional thinker in the service of ideas and not as a person of systematic theological reflection, but as someone who knows how to speak of God authentically. Merton understood discourse (logos) about God (theos). As early as the third-century writer Origen there was a distinction between the intuition of God as creator and sustainer of the world and God who one experienced in prayerful contemplation. The former experience in Greek was called *theoria* but the latter was called *theologia*.

What Merton had to say about contemplative awareness, the life of prayer, and the nexus between social justice and contemplation just rings true. "The theologian," wrote the fourth-century ascetic Evagrius of Pontus, "knows how to pray and the person who really prays is a true theologian." Interestingly enough, Merton quoted those lines in the introduction he wrote for Raissa Maritain's little book of reflections on the Lord's Prayer published in 1964. He had no hesitation at all in applying the Evagrian understanding of the word "theologian" to the writings of the mystical French poet and essayist. Merton associated himself with the understanding of the word "theologian" as it was traditionally understood before the rise of scholastic theology in the universities of the late twelfth century. He was a theologian of the cloister, not of the lecture hall.

What Merton said of the poet mystic Raissa Maritain is surely true of him also. In that sense of the term, if someone were to ask what it means to speak of God in a compellingly real way one might say: read Thomas Merton. Merton himself recognized this task of speaking through his writings of the reality of God. In a preface to a translation of one of his books he wrote that if one "listens, things will be said that are perhaps not written in this book. And this will be due not to me, but to the One who lives and speaks in both." In that fashion the words "theologian" and "spiritual master" become synonyms, which is to say, the theologian in the old monastic sense of the word is someone whose life becomes a "text" that speaks of God; and this person's writings are, as it were, an extension of the text of life.

Merton felt that if the monastic life was to have authenticity monks needed to become theologians in that fundamental sense of the term. It was the task of the monk to pray authentically and, in appropriate ways, to speak of that prayer by his life and his reflection. In a conference Merton once gave, transcribed as "Is the Contemplative Life Finished?" in *Contemplation in a World of Action*, he had some trenchant things to say about this kind of prayer. Prayer was an encounter emerging from our nothingness and our limited freedom at the call of God. Prayer is not only dialogue with God; it is a response of our freedom with God's infinite freedom. Such an encounter should not derive from our sense of abjection and alienation but out of our sense of being called by God. If we are grovelers, Merton insisted, then the Marxist or Freudian critic who calls belief alienation or neurotic projection has won the case. The true person of prayer must insist on the freedom of the true self, who responds to the fulfilling freedom and love that God offers. Otherwise we remain "fixed in our own ego" and "no longer able to go out from ourselves in freedom."

There is one God but many ways to speak of God. Merton did not speak as an academically trained systematic theologian. Indeed, one could argue that his rather perfunctory training in scholastic theology provided by one of the old fathers in the monastery was a benefit for him since it did not constrain either his style or his frame of reference. Merton never felt the need to write as an argumentative apologist nor as an explicator of divine truth rendered in a syllogistic package. The few times he ventured into formal scholastic thought were not among his happiest compositions, as he himself recognized.

189

Merton's great love for the writing of the Swiss theologian Hans Urs von Balthasar (with whom he corresponded) should not surprise. Von Balthasar was a theologian who loved the Bible, the patristic tradition, and the life of prayer; and who in addition organized his theology around the concept of "beauty." Furthermore, like the German theologian Karl Rahner, whom Merton read more fitfully, he tried to keep the life of theology and the life of prayer of a piece. The holistic conjunction of theology as systematic reflection and theology speaking from deep experience was a theme that Merton underscored from the time he wrote *Seeds of Contemplation* in 1949. If today there is a concerted effort to bring theology and spirituality into closer contact, it is an effort that Merton saw as necessary fifty years ago.

Nor was he, except for a certain period in his life, a "devotional" writer, if one understands the word "devotional" in a pejorative sense. In fact, by the middle of the fifties he deliberately chose to get away from the kind of writing (in as much as it was possible; he still had to contend with writing on the demand of his religious superiors) that he produced in the first flush of his conversion to the monastic life. His own preferred way of writing was to find a vehicle or vehicles through which he could focus his deep knowledge of monastic and mystical literature into a vocabulary, drawn from his instincts as a poet, that could strike a chord not only with his fellow believers but with those who were in any way amenable to the life of the spirit. In fact, it may well be his poetic ability to write of God without recourse to the insider's jargon, the language of traditional piety, that makes him most accessible for those who are not predisposed to use that language or find meaning in it.

A basic thesis of this study is that Merton can be understood only if he is understood as a monk who spent twenty-seven years under a monastic rule and within the rich tradition of monastic ascesis, spirituality, and prayer. Apart from those who enjoy a moment of romantic frisson at the thought of monasteries and monks in their close-cropped hair and cowled garments, one must say that Merton's gift was to convey the essential gifts and charisms of the monastic life to a larger world that found nurture in them. Even though he had a deep respect for monastic traditions, he was never beguiled into thinking that the external trappings of monasticism were constitutive of what the life should be about. As he once observed, it would be a tragic mistake to think that a deepening of the monastic life could come by simply re-legislating that life. On the other hand, as he warned his Buddhist hearers in Asia, one should be careful about tossing aside old monastic customs in a desire for "reform" before one had a good understanding of why such customs existed in the first place. There was a vast differ-ence, in Merton's mind, between a tradition and a mere antiquarian custom. He certainly did not want monasticism to exist frozen in tradi-tional amber, but neither did he desire changes to come for the sake of change alone.

At various times in his life Merton would catalog what he found attractive and essential about the monastic life. They were the charac-teristics to which all monks would subscribe: common worship, a life-long meditation on the scriptures, the value of work and community, a countercultural relationship to the world, the interior resources com-ing out of silence, recollection, prayer, study, and compassion for the world. In his provocative essay on the contemplative and the atheist in the volume *Contemplation in a World of Action* he lists silence, solitude, poverty, labor, humility, chastity, fasting, and other monastic disci-plines that "keep ourselves open and attentive to the Spirit of the Liv-ing God." Earlier in his life, he loved to repeat and meditate on words like "purity" or "solitude" or "silence." Such terms were not "ideas" for him; they were markers that underscored the deepest sense of what it meant to be authentically a person of faith. To maintain such terms one needed constantly to go back to discover their true meaning: What could monastic "voluntary poverty" mean in an age of real destitu-tion, he wondered in a letter to Rosemary Ruether.

As he grew in the monastic life these general principles and val-ues became more refined in his life, especially as he began to empha-size, in the face of the turmoil after Vatican II, what the bedrock essen-tials of the monastic life ought to be. Silence could not be reduced to Trappist sign language, or worse, an inability to communicate with others. Labor cannot be equated with mindless commercial activity. Solitude was not crankiness and much less could it be individualism or isolation.

In the notes he developed for his presentation in Calcutta (pub-lished as appendix four of *The Asian Journal*) Merton outlined three fundamental characteristics of what he felt was peculiar to that broad category of what is implied by the term "monastic." He had in mind a broad category here to include the "monastic" traditions found in the world's religions and, parenthetically, those who lived in the spirit of the monastic life. As Merton frequently noted, some people live monastic values deeply without actually living in a cloister.

We can summarize these characteristics briefly and then use those characteristics as a meditation on the ways that Merton fleshed them out. They are:

(1) A certain distance or detachment from the ordinary and secular concerns of worldly life; a monastic solitude of varying intensity and duration.
(2) A preoccupation (Merton's word) with the radical inner depth of one's religious and philosophical beliefs; the grounds of those beliefs; and their spiritual implications.
(3) A special concern with inner transformation and a deepening of consciousness of a transcendent dimension of life beyond the empirical self and of "ethical and pious observance."

The first characteristic of "distance or detachment" is another way of describing the old monastic stance of *fuga mundi* — flight from the world and *contemptus mundi* — which is best read as detachment from the things of the world. It is here that one can see the greatest evolution in Merton's life and thought. When he entered Gethsemani in 1941 his desire was to flee from the horrors he saw in the world in general and in his own life in particular. His entrance into Gethsemani was designed to give him a chance to reject everything secular, worldly, and materialistic in order to live a penitential life "for God alone." In the course of his life he saw that this view, exaggerated as it was, did not pay enough attention to the good of the created world, to his own solidarity with other people, and to his own humanity. Such an attitude, borrowing from the language of Jacques Maritain, led to the error of "angelism" — hatred for the human in the name of a higher and more gnostic perfection. In his maturity he realized that monastic separation from the world, paradoxically, was an invitation to be close to the world in a new but quite different fashion.

He developed his more mature stance both through his own struggles against a false sense of this "angelism," with its denial of bodiliness, as well as his increasing sense of what the Buddhists call "compassion." Compassion, in the Buddhist sense, meant a reaching out in love for all that exists, in order to bring about enlightenment. To translate this concept into Christian terminology is to state the love of Christ as it is understood in the New Testament. The *Bodhisattva*, enlightened though he or she might be, resisted nirvana in order to bring others to enlightenment. The Christian, analogously, would give up everything, including life, for the love of others.

Those who have been deeply influenced by Merton have seen in the evolution of his thinking a resource for their own struggles — whether as monastics or, more frequently, as believers in the world — to live their own lives in a way that would do fair justice to the cultures in which they live without being swallowed up by the false promises of purely materialistic existence. In other words, from Merton it is possible both to say NO to falsity and YES to what is good and true in life. In the broadest sense of the term, as a number of Merton's critics have pointed out, this attitude was very much in the tradition of American writing that goes back at least to Thoreau and finds expression in this century in American writers as different as J. D. Salinger and James Baldwin. It is a countercultural attitude, which Merton found appealing in the writings of the Beats and the lifestyle of the Hippies even if he found their hedonism misplaced and destructive.

Such "detachment" or "distance" permitted Merton to give value to those who, out of religious commitment, lived at the margins or the edges of society. This notion, of course, was not peculiar to Merton alone; it was a concept that in different ways was a theme in the writings of the Protestant theologian Paul Tillich and others who saw that it was at the edges of power and prestige that one could best act in a prophetic manner. And let it be clear: Merton was, in the biblical sense, a prophet. Nobody authorized him to speak truth to power (indeed, his own superiors dissuaded him) but, from his vantage point as hermit, monk, and "watcher," he felt constrained to do so. In other words, as his vision of what flight from the world meant, he felt it natural and proper to speak prophetically to and for the world. Like the monastic life in general, Merton had a strong eschatological sense that oriented him away from the particular demands of quotidian life towards something beyond and "in front of" present concerns. It was, to borrow the language of the New Testament, the "seeking for the kingdom of God."

193

The monastic theme of flight from the world (*fuga mundi*) is closely allied to the monastic emphasis on *contemptus mundi*. The "contemptus" could be understood badly (as it was even by certain strains of monasticism itself) if one took it at its literal meaning of "contempt"; but at its best it signifies the monastic willingness to undervalue success, acquisition, honor, prestige, and those other tokens of worldly accomplishment. In that sense, *contemptus mundi* is another way of saying that monastic life should be humble, hidden, poor, disinterested in wealth, and so on. This contempt for the world was, to use other vocabulary, an ascetic attitude with respect to the values of the world. Part of the motivation of the first desert monks of the fourth century, after all, was to flee the corruption of the cities and the pretensions to power afforded the church after its liberation from persecution and the subsequent corroding influence of the Roman Empire. Such a prophetic stance allowed, as long as it did not corrupt into hatred or envy, for freedom and liberation. Such a stance, further, stood as a countersign to the pretensions and evils of the world they had fled. *Contemptus mundi* is a powerful instrument in the battle against absolutizing any human value in such a fashion as to make it into an idol. Such an instrument desacralizes that which is not God.

If one stands at the edges of culture in order to speak prophetically, one had better have something to say; otherwise, as a person at the edges, one is seen only as a crank or a curmudgeon. The second characteristic of authentic monasticism is a "preoccupation with the radical inner depth of one's religious and philosophical beliefs." This preoccupation is thus intimately linked with the position of being apart from the world. The inner depth of one's religious belief means something like an answer to questions about one's belief: What does it mean to affirm belief in God? What happens in the desire to be "conformed with Christ"? How does one get from the words on the biblical page to the reality towards which those pages point? If one does not have a real sense of the self it is all too easy for other persons, movements, or ideologies to supply one. The monk is first commanded to listen (the opening word of Benedict's Rule is "Listen!") and only then to speak. Prophetic speech comes only after hearing and listening and watching, as both the biblical and monastic vocabulary insists.

These exercises in self-scrutiny are characteristically, although not exclusively, monastic questions. Monastic literature is filled with motifs or metaphors by which one is encouraged to move up ladders or ascend mountains or penetrate mansions or follow steps as one refines mere verbal and conceptual affirmations about one's relationship to God into foundational living truths. To borrow Merton's formulation of the matter: one must nourish and allow for growth those seeds God has planted in every person so that as they mature they may blossom into true contemplatives. At least part of the process of this growth is to cut through accustomed formulations and the ideological use of religious language in order to garner deep and true meanings behind them. The whole gospel message, he wrote in his little book *Contemplative Prayer*, becomes "impertinent and laughable if there is an easy answer to everything in a few external gestures and pious intentions." The final chapters of that excellent little study is a plea not to permit the supposed life of interiority from becoming an evasion from the realities of human existence.

False or superficial or sentimental religious practice is the worse kind of *fuga mundi* — since it constitutes an evasion of reality as such. Such evasions provide evidence for the Freudian charge that religious faith is a neurotic form of illusion, cushioning one from the gritty realities of life. As a long-time director of young monks and monastic aspirants in the novitiate, Merton had ample opportunity both to see religious illusions up close and to supply therapies to disabuse people of them.

A certain detachment from the world and a preoccupation with the ground of one's religious belief have a dialectical relationship. The one makes the other a possibility. From that relationship flows the third essential monastic characteristic: "inner transformation" and a deepening of consciousness towards an "eventual breakthrough and discovery of a transcendent dimension of life beyond the empirical self." Every Christian monk vows what Saint Benedict in his Rule calls a "conversion of life" (*conversatio morum*). This lifelong experience of changing one's life in conformity with the Word of God is the goal of all the other disciplines, labors, and exercises of the Rule. Conversion does not begin when a person enters a monastery; it is in the monastery that a person learns how to be a converted (and converting) person. If that primary goal is not remembered it is all too easy, as Merton repeated frequently, to turn monastic life itself into a false ideology.

It is traditional in monastic spirituality, articulated at length in

195

Cassian's classic work on monastic life, the *Conferences*, to distinguish the means from the goal of the monastic life, which is love of God. To focus only on the means was to mistake them for the goal. As the monastic historian Columba Stewart has written, in his study of the fourth-century monk Cassian, "Cassian knew that obsession with 'perfect' monastic observance can lead to despair and abandonment of the monastic life or anger (a most fatal passion for the monk) or to a judgmental stance towards others. Mistaking the means for the goal can arouse the very 'passions' the monk is meant to shun . . ." (*Cassian the Monk* [Oxford University Press, 1998], p. 44). The monastic life is meant as a conversion process by which a person leaves off a certain way of living in order to enter the life of Christ in the Spirit.

In traditional parlance, this process of conversion or transformation is, in Pauline language, the putting off of the old person and the assumption of the new. Merton often worried in print that religious people — in monasteries or not — went through the motions of religious observance not as a way of changing the self but as a way of erecting masks to evade the radical demands of the gospel. Merton saw such illusions as being part of monastic life as much as in the larger world; nor did he hesitate to use Freud's charge in *The Future of an Illusion* to describe such unreality, such illusion, as a neurosis. The opening pages of *New Seeds of Contemplation* were filled with reflections on the false and true self, on the need to reach the depths of one's being in order to see and live clearly. His conversations with monks, contemplatives, and ascetics in Asia were frequently oriented to his need to see how and what techniques and disciplines were employed to aid in the transformation of consciousness. The goal was never reducible to the disciplines or the techniques; they were only vehicles to reach the goal.

When Merton's reflections on this transformation are read carefully it is clear that he is attempting to give new depth to some very traditional categories of the Christian experience. His goal is to see such terms as "conversion," "new life in Christ," and "rebirth" in the light of the depth of human consciousness. What is the existential meaning of Paul's theme that we are to die to sin in order to live in Christ? What does it mean to live in and see the world through the eyes of a reborn, changed, transformed person? How does that person view the self, the world, and God? This is not a process of mere "self-

196

realization" (he had savage criticisms for such instances of psycho-babble and would no doubt be equally critical of the New Age spiritual banalities current today), but a fundamental attempt to live out an imperative of the gospel. In an article published in 1967 in the student-run journal at Harvard, *The Current*, Merton wrote this about his perception of his solitary life as a monk:

> The Christian solitary, in his life of prayer and silence, explores the existential depths and possibilities of his own life by entering into the mysteries of Christ's prayer and temptation in the desert, Christ's nights alone on the mountain, Christ's agony in the garden, Christ's Transfiguration and Ascension. This is a dramatic way of saying that the Christian solitary is left alone with God to fight out the question of who he really is, to get rid of the impersonation, if any, that has followed him into the woods.

My conviction is that because Merton not only believed but existentially struggled with experiencing and articulating the foundations of belief and the conversion of consciousness in a life set apart from the world, he was able to express some powerfully authentic words that could speak to others in the world who also sought some sense of the transcendent in their own lives as a source of sustenance for authentic living. That he did not always write explicitly of this transformation using the biblical language of "rebirth" or "conversion" is best explained by the fact that he simply assumed it and assimilated its structures in his very worldview.

To that lifelong search was added another facet of his life, which was a kind of freedom from fear or anxiety as he explored new and different expressions of faith (or lack of faith), culture, and experience. At a time when Catholic life in the United States in certain of its aspects was rather parochial, defensive, and shut off, he did not blanch from reading agnostics, writing to Marxists, exchanging letters with such notorious figures as Henry Miller, and sharing in dialogue with people from other religious traditions outside the pale of Christianity.

His frequent diatribes against the facile self-congratulations of "religious" people sprung from his clear-eyed conviction that what often passes for religious faith is a kind of self-congratulation. He would have completely agreed with the wonderful *mot* of the late Flannery

O'Connor that the abiding sin of American Catholics was smugness. He saw clearly that many religious "leaders" could preach, in the name of Christianity, sentiments that were, in fact, ideologies rooted deep in a false sense of culture. The passive or active acceptance of the legitimacy of atomic warfare, to cite an example, sprung not from Christian truth but from the acceptance of unexamined ideologies generated by the propaganda of the state. Closer to home, perhaps, was his disgust with those who thought that Gethsemani's success as a monastery, counted in terms of numbers or products sold through the monks' industry, was somehow a sign of spiritual blessing.

One of the most original contributions that Merton made to contemporary religious practice was his lifelong insistence that one could be faithful to one's religious tradition while being open in a spirit of dialogue to others who did not share one's faith but who were searchers and seekers after authentic transcendent experience. In this study we have noted his desire to engage in an interior form of reconciliation with Orthodox Christians by reading them sympathetically as a first step towards some form of Christian unity. Interior reconciliation was seen as a first necessary step towards a larger, more explicit and public, reconciliation. Likewise, he approached his contacts with Latin and Central American artists, poets, and critics in the same spirit: to bridge the gulf between the southern and northern hemispheres of the Americas. It has hard to think of another American Catholic of the time who ever looked seriously and openly to the southern hemisphere. Reading the Old Testament, he said, demanded that we read it Jewishly or not read it at all. Clearly, when he went to Asia he went as a pilgrim and a learner, asking what these people had to say to him and his tradition.

Merton did not see this strategy of interior dialogue as either a species of indifferentism or as a shameless form of borrowing for merely apologetic reasons. In fact, one of his most attractive characteristics was his ability to profess his Christian faith openly without sounding like a spiritual prig or a rigid apologist. Like the medieval theologians and mystics who found truth in pagan Aristotle and the Jewish thinker Maimonides and the Islamic mystics, so Merton thought, in our age, we must engage those streams of thought and practice that speak to our age without fear or defensiveness.

It is worthwhile remembering that Merton began this practice of both interior dialogue and real exchanges with thinkers of other traditions in the 1950s when such contacts were severely circumscribed in the Catholic Church. He himself felt constrained by the narrow theology he had inherited, and only through meditative openness did he begin to find more elasticity in Catholic theological categories than he previously felt possible. When writing to D. T. Suzuki the Buddhist or Erich Fromm the atheist he worried about whether he ought to be more decisive in trying to convert them, but something deep inside his psyche told him that such an approach was either useless or, at best, patronizing. Something deep within told him that this was not a good or even "Christian" thing to do. It was only after the Second Vatican Council finished its work that the process of dialogue with other Christian bodies, the Jewish tradition, those of the other major world religions, and indeed with atheists, became facilitated through the support of official religious authorities (there are Vatican offices charged with dialogue with other Christian bodies, non-Christians, and nonbelievers) and through the charter of such documents as Vatican II's *Nostra Aetate*. Indeed, the document *Nostra Aetate* explicitly acknowledged God's grace as operative outside the boundaries of Catholic Christianity. At the same time the same document encouraged exchange and dialogue.

This kind of "deep dialogue" is now a commonplace. It is a hallmark of Pope John Paul's encyclical *Ut Unum Sint* (1995) where the pope links dialogue within the context of prayer. The same pontiff insisted, in the same document, that authentic dialogue could only take place where there was an "exchange of gifts" as well as a willingness to examine one's own conscience, and be willing to be more deeply converted to the truth. Writers like the American theologian John Dunne, the Irish Jesuit William Johnston, long resident in Japan, and the French Jesuit Jacques Dupuis have given more systematic theological underpinnings to such exchanges as a result of the encouragement of the work done at the Second Vatican Council and pioneers before the Council like Thomas Merton, Henri LeSaux, and Bede Griffiths. Such dialogue, for example, has been a leitmotif of the writings of Pope John Paul II, as even a cursory reading of his ecumenical encyclical *Ut Unum Sint* so amply testifies. The pope, borrowing the language of continental personalism with which Merton was well acquainted, sees dialogue as a hallmark of humanity — a sentiment one finds abundantly in Merton's writings. Both Thomas Merton and Pope John

199

Paul II have framed their concept of dialogue in the light of the writings of people like Martin Buber and the personalist circle of Gabriel Marcel and Emmanuel Mounier.

A few years before his death in 1984, the noted Jesuit theologian Karl Rahner published an extremely influential and widely reprinted essay entitled "Towards a Fundamental Theological Interpretation of Vatican II." In a somewhat schematic fashion to be sure, Rahner said that the church went through three great paradigmatic shifts in its history. The first watershed came when Paul "won" the argument over how gentiles were to be received into the new assembly of Christian believers. Had Paul not been followed Christianity well could have ended up as a small sectarian movement in Judaism. The second shift occurred when Constantine changed the countercultural church during the period of persecution into the officially approved and supported culture of the Roman Empire. That shift produced legislation, art forms, modes of thinking, conceptual tools, models of jurisprudence, organizational patterns, and all of the other cultural forces that made the church more or less "European."

Rahner then went on to note that at Vatican II, for the first time in Catholic history, an ecumenical council was heavily constituted by representatives from the non-European world. The native bishops of Oceania, the Far East, Africa, etc. were active at the council in significant numbers (at Vatican I in 1869-1870 the representatives from that part of the world were European "missioners"). This new reality, in Rahner's view, represented the emergence of what he called the *Weltkirche* — the World Church. The implications of that shift, however, are yet to be felt. What did the Catholic faith and Catholic practice look like when it was presented in cultural, intellectual, and social forms that sprang, not from Western, but from Chinese or African or Japanese roots? It is only now that these issues are being confronted in a real fashion. It may be safely said that one of the most vexatious problems facing the Vatican is to accommodate the differences demanded by the churches in these parts of the world while maintaining Catholic unity. The issue is both a practical one (i.e., a question of where power is to reside!) and, far more crucially, a theological one. The question goes far deeper than merely using, say, oriental vestments, music, and architecture in the name of inculturation. The more profound questions are these: What does an African christology look like? How does one articulate a Trinitarian faith in a Buddhist or Muslim setting? What does an inculturated clergy look like? Are the models of ecclesial organization pertinent to areas of the world that are not Western?

One aspect of this emerging challenge derived from the continual growth of the *Weltkirche* has been the deep dialogue of common prayer, spiritual exchanges, and mutual study that in the late twentieth century has been seen as one of the more promising arenas of intercultural exchange and understanding. At the level of contemplative exchange, there is an active circle of Christian and Buddhist monks who have been in conversation for two decades, as well as many informal exchanges all over the world involving participants from the various religious traditions.

In this dialogical work, Merton must be seen as a prophet and a pioneer. In the 1960s he seemed to have grasped intuitively the urgency of being open to the larger world that faced the Christian community. That open attitude would not only aid the Christians of other parts of the world but would also increase cross-religious understanding. It is only now, with the perspective of time, that we see how profound his influence was. Only a few years ago, at the request of the Dalai Lama, a group of Buddhist monks and scholars met with their Christian counterparts at the Abbey of Gethsemani to speak about common tasks and to learn from each other about meditative practice, doctrine, and ethics. As the volume entitled *The Gethsemani Encounter,* a collection of the papers and panel discussions from that conference published in 1998, makes clear, Christians were encouraged to speak faithfully of their tradition while Buddhists were to do the same of theirs.

As a number of the participants themselves noted, this historic meeting which the Dalai Lama (who had suggested Gethsemani, once the home of Thomas Merton, as the preferred site for the meeting) himself attended, was possible only because of the pioneering example and efforts of Thomas Merton. Partially as a response to a Merton tribute offered by Abbot James Connor (himself a former monk of Gethsemani and novice of Merton, now the superior of the Trappist monastery in Ava, Missouri) the Dalai Lama, in part, responded:

> As for myself, I always consider myself as one of his Buddhist brothers. So as a close friend — or, as his brother — I always remember

him, and I always admire his activities and his life-style. Since my meeting with him, and so often when I examine myself, I really follow some of his examples. Occasionally, just as at this meeting, I really have a deep satisfaction knowing that I have made some contribution regarding his wishes. And so, for the rest of my life, the impact of meeting him will remain until my last breath. I really want to state that I make this commitment, and this will remain until my last breath. Thank you very much.

While Merton made significant contributions to interreligious dialogue, his continuing impact has been felt more keenly in the area of Christian spirituality, and more particularly, at the place where the life of prayer and the commitment to social action intersect.

First, however, he is widely regarded as a spiritual master, which is to say, someone who through the example of his life and the impact of his writings has taught the current age how to pray authentically. Since his life was shaped by the oldest sources of Christian mystical and ascetical theology, he taught that capacity for prayer and contemplative living in line with what is called, perhaps misleadingly, Christian mysticism.

By writing and living in this neglected vein he was somewhat singular in the English-speaking world of Catholicism. Although it is clear that he wrote as a monk — and there were many monks who were published and read in the first half of this century (e.g., Columba Marmion, Eugene Boylan, Herbert von Zeller, Aelred Graham, Bede Griffiths, etc.), they were, for the most part, regarded as "spiritual writers." Such monk writers certainly did not "count" as theologians since they did not produce that highly technical, scholastic-based theology whose proper audience was the seminary. Nor did many of these writers venture far from the pathways of traditional sources of Christian ascetical and mystical theology.

Some lay writers who did write on the life of prayer were also men of social and political action. Merton was in contact with the most distinguished of those, especially the Arabist Henri Massignon, the sinologist John Wu, the Japanese Buddhist D. T. Suzuki, and the French Catholic philosopher Jacques Maritain. While the latter had a certain readership in the United States, Merton was by contrast almost sui generis, in that he enjoyed an enormous following among both intellectuals and activists, a readership that endures to this day. Massignon, by contrast, is known only to a coterie of scholars in this country; and Maritain has lately become the intellectual prisoner of the restorationist wing of contemporary Catholicism.

In the final analysis, the somewhat "unclassifiability" of Merton is a clue to how he should be understood. The literary scholar Robert Inchausti, in a recent book *Thomas Merton's American Prophecy*, has provided us with an important clue when he notes that as an intellectual, Merton is best understood when he is ordered among those intellectuals who can be considered as "outsiders." The term "outsider," of course, has been canonical since Colin Wilson used it in his precocious study of such figures under that eponymous title fifty years ago. Merton's term for the outsider was the one who stood on the margins or one who was irrelevant or who stood at the edge. Inchausti lists in that group such writers as George Orwell, Albert Camus, Simone Weil, Arthur Koestler, Boris Pasternak, and Czeslaw Milosz (I would add Ignazio Silone to the list) who, in Inchausti's words, "bravely stood up at mid century for the autonomy of the interior life and 'the third position of integrity'."

What this litany of writers had in common was the adamantine conviction that a solitary person could make things different simply by saying the truth, even when the tribe or the crowd or the consensus did not speak the truth. As Merton once remarked to Henry Miller, the individual is a zero but the zero has power once it is understood and according to where it is placed. The paradigmatic expression of that stance of the outsider was Ignazio Silone's observation, uttered through the mouth of his central character in the early antifascist novel *Fontemara*, that when one person had enough courage to write "NO" to the Fascists on the wall of the main piazza of an Italian town that person was, through that gesture, a threat to any totalitarian regime.

It is not insignificant that Merton knew through correspondence or study a number of those listed above. He did a thorough analysis of Camus in the 1960s; he carried on a rather extensive correspondence with Milosz over two decades; in the latter half of the 1950s he read widely in the writings of Arthur Koestler, as his journals from that period testify. Those same journals give a rather complete picture of how fully involved he was with Boris Pasternak even before the publication of *Doctor Zhivago*. Finally, he knew (but did not fully approve of) the

203

writings of Simone Weil, noting with some small irony that the doctor who signed her death certificate in England in 1943 was the same doctor (Tom Bennett) who had been his guardian before he left Cambridge in disgrace.

The "third way of integrity" of which Inchausti speaks is, of course, the attempt to articulate an anthropology that somehow avoids the materialistic determinism of the then regnant Marxism of the intellectuals in the first half of this century, and the Enlightenment individualism characteristic of capitalism, with its dangers coming from human manipulation and its deadening consumerism. It is interesting that all of the "outsiders" had, at one time in their life, been sympathetic to and partisans for some form of Marxism. The "outsider" rubric also helps to place Merton vis-à-vis American culture: he stood outside that culture as a monk but he also stood away from its more elaborate pretensions as leader of the Cold War and its gospel of growth and economic expansion through ever increasing doses of technology.

Merton worked out these lessons not as a survivor of the "God that failed" like Koestler and Orwell nor as an activist like Simone Weil. His starting point was the silent encounter with God as he experienced it within the shelter of the monastery where he spent his adult life. While he had moments of mystical illumination, his vision of what life was like (or: how life ought to be) came through an incremental series of steps as he worked out how, as a contemplative hermit, he could express his compassion for the poor, his desire to communicate at a deep human level, to translate his experience of union with God into some kind of understandable language (even though the language always faltered), and to critique the worst of what he saw in the world he had left.

What Merton did intuit from his study of Marxists was that their main complaint about religion — that it was a symptom of an alienated existence and a palliative against the rigors of the world — had a certain plausibility if one mistook the veils of religious observance, the demands of religious law, and the routines of piety as descriptive of religion. His contrary conviction was that if a person did not come to realize him or herself as a free person with a destiny tied to a transcendently free God who creates, sustains, and liberates us, then the Marxist diagnosis is quite correct; religion did become an opiate. A

204

good deal of his spiritual writing in the final decade of his life was precisely oriented towards a critique of the Marxist description of matters in order to show what a person truly was. In that sense, his whole doctrine on the contemplative life was an ongoing description of a contemplative humanism.

If there is anything "postmodern" about Merton — and who knows what that word really conveys — it was his conviction that rational constructions of the human ego, fashionable since Descartes, were fatally flawed; that rigidly rational analyses of society and culture were conceptual prisons; and finally, that the Enlightenment project turned the human enterprise into an idol instead of a model. If there was an antidote to be had for such a situation there was little profit to be gained in building intellectual systems of argumentation against Enlightenment rationality, even if those systems had the warrant of official scholasticism behind them.

Merton's alternative strategy was to use narrative, or more precisely, personal narrative. One could argue that the vast edifice of his personal writings found in the many volumes of his journals or the books from *The Secular Journal* to *The Asian Journal* crafted from those notebooks, were quite similar to what the Germans call a *Bildungsroman* — a fiction, which is to say, a construction that traces out the education, development, and direction of character.

The Seven Storey Mountian takes its title from Dante's architecture of the mount of purgatory. The metaphor is telling since Dante had to ascend the mount of purgatory undergoing the cleansing of the seven deadly sins whose enumeration, of course, comes directly out of the ancient monastic literature described by Evagrius of Pontus and mediated to the West via Cassian's *Institutes.* It was only through that purgative ascent that Dante could enter the earthly paradise. This Edenic situation of the earthly paradise was a commonplace expression, all through the Middle Ages, for the monastic life. It has not been sufficiently recognized that Merton subtitles the final part of his autobiography "Meditatio pauperis in deserto" ("the meditation of a poor man in the desert"), which is a near perfect allusion to the subtitle of the famous medieval treatise of Saint Bonaventure (which had a profound impact on Dante) called "The Soul's Journey to God." That complex spiritual treatise, as is well known, was an ascent journey as well as an interior one. Bonaventure conceives of this passage to the Sabbath rest in God's love under metaphors of climbing and, simultaneously, of interiority. It is curious, we might note in passing, how few commentators on Merton have noticed the influence of Bonaventure, whose writings Merton read when teaching with the Franciscans in upstate New York before he entered the monastery.

The Seven Storey Mountain, then, is a journey away from the world through the process of purification of those vices that hold the person back from God as well as an interior exploration of the ground of human existence, which is the presence of God through grace. This journey is also a study of a young person's life, a variation of the Joycean portrait of the artist as a young man. In *The Sign of Jonas* Merton utilizes an ancient monastic topos of understanding Jonah in the belly of the sea monster as an allegory of the hidden life of the monk who remains outside of human view, given over to a life of prayer. *The Sign of Jonas* can be understood as the final statement of Merton on the monastic life as a life of retreat and withdrawal from the world. It is a book saturated in the atmosphere of the cloister. The next two published biographies, by sharp contrast, have in their titles allusions to engagement with the world. In *Conjectures,* the bystander is still not in the middle of things but he does see and he is "guilty" because of what he sees and how he is able to witness only by his life and through his words. He is a bystander in the sense that what he sees, he sees from the eccentric vantage point of the cloister. Whether that position is an authentic one is the central question he pursues in the last decades of his life. The posthumous *A Vow of Conversation,* as we noted, has the brilliant double meaning of the monastic vow of conversion (which in Benedict's Latin is *conversatio*) with the implied meaning that the monk must turn to the world and speak. Finally, *The Asian Journal,* posthumously reconstructed from his notebooks, is the only one of the journals (with the obvious exception of *The Secular Journal*) written largely from the perspective of the monk outside the monastery, traveling as a pilgrim-learner to distant lands to learn of their wisdom. Like all the other journals this final book is an interior journey as well as an external one, with the obvious difference that this time he travels not metaphorically up a mountain but to real places far distant from his cloistered hermitage.

The trajectory traced by those works, then, is the journey of one person who was at the edge of much of the Western experience in the first part of the twentieth century. After all, Merton's life is unthinkable except against the background of the events of the two world wars, the wasteland of the *entre deux guerres*, the intellectual turmoil deriving from that setting, and finally, the struggle to find sense and meaning from the detritus of such turmoil. Added to that was Merton's close observations of the technological realities in the Cold War period and the emerging sense of liberation and freedom experienced among African Americans and those people of color from the former colonial lands.

What makes this long personal narrative all the more impressive is that, unlike some of his commentators, Merton himself, by foreseeing the publication of his personal letters and journals, left very little elbow room for the hagiographer. The Merton we get in his writings is Merton, warts and all. He did not resist the eventual publication of his journals and poetry describing his love for M. The journals also reveal his all-too-human failings. There are patches of petty complaints leveled at his superiors. There are breathless spots of enthusiasms soon forgotten. His attempts to obtain a decree of exclaustration from Rome in the late 1950s were not a model of forthrightness. He could be sharply uncharitable in his remarks about some members of his community as well as dismissive of those with whom he disagreed.

The merit of these disclosures is, of course, to be found in the simple fact that every human search after Christian perfection is just that: a human search. One would never guess, for example, from a reading of the various Franciscan legends that Francis of Assisi ever had a bad day. If one can intuit some dark moments in the saint's life one must detect them behind the veil of hagiographic exemplarism. Nor does Merton write from a position of critical distance from the self. Who guesses anything about the life of Thomas Aquinas from his writings or, for a more contemporary example, Karl Rahner? From their corpus all we know is that they were persons of great spiritual depth with highly disciplined work habits. About their personal lives we have next to nothing. What Merton did, by contrast, was to make the personal pronoun "I" an integral part of the human search for God.

Such an observation, of course, does not mean that the monk's writings were totally focused on charting the ego. In some of his most powerful books — notably *New Seeds of Contemplation* and the earlier *Thoughts in Solitude* — the personal voice is more subterranean as he outlines what he sees to be the very heart of the contemplative search for the experience of the presence of God in love. Even in those works, however, there is nothing of the textbook about them. They were not dry expositions of "doctrine" or "dogma" but finely honed reflections that came from his own experience as a person of prayer and as a spiritual director. The model for such works was the pedagogical custom he learned from his early reading of Saint John of the Cross. John would hand out little spiritual fragments or provide short counsels (*avisos*) which he wanted his recipients to ponder, expand, and act on.

In a sense, Merton did the same thing. His finest and most enduring spiritual writing actually began as meditations on fragments he penned as part of his spiritual direction for young monks. The long-term fruitfulness of that strategy is that his spiritual writing had the pledge of experience about it. What he wrote — even in little instructional manuals like the early pamphlet *What Is Contemplation?* or the essays he worked on till his death but have come into use only as discrete essays ("The Inner Experience") — were never exercises in scholastic exposition alone. Readers go to these works and others as well with the recognition that he had the capacity to mediate experience through the use of language. This capacity derived, in turn, from both his poetic gifts and from his long experience as a person of prayer.

In a tribute to Thomas Merton recorded in a film biography of the monk made some years ago by Paul Wilkes, the former Vatican Apostolic Delegate to the United States, Archbishop Jean Jadot, made the telling observation that Merton as a "kind of a prophet" did not discover new things but found old things and turned them into a language that speaks to our age. That strikes me as a very shrewd observation. Like the householder of the gospel who knows how to bring forth "old things and new," Merton took the ancient vocabulary of monasticism — with its practices, asceticism, and discipline — and interiorized them; he then spoke that ancient language in a new and clear way to the people of this age.

That articulation of ancient wisdom for the present age was a task for which he felt a vocation when it was fashionable to think of the monk only as a person who had shunned the world. In 1958, some years before the Second Vatican Council was convened, Merton wrote an introduction to what was projected to be a complete edition (*Obras Completas*) of his works for the Latin American audience. What he

208

wrote there is a sufficiently complete overview of his own fundamental philosophy, and it may serve as the coda to this brief study:

> Contemplation cannot construct a new world by itself. Contemplation does not feed the hungry; it does not clothe the naked . . . and it does not return the sinner to peace, truth, and union with God. But without contemplation we cannot see what we do in the apostolate. Without contemplation we cannot understand the significance of the world in which we must act. Without contemplation we remain small, limited, divided, partial; we adhere to the insufficient, permanently united to our narrow group and its interests, losing sight of justice and charity, seized by the passions of the moments, and, finally, we betray Christ. Without contemplation, without the intimate, silent, secret pursuit of truth through love, our action loses itself in the world and becomes dangerous.

8 Some Bibliographical Notes

I have always wanted to write about everything.

Thomas Merton

WORKS BY AND ABOUT THOMAS MERTON CONSTITUTE A huge body of material. For example, the library holdings at the University of Notre Dame list nearly five hundred items which include books, monographs, essays in books, videos, tape recordings, and so on. What appears below, then, constitutes only a representative sample of Merton's work or studies in him and his work. The criterion used for inclusion in this survey was rather simple: What did the author find useful for his own work in general and his reading for preparing this book in particular?

Frank Dell'Isola's *Thomas Merton: A Bibliography* (Kent, Ohio: Kent State University Press, 1975) has been superseded by *Thomas Merton: A Comprehensive Bibliography (New Edition)*, edited by Marquita E. Breit and Robert E. Daggy (New York: Garland, 1986), which is, alas, now out of print. Publications by and about Merton since then have been chronicled in *The Merton Seasonal*, a quarterly publication of

211

the Thomas Merton Center at Bellarmine College in Louisville, Kentucky. The Center is a major repository of Merton materials, but there are also significant holdings of Mertoniana at the libraries of Saint Bonaventure's University in Olean, New York, as well as at Columbia University, Merton's alma mater, in New York City. The latter institution holds the mss. collection of the late Sister Therese Lentfoehr, who was the recipient of many of Merton's manuscripts.

Various volumes of *The Merton Annual* (first published, beginning in 1988, by AMS Press in New York and now by Liturgical Press in Collegeville, Minn.) regularly review studies on Merton, as does the quarterly journal *Cistercian Studies Quarterly* (formerly *Cistercian Studies Review*) and the relatively new *The Thomas Merton Journal*, which is published in the United Kingdom. Thomas Nelson, C.M., has compiled a *Thomas Merton Bibliography* which traces Merton's writings in chronological order. Unpublished, it is in the archives of various libraries including that of the University of Notre Dame.

Some of Merton's "Orientation Notes" written originally for his monastic students have appeared occasionally in the journal *Liturgy O.C.S.O.* edited by the noted monk-scholar, Chrysogonus Waddell, himself a former novice of Merton. Other selections have appeared in some issues of *Cistercian Studies Quarterly*. Unpublished Merton material, when it comes to light, appears on an irregular basis in the same journal or in *The Merton Annual* or in the *Seasonal*. There are long-range plans to publish editions of the monastic orientation notes through Cistercian Publications. Many of Merton's monastic conferences were tape recorded over the years; the Breit/Daggy bibliography has a list of the titles and the recording companies that produced them for commercial use. Many such tapes are distributed through Credence Cassettes at the National Catholic Reporter Company in Kansas City, Missouri.

The authorized biographer of Thomas Merton was to be the noted writer, photographer, and friend of the monk, John Howard Griffin. Griffin, due to bad health, never finished the project. What he had worked on while living in Merton's hermitage doing research was published under the title *The Hermitage Journals* (Garden City, N.Y.: Doubleday Image, 1983). Griffin earlier also contributed the text to a collection of photographs taken by himself and Merton in *A Hidden Wholeness: The Visual World of Thomas Merton* (Boston: Houghton

212

Mifflin, 1970). A biographical sketch of Griffin can be found in Robert Bonazzi's *Man in the Mirror: John Howard Griffin and the Story of "Black Like Me"* (Maryknoll, N.Y.: Orbis, 1998). Michael Mott, the British-born poet, essayist, and fiction writer, then took the place of Griffin as the authorized biographer. His book *The Seven Mountains of Thomas Merton* (Boston: Houghton Mifflin, 1984) is the designated authorized biography.

There have been many biographies of Merton of the "life and work" variety listed in the Breit and Daggy bibliography, but they vary widely in quality. Edward Rice's *The Man in the Sycamore Tree: The Good Times and Hard Life of Thomas Merton* (Garden City, N.Y.: Doubleday, 1970) is a somewhat iconoclastic memoir by a close friend. Monica Furlong's popular *Merton: A Biography* (San Francisco: Harper, 1980) is rather tendentious in some of its interpretations. William Shannon's *Silent Lamp: The Thomas Merton Story* (New York: Crossroad, 1992) is a reliably readable work by an author who has a thorough knowledge of the Merton corpus. *Merton by Those Who Knew Him Best*, edited by Paul Wilkes (San Francisco: Harper, 1984), is a companion to the highly regarded film "Merton" made by Wilkes in the same year. Basil Pennington in *Thomas Merton Brother Monk* (San Francisco: Harper, 1987) writes of Merton through the eyes of a fellow Cistercian monk.

Merton's own *The Seven Storey Mountain* (New York: Harcourt, Brace & Company, 1948) tells of his life, in a somewhat circumscribed fashion, until he enters Gethsemani Abbey in 1941. That story and his subsequent life is fleshed out by the publication of Merton's own personal notebooks, which have now all been published. Those personal journals and notebooks constitute the raw material that aided Merton in the publication of his journals. *Run to the Mountain: The Journals of Thomas Merton, 1939-1941*, edited by Patrick Hart (San Francisco: Harper, 1995), was partially published by Merton as *The Secular Journal of Thomas Merton* (New York: Farrar, Straus & Cudahy, 1959). *Enter the Silence: The Journals of Thomas Merton, 1941-1952*, edited by Jonathan Montaldo (San Francisco: Harper, 1996), is the source for much of *The Sign of Jonas* (New York: Harcourt, Brace & Co., 1953). *A Search for Solitude: The Journals of Thomas Merton, 1952-1960*, edited by Lawrence S. Cunningham (San Francisco: Harper, 1996), and *Turning Toward the World: The Journals of Thomas Merton, 1960-1963*, edited by Victor A.

Kramer (San Francisco: Harper, 1996), provided material for Merton's *Conjectures of a Guilty Bystander* (Garden City, N.Y.: Doubleday, 1966). *Dancing in the Waters of Life: The Journals of Thomas Merton, 1963-1965*, edited by the late Robert E. Daggy (San Francisco: Harper, 1997), was used by Merton in a volume posthumously published: *A Vow of Conversation*, edited by Naomi Burton Stone (New York: Farrar, Straus & Giroux, 1988). *Learning to Love: The Journals of Thomas Merton, 1966-1967*, edited by Christine Bochen (San Francisco: Harper, 1997), contains crucial material about his love for M, which Merton wished to be sealed until twenty-five years after his death. The seventh and final volume entitled *The Other Side of the Mountain: The Journals of Thomas Merton, 1967-1968*, edited by Patrick Hart, OCSO (San Francisco: Harper, 1998), was published in part as *The Asian Journal* (New York: New Directions, 1977). Two small journals from the year of his travels (1968) have also been published, even though most of the material can be found in the final volume of the notebooks: *Thomas Merton in Alaska*, edited by Robert Daggy (New York: New Directions, 1988), and *Woods, Shore, and Desert* (Albuquerque, N.M.: Museum Press, 1988).

We have five volumes of Thomas Merton letters which, alas, have not been published in chronological order but grouped under various themes according to the correspondents. That arrangement makes it difficult to see the correspondence in any coherent fashion without thumbing through several volumes. Matters are made more difficult in that most of the volumes do not arrange the letters in strict chronological fashion. All of those volumes have been published by Farrar, Straus & Giroux in New York. The published correspondence, however, does not represent the whole of Merton's extant letters. The five volumes are:

- *The Hidden Ground of Love: Letters on Religious Experience and Social Concern* (ed. William Shannon) [1985]
- *The Road to Joy: Letters to Old and New Friends* (ed. Robert E. Daggy) [1989]
- *The School of Charity: Letters on Religious Renewal and Spiritual Direction* (ed. Patrick Hart, OCSO) [1990]
- *The Courage for Truth: Letters to Writers* (ed. Christine Bochen) [1993]
- *Witness to Freedom: Letters in Time of Crisis* (ed. William H. Shannon) [1994]

Patricia Burton of the International Thomas Merton Society's Rochester, New York, chapter has compiled an *Index to the Published Letters of Thomas Merton* which was published by the society in 1996.

In addition to the five volumes of correspondence, there are also some discrete volumes of letters addressed to specific persons. *A Catch of Anti-Letters* (Kansas City, Mo.: Sheed, Andrews, and McNeel, 1978) represents the correspondence between Merton and his close friend Robert Lax. David Cooper has recently edited *Thomas Merton and James Laughlin: Selected Letters* (New York: Norton, 1997), which represents the correspondence between the monk and his long-time friend and editor at New Directions. R. Faggen has edited *Striving Towards Being: The Letters of Thomas Merton and Czeslaw Milosz* (New York: Farrar, Straus & Giroux, 1997). *At Home in the World: The Letters of Thomas Merton and Rosemary Radford Reuther,* edited by Mary Tardieff, OP (Maryknoll, N.Y.: Orbis, 1995), is an extremely interesting collection of exchanges between the noted feminist theologian and the monk. Wilbur Ferry published his personal collection of Merton letters in *Letters from Tom* (Scarsdale, N.Y.: Fort Hill Press, 1983). All of the published letters represent only a selection of the extant correspondence with more publication promised (e.g., the exchange of letters between Merton and Dom Jean Leclercq as well as the complete correspondence between Thomas Merton and Robert Lax are in preparation).

With the exception of a few items like the eighteen poems he wrote for M (published in a limited edition under the title *Eighteen Poems* by New Directions in 1985), the poetry of Merton, scattered in many journals and published as a number of books at various times during his life as well as his translations of other poets and some hitherto fragments and marginalia, is available in the one volume *The Collected Poems of Thomas Merton* (New York: New Directions, 1977). Merton's literary essays have also appeared in a single comprehensive volume: *The Literary Essays of Thomas Merton* (New York: New Directions, 1981). *Monks Pond* (Lexington, Ky.: University of Kentucky Press, 1989) is a facsimile edition of the four issues of the literary journal edited by Merton in 1967-1968. Ron Seitz's memoir *Song for Nobody* (Liguori, Mo.: Triumph, 1993) describes Merton's friendship and help given to the young Kentucky poet.

Passion for Peace: The Social Essays, edited by William Shannon (New York: Crossroad, 1995), gathers together a significant selection of his disparate writings on social justice. A wide sampler of Merton's writings are available in the expanded *A Thomas Merton Reader*, edited by Thomas McDonnell (Garden City, N.Y.: Doubleday, 1974, rev. ed.). *Thomas Merton: Spiritual Master*, edited by Lawrence S. Cunningham (Mahwah, N.J.: Paulist, 1995), provides a generous sampling of his spiritual writing with a long introduction. Those requiring the original publication sources of his published poems and essays will find help in the Breit/Daggy bibliography.

In the body of this study many works of Merton have been cited. Some of these works have been reissued in various formats and from different publishers over the years (most of Merton's major works are still in print). The following prose works, mentioned in the text of this book, were published in Merton's lifetime. *The Spirit of Simplicity* was published under Gethsemani's own imprint in 1948. After *The Seven Storey Mountain* (1948) Merton published a history of his religious order entitled *The Waters of Siloe* (New York: Harcourt, Brace & Company, 1949). His next major work was his study of Saint John of the Cross, *The Ascent to Truth* (New York: Harcourt, Brace & Company, 1951), with *The Sign of Jonas* coming from the same publisher in 1953. *The Last of the Fathers* (New York: Harcourt Brace & Company, 1954) was a brief volume celebrating the papal encyclical devoted to Saint Bernard of Clairvaux. *No Man Is an Island* (New York: Harcourt, Brace & Company, 1955) is a collection of essays on spiritual topics. *The Living Bread* (New York: Farrar, Straus & Cudahy, 1956) was a meditative volume on the Eucharist. In that same year Merton wrote his rather now dated study of various forms of monasticism, *The Silent Life* (New York: Harcourt, Brace, 1957). In 1958, from the same publisher, he published his important and influential *Thoughts in Solitude*. The following year saw the appearance of *The Secular Journal of Thomas Merton* (New York: Farrar, Straus & Company, 1959). The collected essays *Disputed Questions* (New York: Farrar, Straus & Company, 1960) marked a departure in his writing with a new emphasis on social consciousness. The anthology of essays under the title *The New Man* (New York: Farrar, Straus & Cudahy, 1961) is a volume whose interests are in tandem with *Disputed Questions*. *The Wisdom of the Desert* (New York: New Directions, 1961) was a selected translation of some of the sayings of the early desert fathers with an introduction by Merton. *New Seeds of Contemplation* (New York: New Directions, 1961), a complete overhaul of the original *Seeds of Contemplation* (1949), is generally regarded as one of the most enduring classic spiritual works of our age. In the early 1960s Merton saw published two books which, given his new orientation, he saw as pious and somewhat peripheral to his new concerns; they were *Life and Holiness* (New York: Herder, 1963) and his essays on the liturgy, *Seasons of Celebration* (New York: Farrar, Straus and Company, 1965). Of far more importance to Merton himself were books like the essay collections *Seeds of Destruction* (New York: Farrar, Straus and Company, 1964) and *Raids on the Unspeakable* (New York: New Directions, 1966).

It was also in 1966 that Merton published the reworked excerpts from his private journals under the title *Conjectures of a Guilty Bystander* (Garden City, N.Y.: Doubleday, 1966). In the last three years of his life, he also published three titles that reflected his increasing interest in the religions of the East: *The Way of Chuang Tzu* (New York: New Directions, 1965); *Mystics and Zen Masters* (New York: Farrar, Straus and Company, 1967); and *Zen and the Birds of Appetite* (New York: New Directions, 1968). Also, in 1968 the collection of essays appeared entitled *Faith and Violence* (Notre Dame: University of Notre Dame Press), testifying to his continued interest in social issues.

In the period after his death a number of books, quite apart from the letters and the journals, appeared under Merton's name which were mainly collections of his essays or manuscripts that were being edited before his departure for the East. *The Climate of Monastic Prayer* (Kalamazoo, Mich.: Cistercian Publications, 1969) was reissued under the title *Contemplative Prayer* (Garden City, N.Y.: Doubleday Image, 1971) in order to make the book more attractive to non-monastics. *Opening the Bible* (Collegeville, Minn.: Liturgical Press, 1971) is a pamphlet-sized reflection on the contemplative reading of sacred scripture. The same press had published another Merton pamphlet during the monk's lifetime called *Praying the Psalms* (1956). *Ishi Means Man* (Greensboro, N.C.: Unicorn, 1976) has four essays on Native Americans. *The Monastic Journey*, edited by Patrick Hart (Kansas City, Mo.: Sheed, Andrews, 1977), is a fair sampling of his monastic studies. *Love and Living*, edited by Naomi Burton Stone and Brother Patrick Hart (New York: Farrar, Straus & Giroux, 1979), gathers together some of his occasional writings, including his tribute to the education he received at Columbia University. *The Non-Violent Alternative* (New York:

Farrar, Straus & Giroux, 1980) was a revised version of the monk's earlier *Thomas Merton on Peace* done by the noted pacifist thinker, Gordon Zahn. *The Geography of Holiness: The Photography of Thomas Merton,* edited by Deba Prasad Patnaik (New York: Pilgrim Press, 1980), reproduces the better results of Merton's camera work. *Thomas Merton — "Honorable Reader" — Reflections on My Work,* edited by Robert E. Daggy (New York: Crossroad, 1989), is an extremely valuable book that reproduces prefaces and introductions written by Merton for foreign translations of his work. *Thomas Merton: Spiritual Master,* edited by Lawrence S. Cunningham (Mahwah, N.J.: Paulist, 1992), mentioned above, offers a generous cross-section of his spiritual writing. *Springs of Contemplation* (New York: Farrar, Straus & Giroux, 1992; reprinted by Ave Maria Press, 1997) is a transcription of the conferences Merton gave to religious women in 1967-1968. *Thomas Merton on Saint Bernard,* edited by Patrick Hart (Kalamazoo, Mich.: Cisterican Publications, 1980), gathers some essays Merton wrote on one of the founders of the Order. A more complete version of the collected essays under the title *Contemplation in a World of Action* with a prefatory note by Robert Coles, M.D., is forthcoming from the University of Notre Dame Press in 1999. This edition will replace the Doubleday Image volume first published in 1971. Apart from the above anthologies one should also note the posthumous publication in 1969 of *My Argument with the Gestapo: A Macaronic Journal* (Garden City, N.Y.: Doubleday, 1969) — Merton's youthful novel.

A New Charter for Monasticism, edited by John Moffitt (Notre Dame: University of Notre Dame Press, 1970), has a report on Merton's death, a transcript of the memorial service in Thailand, and the papers given at the conference at which Merton spoke. The late Walter Capps published a transcription of the dialogues Merton entered into at the Center for the Study of Democratic Institutions before his Asian journey: *Thomas Merton: Preview of the Asian Journey* (New York: Crossroad, 1989).

The number of works on Merton is vast, of wildly varying quality, and ranging from the popular to the scholarly. Listed here are only those that seem to be the most helpful from a critical point of view. James Baker's *Thomas Merton: Social Critic* (Lexington, Ky.: University of Kentucky Press, 1971) is an early study interesting if for no other reason than that Merton had read the book in manuscript before its publication. Ross Labrie's *The Art of Thomas Merton* (Fort Worth, Tex.: Texas Christian University Press, 1979) was an early attempt to focus on Merton's many artistic interests. Elena Malits's *The Solitary Explorer: Thomas Merton's Transforming Journey* (San Francisco: Harper, 1980) analyzes the use of the "I" in Merton's theology. Gerald Twomey's *Thomas Merton: Prophet in the Belly of a Paradox* (New York: Paulist, 1978) is a reliable analysis. Victor Kramer's *Thomas Merton: Monk & Artist* (Kalamazoo, Mich.: Cistercian, 1987) is a reprint of the author's volume in the Twayne World Authors series. Jim Forest's *Thomas Merton: A Pictorial Biography* (New York: Paulist, 1980) is just that; it has been recently reissued as *Living with Wisdom* (Maryknoll, N.Y.: Orbis, 1991). *Father Louie: Portraits of Thomas Merton,* edited by Ralph Eugene Meatyard (New York: Tinken, 1991), reproduces pictures taken in the 1960s, mainly at the abbey and its environs. Anthony Padovano's *The Human Journey: Thomas Merton, Symbol of a Century* (Garden City, N.Y.: Doubleday, 1982) is useful for its attempt to situate Merton in the context of American literature. *Thomas Merton: Monk,* edited by Patrick Hart (New York: Sheed and Ward, 1974), is valuable because the contributors, themselves monastics, study Merton's significance from that perspective. Therese Lentfoehr's *Words and Silence: On the Poetry of Thomas Merton* (New York: New Directions, 1979) is somewhat adulatory but important since she, a poet in her own right, had been a longtime correspondent of Merton's and a keeper of many of his manuscripts. Her collection of Merton materials is now in a depository at New York's Columbia University. Lentfoehr's books should be supplemented by George Kilcourse's *Ace of Freedoms: Thomas Merton's Christ* (Notre Dame: University of Notre Dame Press, 1993), which is a study of Merton christology mainly through the poetry. One may also profitably consult the earlier work of the Canadian critic George Woodcock, whose *Thomas Merton: Monk and Poet/A Critical Study* (New York: Farrar, Straus & Giroux, 1978) has some incisive things to say about the classification of Merton's poetry. David D. Cooper's *Thomas Merton's Art of Denial: The Evolution of a Radical Humanist* (Athens, Ga.: University of Georgia Press, 1989) has the particular merit of providing a full account of Merton's (failed) attempt to write persuasively on the visual arts. Cooper's book is also the most ambitious attempt to understand Merton as a man of letters and humanist. *Thomas Merton: Poet-Monk-Prophet,* edited by Paul Pearson et al. (Abergavenny, U.K.:

Three Peaks Press, 1998), reproduces the papers given at the second annual meeting of the Thomas Merton society of Great Britain and Ireland.

There have been a number of studies of Merton's spirituality and theology of prayer. John J. Higgins's *Merton's Theology of Prayer* (Spencer, Mass.: Cistercian Publications, 1971) is an early synthetic work. Raymond Bailey's *Thomas Merton on Mysticism* (Garden City, N.Y.: Doubleday, 1975) is a helpful discussion. Both can be supplemented by Anne Carr's *The Search for Wisdom and Spirit: Thomas Merton's Theology of the Self* (Notre Dame: University of Notre Dame Press, 1988), which is a fine study of the concept of the "self" in relation to God. William Shannon's *Thomas Merton's Dark Path* (New York: Farrar, Straus & Giroux, 1987, rev. ed.) is an excellent work that pays full attention to the material in Merton's unfinished studies of "The Inner Experience" as well as Merton's major spiritual books from the early pamphlet "What Is Contemplation?" The late Henri Nouwen's *Thomas Merton: Contemplative Critic* (San Francisco: Harper, 1981) is a sympathetic but broadly impressionistic reflection by the well-known spiritual writer. Donald Grayston's *Thomas Merton: The Development of a Spiritual Theologian* (New York: Mellen, 1985) is a densely argued study of the evolution of Merton's spiritual doctrine from the publication of *Seeds of Contemplation* through *New Seeds of Contemplation*. Thomas King's *Merton: Mystic at the Center of America* (Collegeville, Minn.: Liturgical Press, 1992) focuses on Merton as an American prophetic figure. James Finley's *Merton's Palace of Nowhere* (Notre Dame: Ave Maria, 1978) focuses on Merton's theology of prayer and contemplation.

Towards an Integrated Humanity: Thomas Merton's Journey, edited by Basil Pennington (Kalamazoo, Mich.: Cistercian, 1989), contains essays and studies devoted to Merton on the twentieth anniversary of his death. That volume can be seen as the companion to the earlier *The Message of Thomas Merton*, edited by Patrick Hart (Kalamazoo, Mich.: Cistercian, 1981), which contains papers given at Columbia University to observe the tenth anniversary of the monk's death.

As background for an understanding of the Christian contemplative tradition, one should consult the ongoing work of Bernard McGinn, who as of this writing has finished three volumes of his history of Christian mysticism: *The Foundations of Mysticism* (New York: Crossroad, 1991), *The Growth of Mysticism* (New York: Crossroad, 1994), and *The*

Flowering of Mysticism (1998); the second volume studies the early Cistercians with an especially rich chapter on Bernard of Clairvaux. All three of these volumes contain ample bibliographies.

Thomas del Prete's *Thomas Merton & the Education of the Whole Person* (Birmingham, Ala.: Religious Education, 1990) views Merton under the rubric of pedagogical theory. Ronald Powaski's *Thomas Merton on Nuclear Weapons* (Chicago: Loyola, 1988) sees Merton in his role as peace maker. Merton's teachings about nonviolence receive attention in Robert Givey's *Social Thought of Thomas Merton* (Chicago: Franciscan Herald, 1983). Robert Inchausti's recent *Thomas Merton's American Prophecy* (Albany, N.Y.: SUNY, 1998) is a valuable (if somewhat eclectic) contribution in its attempt to see Merton in the light of postmodernism.

For a general background of religious history during Merton's life one might consult the following: Jay Dolan, *The American Catholic Experience* (Garden City, N.Y.: Doubleday, 1985); Margaret Mary Reher, *Catholic Intellectual Life in America* (New York: Macmillan, 1989); and Eric Hanson, *The Catholic Church and World Politics* (Princeton, N.J.: Princeton University Press, 1987). Patrick Allitt's *Catholic Converts* (Ithaca, N.Y.: Cornell University Press, 1997) is very useful for historical background of Catholic converts in the English-speaking world, but the pages on Merton are rather pedestrian.

*   *   *

In various letters during the 1960s Merton wrote to various people indicating which of his books he thought to be most satisfactory. In 1965, borrowing a phrase from the poet Rainer Maria Rilke, Merton said that some of his writing came from necessity (he listed *Chuang Tzu; Guilty Bystander;* some of the poems in *Emblems;* "Philosophy of Solitude" in *Disputed Questions; Sign of Jonas; The Seven Storey Mountain;* and *Thirty Poems*); the rest was "trash," he said; but then he hastily added that some of the writing on Zen and some of *The Behavior of Titans* was also "necessary." In a 1968 letter to a nun, Sister John Marie, he divided his work into three large periods: writings done from his conversion until his ordination to the priesthood in 1949; the second period ended with the publication of *Disputed Questions* in 1960; the third period, of course, extended from that time onwards. In that same letter he characterized the first period as being one of piety; the second as one that was more open to the world; and the third was marked by an evolution in which he attempted more experimental forms of writing. In the course of our study we have noted those shifts in some detail.

He did not always list the same books, but the omissions were the same. On February 6, 1967, he made a graph of his books on a single sheet of paper ranking them from "awful" to "best." One book made the bottom of the list *(What Are These Wounds?)* And none made "best." Here are Merton's own rankings according to his sliding scale:

Awful: *What Are These Wounds?*

Very Poor: *Exile Ends in Glory*

Poor: *Figures for an Apocalypse*

Less Good: *Man in a Divided Sea; Bread in the Wilderness; Ascent to Truth; The Last of the Fathers; Living Bread; Spiritual Direction & Meditation; Life & Holiness*

Good: *No Man Is an Island; The Strange Islands; Seeds of Destruction; Seasons of Celebration*

Better: *Thirty Poems; The Seven Storey Mountain; Seeds of Contemplation; Tears of the Blind Lion; Sign of Jonas; The Silent Life; Thoughts in Solitude; Wisdom of the Desert; Disputed Questions; New Seeds of Contemplation; Chuang Tzu; Emblems of a Season of Fury; Conjectures of a Guilty Bystander*

Best: None named.

*   *   *

The question has often risen whether potential readers of Thomas Merton should follow his ranking by beginning with his "better" list and perhaps working downward? Or focus on the works written "out of necessity"? Perhaps one should be suspicious of a writer who too

222

easily dismisses his early work as he falls in love with his later efforts. Of course, when he made this list in an idle moment a good deal of what he eventually produced had not yet been published, such as the popular collection *Zen and the Birds of Appetite*. In short, Merton may not be the very best judge of how enduring and influential his work might be.

There is the further question of *which* Merton one wants to read. Is it Merton the poet? The mystic? The social critic? The monastic apologist? As we have seen, there are many Mertons. The suppositions that follow assume not the specialist, but one who would like to get a broad view of this many-faceted writer and spiritual master.

When that question of how to read Merton has been asked of me by students my ready response has been to read the "autobiographical" works beginning with *The Seven Storey Mountain* and ending with *The Asian Journal* to get a sense of the sweep of Merton's life. Those less interested in that more personal and chronological approach to reading Merton would perhaps benefit from a slow meditative reading of the two great spiritual works: *Thoughts in Solitude* and *New Seeds of Contemplation* along with some of the works written "out of necessity" such as his essay "A Philosophy of Solitude," which he himself thought was one of his better efforts.

Anyone who wishes a systematic guide to a thorough study of Merton might wish to consult a recent book written for the neophyte reader that offers a reading plan for a study of the Mertonian corpus: William H. Shannon, *Something of a Rebel: Thomas Merton, His Life and Works; an Introduction* (Cincinnati: St. Anthony Messenger Press, 1997).

*   *   *

1998 marked the nine hundredth anniversary of the founding of the Cistercian Order and the 150th anniversary of the founding of the monastery of Our Lady of Gethsemani where Merton lived his monastic life. To mark the monastery's anniversary Dianne Aprile wrote a history of the monastery: *The Abbey of Gethsemani: Place of Peace and Paradox* (Louisville, Ky.: Trout Lily Press, 1998). Her book advances the story of the monastery first told by the young Thomas Merton in his book *The Waters of Siloe* in 1949. It is particularly good in highlighting the various emphases insisted on by the various abbots under whom Merton lived as a monk.

The standard history of the Cistercian Order is Louis Lekai's *The Cistercians: Ideals and Reality* (Kent, Ohio: Kent State University Press, 1977), although much research has been published since its publication. Also very useful and illuminating is André Louf, *The Cistercian Way* (Kalamazoo, Mich.: Cistercian Publications, 1983). The classic study of traditional monastic culture is Jean LeClercq's *The Love of Learning and the Desire for God* (New York: Fordham University Press, 1961). Esther De Waal's *The Way of Simplicity: The Cistercian Tradition* (Maryknoll, N.Y.: Orbis, 1998) is a brief study of Cistercian spirituality. *The Cistercian World: Monastic Writings of the Twelfth Century,* edited by Patricia Matarasso (New York: Penguin, 1993), provides a brief taste of some classic Cistercian texts from the early founders and writers. James France's *The Cistercians in Medieval Art* (Kalamazoo, Mich.: Cistercian Publications, 1998) has an informative text that enhances the illustrations and describes early Cistercian life. Raimundo Pannikar's *Blessed Simplicity: The Monk as Universal Archetype* (New York: Seabury, 1982) attempts to understand monasticism as a universal phenomenon. With contributions by some Cistercians, it is an illuminating attempt to describe monasticism as a broad religious phenomenon. The video *Trappist,* made at the Cistercian monastery at Mepkin, South Carolina, and available from Paulist Communications, interweaves monastic history and contemporary Trappist life at an American monastery.

During Merton's own lifetime he supplied the written text for a number of books on Cistercian life at Gethsemani. *Gethsemani Magnificat* (published by the abbey in 1949) celebrated the centenary of the monastery. Merton supplied the foreword to Shirley Burden's book of photographs *God Is My Life: The Story of Our Lady of Gethsemani* (New York: Reynal, 1960). He also authored two small pamphlets on Trappist life both published and distributed by the abbey: *Guide to Cistercian Life* (1948) and *Gethsemani: A Life of Praise* (1966). Variations of that guide have appeared in pamphlet form for the various monasteries of the Order in the United States of America. *Why We Live in Community* (New York: Plough, 1995) is an interesting set of reflections in which the Anabaptist Bruderhof community leader Eberhard Arnold dialogues with Merton on the meaning of religious community.

Understanding the Rule of Saint Benedict is made easier by the splendid bilingual Latin/English edition *The Rule of Saint Benedict*, edited by Timothy Fry, O.S.B. (Collegeville, Minn.: Liturgical Press, 1981), which also provides glossaries, running commentaries, and useful background essays.

For a theoretical grasp of autobiography, James D. Fernandez's *Apology to Apostrophe: Autobiography and the Rhetoric of Self-Representation in Spain* (Durham, N.C.: Duke University Press, 1992) and *Autobiography: Essays Theoretical and Critical,* edited by James Olney (Princeton, N.J.: Princeton University Press, 1980), provide useful frames for discussion.

Index